The Poet's Notebook

The POET'S NOTEBOOK

Excerpts from the Notebooks of Contemporary American Poets

EDITED BY

Stephen Kuusisto

Deborah Tall

David Weiss

W. W. NORTON & COMPANY
New York   London

The text of this book is composed in Electra with cursive
with the display set in Mistral and Atrax.
Composition by PennSet, Inc.
Manufacturing by Courier Companies, Inc.
Book design by Charlotte Staub

Library of Congress Cataloging-in-Publication Data

The poet's notebook / [edited by] Stephen Kuusisto,
Deborah Tall, and David Weiss.
p.   cm.
1. American poetry—20th century—History and criticism—
Theory, etc. 2. Poetry—Authorship. 3. Notebooks. 4. Poetics.
I. Kuusisto, Stephen. II. Tall, Deborah. III. Weiss, David.
PS325.P63   1995
811'.509—dc20   95-1827

ISBN 0-393-03866-1
ISBN 0-393-31655-6 pbk.

W. W. Norton & Company, Inc.
500 Fifth Avenue, New York, N.Y. 10110

W. W. Norton & Company Ltd.
10 Coptic Street, London WC1A 1PU

1 2 3 4 5 6 7 8 9 0

Acknowledgments

Many of the notebook excerpts included in this volume previously appeared, sometimes in shorter versions, in *Taking Note: From Poets' Notebooks*, edited by Stephen Kuusisto, Deborah Tall, and David Weiss and published as a special edition of *Seneca Review* by Hobart and William Smith Colleges Press in 1991. The editors wish to express their gratitude to Hobart and William Smith Colleges for their support of the original project.

We also thank John D'Agata and Suzanne Yates for their help in assembling the current manuscript.

And we thank the following for permission to reprint previously published material:

Marvin Bell's notebook excerpts previously appeared as "Pages #2" in *The Marvin Bell Reader*, copyright ©1994 by Marvin Bell, and are reprinted by permission of the University Press of New England.

Marvin Bell's poem "The Book of the Dead Man (#1)" is reprinted from *The Book of the Dead Man*, copyright ©1994 by Marvin Bell. Reprinted by permission of Copper Canyon Press, P.O. Box 271, Port Townsend, WA 98368.

Rita Dove's poem "Ozone" is reprinted from *Grace Notes: Poems by Rita Dove*, by permission of W. W. Norton & Company, Inc. Copyright ©1989 by Rita Dove.

A portion of Stephen Dunn's notebook excerpts, reprinted from *Walking Light: Essays and Memoirs* by Stephen Dunn with the permission of W. W. Norton & Company, Inc. Copyright ©1993 by Stephen Dunn. Originally published in *Seneca Review*.

Stephen Dunn's poem "Some Things I Wanted to Say to You" is reprinted from *New and Selected Poems: 1974–1994* by Stephen Dunn, by permission of W. W. Norton & Company, Inc. Copyright ©1994 by Stephen Dunn.

Donald Hall's notebook excerpts were previously published as "Working Journal" in *Antaeus* 61.

Joy Harjo's poem "The Naming" is reprinted from *The Woman Who Fell from the Sky: Poems by Joy Harjo,* by permission of W. W. Norton & Company, Inc. Copyright ©1994 by Joy Harjo.

Anselm Hollo's poem "Sonnet IV from NOT A FORM AT ALL BUT A STATE OF MIND" was first published in *Exquisite Corpse,* a journal of books and ideas.

Garrett Hongo's poem "Obon: Dance for the Dead" is reprinted from *The River of Heaven,* copyright ©1988 by Garrett Hongo. Reprinted by permission of Alfred A. Knopf, Inc.

X. J. Kennedy's poem "The Devil's Advice to Poets" is reprinted from *Cross Ties: Selected Poems* (University of Georgia Press, 1985) by permission of the author.

Yusef Komunyakaa's poem "A Reed Boat" was first published in *The Threepenny Review.*

Heather McHugh's poem "What Hell Is" is reprinted from *Shades,* copyright ©1988 by Heather McHugh, Wesleyan University Press. Reprinted by permission of the University Press of New England.

Susan Mitchell's poem "Music" was first published in *Antaeus* 75/76.

Mary Oliver's notebook excerpts are used by permission of the Molly Malone Cook Literary Agency. Copyright ©1991 by Mary Oliver.

Mary Oliver's poem "Toad" is reprinted from *White Pine: Poems and Prose Poems,* ©1994 by Mary Oliver, by permission of Harcourt Brace & Company.

Liz Rosenberg's poem "The Poem of my Heart" is reprinted from *Children of Paradise,* by Liz Rosenberg, by permission of the University of Pittsburgh Press. Copyright ©1994 by Liz Rosenberg.

Laurie Sheck's poem "The Book of Persephone" was first published in *Agni.*

Charles Simic's notebook excerpts appear as "The Minotaur Loves his Labyrinth" in *The Unemployed Fortune-Teller,* ©1995 by Charles Simic, and are reprinted by permission of the University of Michigan Press.

William Stafford's poem "The Trouble with Reading" is reprinted from *Passwords,* ©1991 by William Stafford, by permission of HarperCollins Publishers.

Rosanna Warren's poem "Poetry Reading" was first published in the *Washington Post,* December 13, 1992.

In Rosanna Warren's notebook excerpts, the quoted haiku are reprinted from *The Zen Wave,* translations by Robert Aitken, by permission of Weatherhill.

The annotations and sources of quotations within the poets' notebook excerpts have been left as in the original notebooks in order to preserve each poet's style of notation.

Contents

Preface, by Charles Simic   ix
Editors' Introduction—
  "The Note-Taking Habit"   xiii

Marvin Bell   3

Rita Dove   13

Stephen Dunn   22

Carolyn Forché   31

Alice Fulton   43

Donald Hall   65

Joy Harjo   77

Anselm Hollo   89

Garrett Hongo   102

Donald Justice   110

X. J. Kennedy   121

Yusef Komunyakaa   134

William Matthews   144

J. D. McClatchy   153

Cynthia Macdonald   164

Heather McHugh   178

James Merrill   190

Susan Mitchell   198

Lisel Mueller   212

Mary Oliver   222

Liz Rosenberg   233

Peter Sacks   245

Laurie Sheck   257

Charles Simic   269

William Stafford   285

Rosanna Warren   291

Notes on Contributors   303

Preface

> But the POETRY *notebook, while it hasn't helped my powers of observation worth a hoot, has been for the last forty years a place to vent steam in private, a seedbed for critical articles, and a parking lot for notions to retain.* —X. J. Kennedy

> *Notebooks are dedicated to a perpetual sketchiness, and that's their charm.* —Alice Fulton

*N*otebooks? In the age of the laptop? What is it with these poets, you're probably asking yourselves? How ridiculous can they get? Almost every household can choose from a hundred TV channels, and here they are shuffling off to the kitchen, looking for something to sharpen their stub of a pencil with. Do they lick the lead once before they start writing? You can bet on it that some of them do.

Still, the question remains: Why write things down?

The answer is simple: Trusting memory is a bad idea.

My father used to remind us often that his life's biggest regret was that he never had anything to write with whenever a terrific idea struck him. He expected us to sigh with him for the great loss to humanity; instead we just laughed until he got mad and left the dinner table. Luckily, for us, the poets in this anthology walk around with pockets and purses containing not one but several writing implements and notebooks.

What Deborah Tall, David Weiss, and Stephen Kuusisto have collected here are examples of journal writings, notebook jottings, scraps, diaries connected with literary projects, memorable quotes, workbook fragments, some of which have already found their way into poems and others that have not and never will. What is amazing about the entries is how varied and how entertaining they are. It's the unsystematic, odds-and-ends quality about them I find especially attractive.

The habit of note taking is obviously compulsive, like biting one's fingernails. Our culture's need to pigeonhole everything is defeated in these notebooks. Spontaneity rules here. The writer incorporates chance and makes do with the unforeseen. The head of a poet is more like a town dump than a town library.

Oracles are brief and so are poems. The deepest belief of every poet is that less is more. Poems, despite their obscurity, tend to be attempts at clarifications. That aesthetic and philosophical premise of poetry makes poets the ideal note takers among us. As I read these entries, it occurs to me that most literary essays, columns, and even novels would benefit by being cut down to a few sentences.

Schoolteachers, clergymen, and other policemen of virtue have always been in complete agreement with philosophers. No model of the ideal society since Plato has ever welcomed poets, and for excellent reasons. Poets have no respect for the authority of church and state. They are always corrupting the young, making them lazy and dreamy. Irreverence, as you'll see for yourselves as you read this book, is what they are peddling. From the point of view of group-think, such manifestations of individualism are, of course, perverse, but what fun you'll have as a reader!

"So much of what Woolf wrote she wrote not because she was a woman, but because she was Woolf," concludes Mary Oliver. Would one want a two-volume study elaborating the idea? Of course not.

"Also I write in order to make God repent of His sins," says Liz Rosenberg.

A good notebook entry must shock us into thinking.

"Something totally unexpected, like a barking cat," writes Oliver.

"All is transitory," said Buddha, who knew wisdom is not systemizable. Long-drawn-out works conflict with the fragmentariness of our consciousness. What is recorded here is the sense of the unique and unrepeatable experience of those rare moments of clarity. All of a sudden words come to us out of nowhere, true words, words that for some reason we can't find when we want them, when all we get are words that sound hollow. There are insights one either seizes quickly or not at all. It's like catching flies. It's not by cunning calculation that one captures the flavor of life.

Perhaps we all have a secret belief that lives are more revealing in their casual detail than in their broader outlines? If that were not true, who would care about the private lives of the famous. Individual eccentricities are fascinating. To eavesdrop, to peep through the keyhole on the human comedy—that's what poetry lets us do.

The commonplace is where poetry hides. Every art depends on nuance, detail, and lightness of spirit. There are as many ways to touch a single piano key as there are to use a word.

Will the computer ever replace the fetishism of the notebook? It's possible, but I doubt it. To hear the poets tell it, the small, handsome notebook and a special pen or pencil are half the work. They are an invitation to write in a certain way. They demand from us absolute conciseness, an aesthetic of modesty. If you write poems on the back of old envelopes and garage sale announcements, as I often do, you don't write epics.

"Whoever has two pairs of pants, sell one and buy this book," said the great German aphorist Lichtenberg more than two hundred years ago. I could not agree more.

This is a kind of book in which you'll want to underline a lot. There are good stories here, quirky observations on life and literature, jokes, wonderful quotes, and even passages of sensible advice and wisdom that will delight your grumpiest friends.

Perhaps you'll even get a notebook of your own and an old-fashioned fountain pen and make your first bold entry in red ink? Just remember, "You got to lie to stay halfway interested in yourself." The novelist Barry Hannah said it, and I can't think of any better advice to give to all the future notebook writers.

—Charles Simic

The Note-Taking Habit

*It is a long time since I have kept any notes, taken
any memoranda, written down my current reflections, taken a sheet of paper, as it were, into my
confidence. Meanwhile so much has come and gone,
so much that it is now too late to catch, to reproduce, to preserve. I have lost too much by losing, or
rather by not having acquired, the note-taking habit.*
—Henry James

There are probably as many kinds of notebooks as
poets who keep them. Called commonplace books, journals, diaries,
they house under one cover lines of poetry, reflections, ideas, observations, feelings, quotations, impressions, confessions, aphorisms,
sketches, speculations, intuitions, responses. "To catch, to reproduce,
to preserve," writes James, nicely summarizing the impulse. In the
verb "preserve," one feels the upstream swim against things passing;
in "catch," that swipe at the will-o'-the-wisp of passing thought and
sensation.

Anyone who has read the published notebooks and journals of writers will no doubt have been struck by the rich vein of thought and
feeling mined from the mountain of daily living. Sift through almost
any page, and nuggets of ore will lie glinting there in the pan. The
notebook brings us face to face with its writer in an unmasked
guise—although there is no getting away from guises, the semblance
of undisguise is what we prize. As Stephen Dunn describes it, the
journal "is offered in the spirit of someone open and vain enough to
let you in his house. It's possible that a part of him always had you
in mind."

In the fragmentary nature of notebook entries, the reader can sense the immediate, provisional, and searching presence of the writer. Indeed, the French poet Paul Valéry, a great keeper of journals, called diarists "amateurs of the unfinished." That unfinished quality may be what, beyond brilliance of idea or observation, we seek them out for.

Or maybe it's for the immersion in the densities of the writer's sensorium, the mind tireless in its ruminations and self-scrutiny. There have been remarkable journals and notebooks published this century, among them Franz Kafka's, Cesare Pavese's, Ivo Andrić's, May Sarton's, Theodore Roethke's, Paul Valéry's, Max Frisch's, and Fernando Pessoa's. We wondered if the notebooks of contemporary American poets would prove as valuable and compelling, and so we decided to seek them out.

The excerpts gathered here are the result. Some cover many years of jottings; others record a particular, intense period in the poet's life. Some include a poem that derives in some way from the entry. And the poets have written introductory notes that address their own use of notebooks. "I keep a journal when my brain is killing me," writes Marvin Bell. The notebook is where "the writer is free to make indefensible utterances," says Anselm Hollo.

Because the notebook or journal is not strictly a form or a genre, more aptly the quarry of the writer's working life, one rarely finds it in print. ("A novel is released, but a notebook is kept," as Heather McHugh describes it.) In bringing the notebooks of some of our best contemporary poets to light, we hope to illuminate the poet's temperament and process, to reveal the blue out of which poetry arises.

—David Weiss, Deborah Tall, and Stephen Kuusisto

The Poet's Notebook

Marvin Bell

Why a journal? Well, I like writing that spills over. I want to live as much as possible at the ends of my fingertips rather than, say, in the capillaries of the brain. I like it when the soup simmers, the kettle hisses. I want it, I require it, I trust it. Therefore, once in a while I take up with prose as if it had nowhere in mind. Do I keep a journal? —No. —Yes. —Sometimes. Do I plunder it for poems? —Never. What's its use? —Peacock feathers. —Bandages. Journals are useful in emergencies, but tricky: a journal can provide artificial respiration, or it can turn living art into a finely etched corpse. As to the nuances of certain American terms for such an enterprise—I tend to apply "journal" to my prose spillover because it sounds helpless and private, whereas "notebook" sounds civic and civil. On the other hand, "diary" suggests the writings of someone awaiting rescue. I don't keep a diary. "Daybook" suggests an annotated calendar. "Chronicle" suggests reportage. I suppose the common denominator is that all such are thought to consist of scraps, pieces— the tip of the iceberg, as it were. I keep a journal when my brain is killing me. The poem that seven years later was to become #1 in The Book of the Dead Man was written the winter I kept this journal. I titled it "from: The Book of the Dead Man," though there was no such.

—July 28, 1994, Port Townsend

3

In the winter of 1986–87, while residing alone in a small house in the Northwest, near a bluff above Port Townsend Bay, I kept a notebook of personal struggle not intended for publication. Sometimes, a page would begin in the language and feeling of a journal, move toward that of the essay, and finish in that of poetry. During the same period, I was compiling a *Selected Poems* and, as is my habit, obsessively rethinking matters of thought, emotion, and language. These pages are some that lingered there, whatever their true subject.

The Journal of a Few Minutes to Midnight. Saturday, 13 Dec 86. First night in the house on Polk Street. Off the bluff, the gulls swoop and veer, taunting the old man who owns the big house at the edge with his earthiness, his mere flightlessness. Below, the car ferry makes its way in winter-roughened waters. Three sailboats have ventured forth but stay near shore. I understand both motives: the one that made these sailors take to choppy seas and the one that keeps them within easy reach of land. In the BayView, over breakfast, the local men at the next booth agreed that it was a foolish thing to sail out in the current weather. I have just driven three and a half days to reach this small port town on the tip of the Quimper Peninsula, which itself juts out from the better-known Olympic Peninsula. Here, in the far corner of the country, as far as one can go in the contiguous United States from the weight of literary power, I will live for eight months, beginning in the rainy season when the light fails at four in the afternoon and the night lasts sixteen hours. I love it here. For three to four months, the days will be windy and wet, and this town of six thousand, much of it unemployed, will live on its pennies until warmer weather brings in tourist dollars. And I will be counting my pennies, too, trying by sustained attention and solitude to determine for myself the value of my art.

*

21 Dec 86.   The question of what I am up to. I am carving my own face. I am taking responsibility for the furrows on the hillsides and the wheel marks in the grass. I am absorbing all the moisture of a Northwest seaside winter. I am closing the walls of my feelings about the deep, insistent winds that ride the bluff. I am in the distance and at home, hurrying to move and hurrying not to move. I often write, now, some prose on a page of poetry, or some lines on a page of prose. Afterwards, I find I want to keep the lines of poetry and the paragraphs of prose together. There is something about the prose, the more so if it is journal-prose rather than prose-poetry—something (intimacy? the raw?) that lends specific gravity to the poetry. If the foundation of a poet's argument is shabby, a loud style and a skillful use of interval can distract the reader from basic considerations. Prose, however—at least the kind of journal-prose I am thinking of —is so properly and obviously the home of sustained attention and loyalty to argument that the poets of theory and willful imprecision must avoid it. In any case, the key to William Carlos Williams' "triadic stanza" is the sentence. The essence of the poetic sentence is the phrase as it holds hands with the line. And the secret that contains the poem made of sentences composed of phrases distributed in lines is just this: prose was always poetry. Today, prose has the greater freedom to be poetry, because poetry is the victim of its own conventions. Most poems today are written to sound like poems; hence, written according to vaguely understood, ill-defined conventions of theme, development, what constitutes a beginning of a poem, what constitutes an ending, how does a poem sound and proceed, etc. It would be a happier and more productive circumstance if poets tried to write bad poems, without being silly or nonsensical. For then every move made by the poet to make the poem less like other poems would only make the poem more and more interesting. One must constantly understand the hidden rules of poetry so as to better violate them. There is no hope for the numbers on the pages. And it is always the hottest day of the year for the globe of the world that sits on a table underneath a lamp. So much is the constant rain outdoors against the artificial suns inside. The white balls of light flood my plate and my page. If the intention of such circumstance is to keep at least a few thoughts from leaving prematurely, then circumstance must be given its due, and the prose kept by the poetry to absorb much of the otherwise blinding light.

*

25 Dec 86. It's a yo-yo life at the end of one's fingertips. All bitterness (just an example) is of the emotions. It, and its raucous pals— good fellows all—live in the biology of the blood, in the chemistry of the body. The mind knows better. It can say, "I am angry," but it can also say, "I understand." Thought, I think, is of the electricity of the body, the binary jungle of the brain. Thoughts are not threatening. Censorship is not aimed at thought, although it *thinks* it is, but at the emotions. Mobs aren't a response to dialectics but to flags.

My question: is it possible to live among emotions—a life at the end of one's fingertips—as one can live among one's thoughts, without the chemical extravagances of helplessness and cruelty? Surely it is a matter of conditioning and, too, of abandoning one's willfulness. When Williams writes that there is "only one solution: to write carelessly so that nothing that is not green will survive," he has caught on to the limitation, the fatal flaw, in willful aesthetics, in any theory of writing, in any method that claims to know good from bad, appropriate from inappropriate. I would go further, as the woman of *Paterson* does, the young Marcia Nardi who writes to "Doctor P." Her language simmers. Her whole being is pressed against the glass. Williams has it in him to be like her. In his secret life, he dances naked before the mirror in his north room. He would go further, but he is not in a position to. He cannot fall far enough. He cannot fall at all. To live more in the emotions is to fall. One must literally take on weight. The ethereal life of the brain, with its vain assertions of purity, is like water on all sides. It looks as if one could simply step through, but the surface tension is very great. If anyone can break through so thick a glassy wall, there will be a flood made up of unrehearsed emotion, a cascading greater than Niagara's, on which one's being must drop to the very bottom of a gorge before a single thought can intervene. Williams instinctively knew the power of the falls, central to *Paterson*. *Paterson* without the falls is a silly metaphor for critics. If Williams could only have been that young woman, and himself as well! He wanted to be. He came as close as he could to the idea, incorporating her letters into the body of his poem, making her a part of the dance of his poetry. Now I would apply his discovery to the emotions: only one solution: to feel (live) carelessly so that nothing that is not life-giving will survive. It takes a certain helplessness. It takes a fall. And sometimes there is no music present to put a limit on solitude.

*

25–26 Dec 86. Journal of the Perverse Nature of Ice. Watch for it, says the sign next to the highway, "Watch for Ice." That's black ice, those otherwise glassy irregular shapes that look like shadows on the black roadway during the day. Now, it is necessary to note that many have traveled the line to reach the paragraph, but it is rare that anyone successfully travels the paragraph to reach the line. The novelist who ends up as a poet began as a poet. It is at least as necessary now to establish the difference between loving and believing in. In the middle of a busy street, against the traffic, a young woman stopped to say that she was unable to decide which she wanted most: to be loved or to know the truth. For the moment, she wanted only orgasm and repose. As for the truth . . . as another woman said to me during a walk in the woods, "There are people who get it, and there are people who don't." The first of these became an experimental prose-poet of delightful, yet frivolous, sensuality. The second became a formalist whose meters and rhymes served with great skill the poetic conventions of intellectual detail and regret. I loved her for her laugh, not for her sense of humor. Thus, it may be worth noting that the headlights of an approaching car as it climbs a hill under a fog only slightly risen above the roadway light up the mist with an angelic glow, as if a pocket of illumination were soon to descend to earth, bearing belief and love, arriving like lightning inside a white cloud. And across the long, low stretch of the bridge on the Hood Canal, one day turns into another on the clock, and the first news of the day leaves a series of accidents in the air.

*

12 Jan 87. I had forgotten, living for decades in a house with children, on a neighborhood street along a bus run, in a town of students and their renewable sources of energy, how much less sound there had been throughout my youth. Here, I am reminded. Nights, Polk Street suffers little interruption. My neighbor says she can sometimes hear the thump of the foundry at work at the edge of town. Once, three sonic booms in quick succession startled me into thinking that someone at the door was using his forearms to knock. Most of what one hears, however, is indoors, some of it in the inner ear. The jabbing sounds of rainwater falling from the roof and the rush of wind encircle the rooms of isolated light in which I am awake. Outside, I have heard the closed-lips hum of a float plane easing down into the bay by the boat yard, and the sizzle of the street light. And this night I must include the would-be voice of a clouded moon flat against Earth's shell of vapor. Inside, there is the nasal hum of electricity making heat and ice, the clucking of metal panels inside the baseboard heaters as they warm up at irregular intervals, the syncopated creaking of a hinge on a door left ajar. I know there to be the usual musketry and bee-sounds of the actual inner ear: source of dream imagery. In moments of whole quiet, the shell of my ear catches the

full-wave sound of a universal ocean. For the rest, here is a resonant cavity, a chamber of indeterminate frequency, the body of a man temporarily inhabited.

In poetry, what is sometimes mistakenly called "silence" is, in fact, interval. Cage, attributing his sense of composition to a remark by Thoreau: "Music is continuous; only listening is intermittent." A silence that is not an interval will be available to all of us soon enough. We interrupt it with our lives. I would prefer a poetry that knows this without taking it for its subject. Give us the drone of death, and we will work enough variations in the higher notes to make you forget there was ever a night in which you were asleep.

Wrapped in the cold, now the clock in the courthouse tower lets loose its twelve solid bell tones—loud tonight, heavy tonight, falling with the weight of a hammer upon an anvil. The sound could be the clanking of a broken machine except for the music of it, made to ring out the emptiness of its shape.

Here's a jar to drop a pencil into, and again.

*

31 Jan 87. The ceaseless wind of a day has blown down the beach grass, but a rose blooms on the calm side of the tree line. I continue to work best mornings just after rising and late nights, while the late afternoon as the light fails will do for willful beginnings that can be given their heads. Morning and late night—times closest to sleep and dreams. Time and no-time connected at both ends. Just so, rhetoric without sensory equivalents becomes the distortion of runaway grammar. The logic of it "makes sense," but the sense is wrong. Hence, the importance of the physical world in poetry, the lasting influence of imagery, the apparent sincerity of the story, etc. But the sentences that contain these things lie just because they are sentences. Nature is not a list, yet nature contains no prepositions, articles, conjunctions, and the like. What some people call "the irrational" must needs be placed among the rhetorically sound and the rational to complete the truth of life. Hence, the shine of the violin must accompany the dull sleeve of the musician as he saws a continuum of sound into portions of pitch and length. Adagio of thumbtacks. Andante of the slide rule. Allegro of the turning compass. No poem will stand up to the unprogrammatic in music unless it first soak itself in an unselective yet localized paste to which all adheres. For this, rain will suffice. Inside, the musicians tune up against the moisture in the air. Outside, crows and gulls stand in under eaves, hiking up their wings now and then without persuasion.

*

1 Feb 87. High tides, wind and rain have undercut two waterfront houses on Vashon Island. I often saw the same thing on the East Coast: on Fire Island, homes built on stilts to let the dunes move underneath, one day after a storm out in the water on their poles and the soft ground underneath them sinking lower. The concert pianist who survived certain death in a plane crash (broken back, severed aorta) returns to his music by way of Bach (unable to employ his pedal foot), saying that now he is most interested in "direct communication." There in a nutshell is the dilemma of experiment. Two things must go on at the same time—that which is experimental and that which is not—so that the experiment may go unnoticed. The conjunction "and" and its reverse "d-n-a" are a fair representation of the related and the discrete. Poetry has seen heavy labors to connect all things, to represent the universe, to mouth the sound that contains all other sounds, to calculate the transformation of thing into image, image into symbol, and symbol into archetype. In conversation, we are able to look to the side and back again. We are able to follow the red thread of our words while we recognize other things to say which are not, existing as they do inside our minds, interruptions of the moment but whole components of it. The poem, so far exteriorized in the convention of the poetry reading, must retain for itself the irregular, the aside, those phrases and sentences which seem to be spare parts for other pieces. The selectivity of poetry has been identified with a "normal" range of association and logic, whereas sufficient force may, in time, extend the range of normalcy. The notion of "closure" has not been helpful. After the fact, in any case. Tie a knot in your lasso and see what you catch. Those people who got out just before the mud slid and the bank fell spoke to the camera as if they felt saved. Money can make you dumb, but not *that* dumb. Direct communication: alive or dead. Meanwhile, the lunch meat gets slippery, the milk thickens, yesterday's bread already blackening—just before the whole house falls to its knees before nature.

*

10 Feb 87. Journal of the Night of Blue Light. Pairs of three-second blasts from a foghorn separate the evening. Such a small town still that elementary school teachers bring their students to the post office to learn to mail a letter. The long line snakes past the bulletin board and up to the stamp window. I prefer this post office way of picking up one's mail at a box in the lobby to home delivery on someone else's schedule. Small-towner myself, I only regret that there is but one delivery—and that sorted by 9 a.m. Letters are the reason the woods quake when a highway is extended. Letters open the eyes of the mermaid nailed to the prow of the boat roughed up by distance. Well, one day when I was wondering if bird song would ever be my song, an old curse came to me: the curse of leaving. First, losing; then, leaving. I had it wrong when I thought that little losses are the forerunners of a final loss. In truth, losing is the preparation for leaving. We have trouble with the concept of leaving. Our language stops at the thought of death. Our sentences depend on an unending future. The vanity of clocks. So a letter gains importance as words left behind. In it, the past coils back around the present. As the years pass, one gives up without losing touch. The blue light of an evening is a curiosity one can hold in the globe of an eye. The shouts of the ship's horn can lie in the chamber of an ear like a sleeper who turns periodically in his sleep and, as he moves, smooths the sheet before him with his hand. Is it preposterous to liken these things to one another? Then the glass sea is preposterous and compassion impossible, and it is ridiculous to carve eyes in the head of a wooden mermaid. The lowest recorded temperature of all time is still something to write home about. Next to a thermometer, with its ruler of discipline, the face of a clock is a wheel of vain permission. I do not ask of a letter that it seem to suspend the passing of time, but only that it be aware that it has been sent to a future with the big hands of an Antarctica. Of all blues, it is the blue of ice that best matches the night.

*

15 Feb 87. Finally, I always feel more alive for writing, and writing in paragraphs goes on longer than writing in lines. Shall we call this an aesthetic? Tonight the light from the Navy refueling station on Indian Island is pinned against a low strip of cloud. The moon is white-faced to be seen through those thin fabrics that make the sun's light seem to stream away to reach people. It is not true. The moon hasn't cried since 1954. All the long tears of its defeat have fallen into places no one now remembers or would understand. The moon was the invincible cache of our romance.

*

Undated pages.   Already (three days) the manuscript so many years in the making seems far away and lifeless to him. He means it: lifeless! First, one's children are always home. Next, they leave occasionally. By seventeen, they are seldom home when anyone else is awake. Still it seems as if they are there—tangibly present—when they are not. But let them leave, actually move their bed and board, even to the other side of the same small town, and they are as gone as a stone thrown into a river, the memory of them as wistful and hopeless as a brilliant musical chord disassembling in the wind. How new our lives are when we are left with only ourselves—those of us of whom intimacy has produced one person where there were two to begin. How we struggle to regain the old life. We would, if the truth be known, crush the spark that took them from us if we could have them back. We would gladly live in the ashes of the house that burned. Not to do so will take the effort of an Houdini under water wearing a strait jacket, but it will not be a trick. It will be a birth—a bloody, unlovable birth defying the laws of hygiene.

THE BOOK OF THE DEAD MAN (#1)

1. *About the Dead Man*

The dead man thinks he is alive when he sees blood in his stool.
Seeing blood in his stool, the dead man thinks he is alive.
He thinks himself alive because he has no future.
Isn't that the way it always was, the way of life?
Now, as in life, he can call to people who will not answer.
Life looks like a white desert, a blaze of today in which nothing
   distinct can be made out, seen.
To the dead man, guilt and fear are indistinguishable.
The dead man cannot make out the spider at the center
   of its web.
He cannot see the eyelets in his shoes and so wears them
   unlaced.
He reads the large type and skips the fine print.
His vision surrounds a single tree, lost as he is in a forest.

From his porcelain living quarters, he looks out at a fiery plain.
His face is pressed against a frameless window.
Unable to look inside, unwilling to look outside, the man who is
    dead is like a useless gift in its box waiting.
It will have its yearly anniversary, but it would be wrong to call
    it a holiday.

2. *More About the Dead Man*

The dead man can balance a glass of water on his head without
    trembling.
He awaits the autopsy on the body discovered on the beach
    beneath the cliff.
Whatever passes through the dead man's mouth is expressed.
Everything that enters his mouth comes out of it.
He is willing to be diagnosed, as long as it won't disturb
    his future.
Stretched out, he snaps back like elastic.
Rolled over, he is still right-side-up.
When there is no good or bad, no useful or useless, no up, no
    down, no right way, no perfection, then okay it's not necessary
    that there be direction: up is down.
The dead man has the rest of his life to wait for color.
He finally has a bird's-eye view of the white hot sun.
He finally has a complete sentence, from his head to his feet.
He is, say, America, but he will soon be, say, Europe.
It will be necessary merely to cross the ocean and pop up in the new
    land, and the dead man doesn't need to swim.
It's the next best thing to talking to people in person.

Rita Dove

I couldn't live without my notebooks. I collect them like fetishes: my favorites are black-and-red bound notebooks that come in a variety of sizes from the People's Republic of China. Into my notebook goes anything that is interesting enough to stop me in my tracks—the slump of a pair of shoulders in a crowd, a newspaper entry, a recipe, "chewy" words like raga-muffin or Maurice. I refer to my notes (on my desk right now are over fifteen different notebooks) at the start of each writing day: sometimes I copy several entries onto a sheet of lined note-book paper just to see how they work together. Poems evolve slowly, in spurts and sputters, on these college-ruled pages; a small stack of notebooks is always at the ready for browsing. For me, it all begins with a notebook: it is the well I dip into for that first clear, cool drink.

1980

Strike a stone
to see if it's thinking of water.

*

IVORY GATE

Tom sleepwalking—when are you going to take me fishing?

I love you and you (don't) love me
It is not exactly like
drinking the sea.

Here we go round the
coconut tree
It is not exactly like
drinking the sea.

*

THE PROJECTS.

Washing lines of the poor—the banners.

      shut you up & out.
      brick, housing art.

*

Arson: houses mysteriously bursting into flame.

      language is identity.

It was hotter: they wanted it hotter.

*

I was so handsome women cried.
I got shot but never died.
        —Cher, "A Cowboy's Work Is Never Done"

*

The buffalo faces the storm from the west;
therefore its hair is thicker in front,
and he gets out of the storm quicker.

*

We drove through olive
    fields quartz and dust,

their petticoats hiked up
above our heads; small reward
for the assiduous, small gain
for aesthetics, this dive
     thru butterflies
& dust.

*

Purse as womb.

*

A porcelain cup overturned on a plate: an iridescent igloo.

*

1987–89

"When you begin to write, you're in love with the language, with the act of creation, with yourself partly; but as you go on, the writing— if you follow it—will take you places you never intended to go and show you things you would never otherwise have seen. I began as a profoundly apolitical writer, but then I began to do what all novelists and some poets do: I began to describe the world around me."

—Margaret Atwood, in an interview
with *Ms.* magazine, January, 1987.

*

Jerusalem as interpreted by Zali: 12/4/87

First to the graves from 8 B.C., behind the Scottish Hospice. Incredibly chaotic traffic. Z. explains that the valley between us and the Old City was called *Gehenna*, or Hell, and was the place where human sacrifices were made. The graves, vaults carved from rock, are on a slope called Kebet (?), or the Shoulder of Hell. There are light bulb–shaped hollows for the heads, and a vault situated between an L-shaped cadaver cache that had been filled with treasures—vases, urns, oil lamps, etc.

Here you can see the absence of bodies more vividly than the bodies themselves must have been. The entire area is littered with shit— literally curlicues of shit, garbage, Pepsi ringtops, plastic bags in all colors. And then one looks straight up into the blond foundations of the hospice, its stalwart honey-colored cross on top.

Zali tells us about his personal relationship to the Burnt House, discovered in the Old City in the Jewish Quarter, directly across from the Wailing Wall. Many many meters below today's surface, a ruin of a house was found—carbon-dating sets its destruction at 70 A.D., the same year that the Romans destroyed the Temple. Found were the implements of daily life, plus an arm bone of a man, plus a sword that, judging from its position, was thrust into the body belonging to the arm. And a nameplate was found, carved into stone with the name of a priestly family mentioned in the chronicles of Josephus Flavius.

Zali says he learned about the Burnt House upon his return from Berkeley, and he feels as if he is fated, that he carries the Burnt House inside him, that his communion with 70 A.D. and Josephus Flavius has been burnt into him.

This is the direct time axis that only Jerusalem has—eons piled on top of eons, so many eons that it is impossible to fence them off and charge admission. Hence these sights are the true discoveries, *real* artifacts at dirt level, clear and clean as the shapes of bodies outlined in the rubble and donkey droppings.

(The idea of the Burnt House, a plunge into History, a telescoping of time on the one hand and the smoldering grief that inures on the other—this is contained in the appelation:
The Burnt House—
a heartbreak.

The Burnt House: a rebellion of a neighborhood—
Firetraps on fire, determined to turn into their names.)

Then we go to the newly built promenade in Talpiot with its magnificent view of Jerusalem, where one understands the phrase *Jerusalem, mountains around her*—for the Old City (which is the only Jerusalem) is surrounded, set off by hills, like a jewel that draws all sight to it: it shines. Here, Z says, you can see what makes Jerusalem different, for it is a city that draws its inhabitants inward—the very setting is a centripetal force drawing all thought, all contemplation, inward. A city of introspection . . . whereas Tel Aviv looks outward, toward the sea. Z tells us of the time he flew over Mt. Scopus in a plane while on reserve duty. As a professor, he had always simply driven up the hill, parked and gone into the university; the hill was part of the city, of his daily life. From the air, however, he could see that Mount Scopus (named so because it was the vantage point citizens—including Josephus Flavius—climbed up to in order to look down upon the Temple, which in those days had been covered in gold) was the last ridge before desert, desert, desert. From the air he realized that Jerusalem was *in* the desert, that it *was* a desert town. And the original Israelites who had moved in and built the first temple, were a desert culture—they didn't like nature with its trees and bushes, they didn't like sex or good food—they liked meat without the sauce.

So Z calls forth another axis in Israel—the cultural axis. Tel Aviv to Jerusalem, a mere 70 kilometers but really a swing from Mediterranean to desert.

Another axis is the nature axis, north to south, from vegetation to barrenness. And so Jerusalem (my interpretation) is the original Axis Mundi, the earth rotating on a spit like a *Baumkuchen* that grows crust after crust.

*

Jean Follain: often had nightmares that he could have been born two years later and would not have remembered the time before the first World War . . . when the archetypes were clear.

    a) The soldiers would meet people who had experienced this great calm, and for whom the world made no sense anymore.

    b) The soldiers, though, come from a world without a backyard (back porch); they know a world that is senseless.

Don't forget all the plays of colloquial language.

Check book for direct quotes from soldiers.

You must learn French.

—The March to the Rhine
—Lt. James Europe's Jazz Band

Our terrible century (W.S. Merwin)

The Romans were a race of travellers/tourists

*

Ars Poetica—"Build a cell in your mind, from which you can never escape."   —Catherine of Siena

*

Overheard on stewardesses' P.A. system, in between flights—Phoenix-Dallas-LaGuardia:
    Pilot: Ladies, we're ready to board now, we'll need two pluckers up front. (Pause) Ladies *and* gentlemen . . .
    Chief Stewardess: It's show time.

*

Ample make this bed
Make this bed in awe
In it wait till Judgement break
Excellent and fair

Be its mattress straight
Be its pillow round
Let no sunrise yellow noise
Interrupt this ground
            —Emily Dickinson

(Written out by Bruce Weigl during a heated discussion at the April 1988 AWP board meeting)

*

"Christianity is, from its inception (Paul), the romantic religion. The cult of love in the West is an aspect of the cult of suffering—suffering as the supreme token of seriousness (the paradigm of the Cross)."
                        —Susan Sontag
                        The Artist as Exemplary Sufferer

"The writer is the man who discovers the use of suffering in the economy of art—as the saints discovered the utility and necessity of suffering in the economy of salvation."   —Susan Sontag, *ibid.*

*

Title for a section (poetry)—"The low grounds of sorrow" from
G. W. Carver, referring to the poor farmland given to the poor blacks.

*

14th c.—Venetians cut down Yugoslavian forest for their fleets—
which destroyed the land (topsoil blown away) and changed the
climate.

*

Ozone layer

Now you see it
Now you don't

The glass is tipped
The plug pulled

Afghani—knitting is too intricate, too microsopic and small town/
world.

Terraces of the Doge—from far they look like quiltwork, but they,
too, are more like knitting, weaving the rocks without mortar into a
wall to stand 400 years.

And the wake of the motorboat
braiding, braiding
And the world tipped upside
down, the plug pulled,
draining out its vital fluid
            (ozone)

*

Afghani Nomad Coat

A beastiary
A breviary

*

Jet lag, and the home space
stapled onto the bow of the world;
each desert papery bloom a fluttery paste-up,
purple trumpets of sage,
tiny mustard pockets of sage purses

*

As my daughter said on the way to K-Mart: "Everyone was inside
someone else once."

*

[Thomas Hardy] told a friend that he wanted to avoid "the jeweled
life"; his awkwardness, often an ostentation, laboriousness, was both
natural and cultivated. He is the first of the poets, so numerous now,
who are suspicious of writing well.

*

. . . he said that "Art is a disproportioning of realities, to show more
clearly the features that matter in those realities."

OZONE

> . . . Does the cosmic
> space we dissolve into taste of us, then?
> —Rilke, *The Second Elegy*

Everything civilized will whistle before
it rages—kettle of the asthmatic,
the aerosol can and its immaculate awl
perforating the dome of heaven.

We wire the sky for comfort;
we thread it through our lungs for a perfect fit.
We've arranged this calm, though it is constantly
unraveling.

> *Where does it go then,*
> *atmosphere suckered up*
> *an invisible flue?*
> *How can we know where it goes?*

A gentleman pokes blue through a buttonhole.

> *Rising, the pulse*
> *sings:*
> *memento mei*

The sky is wired so it won't fall down.
Each house notches into its neighbor
and then the next, the whole row scaldingly white,
unmistakable as a set of bared teeth.

> *to pull the plug*
> *to disappear into an empty bouquet*

If only we could lose ourselves
in the wreckage of the moment! Forget
where we stand, dead center, and
look up, look up,
track a falling star . . .

> now you see it

> now you don't

Stephen Dunn

In my case, function followed form. For Christmas, some eight or nine years ago, my wife gave me a small, handsomely bound notebook, and I became a note keeper. Before, I'd jot things down on scraps of paper, and eventually lose or misplace them. Mostly I'd trust my memory, which was also a bad idea. But this notebook and its blank, unlined pages was a kind of invitation. And it was small. It would accept small things.

My first entries were the pithy sayings of others, largely taken from my reading, some from conversation. Gradually, I interspersed notions of my own. I was and am both collector and utilitarian; I liked being my own Bartlett, but I'd keep an eye toward how this might spur a poem, how that might be used in an essay. It became a writer's day book—a place to record both what presented itself to me and snatches of what was on my mind. I had no diarist's fidelity to periodicity.

Because the majority of my entries are the writings of others (seemingly inappropriate en masse for this occasion), I've put together a smattering of those mixed with a smattering of my own. In a sense, of course, I understand that everything is my own—in the way we are known by the stories we choose to tell or the art we keep in our living rooms. What follows is offered in the spirit of someone open and vain enough to let you in his house. It's possible that a part of him always had you in mind.

One perception must immediately lead to another perception, as Olson said, is another way of saying that a poem should be interesting *all* the way through.

*

When people praise a poem that I can't understand I always think they're lying.

*

The problem with most nature poetry is that it doesn't sufficiently acknowledge Nature's ugliness and perversity. It is as falsifying as most poems about happy marriages.

*

Poems about happy marriages need to be mysterious. A successful happy-marriage poem, like a happy marriage itself, is a triumph over the unlikely. You must write it with the inventive care with which you would write science fiction.

*

Every male has a stake in feminism. Obviously it is not a good situation for anybody when one sex has earned the greater right to complain. And don't happy women tend to be generous? Self-interest, if not basic decency, should convince men that a fair-minded feminism is also their liberation. All of us, finally, free enough to be scoundrels.

*

Poets who defy making sense and do it deliberately and often brilliantly (as Ashbery can) *are* making a kind of sense, and may be extending the range of what poetry can do, though they ensure that poetry's audience will be small and chiefly academic: i.e., composed of people inclined to equate a puzzle with that which is meaningful.

*

Mystifications protect power. Mysteries protect the sacred.

—John Berger

*

Authenticity in literature does not come from a writer's personal honesty. . . . Authenticity comes from a single faithfulness: that to the ambiguity of experience. . . . If a writer is not driven by a desire for the most demanding verbal precision, the true ambiguity of events escapes him.   —John Berger

*

When I've had an interesting or haunting dream, I know I'd better not try to write about it until it has begun to bore me a little.

*

A perfectly modulated sentence, one that discloses its information at just the right pace, is a victory over what is crude and easy and care-less about the way we think and feel. A paragraph of such sentences has the sufficiency of a well-made sculpture. About its content, we're likely to say, "That's true." What we mean is how persuasively the meaning is being displayed and held.

*

When a poem's rhythm is right, the body is saying to the head, Good job, you haven't falsified my role in this enterprise.

*

After the superb dance concert (Momix) the other night, I felt so elated and enlarged that I knew what I should expect of poetry readings.

*

"Sometimes," said Whitey Ford, the great Yankee curveballer, "you need to put one right down the middle." He was speaking of sur-prises. I've always thought that poets, especially abstruse poets, could profit by his remark.

*

I dream of an art so transparent that you can look through and see the world.   —Stanley Kunitz

*

Finally, what I want from poetry is akin to what Flaubert wanted from novels. He thought they should make us dream. I want a poem, through its precisions and accuracies, to make me remember what I know, or what I might have known if I hadn't been constrained by convention or habit.

*

In a sense, my father was a Willy Loman. He was my introduction to the pathetic and to sadness and heroism. I don't know how I escaped Biff's escapism, his self-destructiveness. But I did. Perhaps it was because when things went bad I still had the esteem of the schoolyard. For a long important while I didn't have to think, except as an athlete does. I just played ball. Sweet moves and the ball in the hole. The pure poetry that satisfies when you're young.

*

My maternal grandfather's name was Montefiore Fleischman. He was a storyteller, a lover of women, and, depending on how many mistakes we allow someone before his stature is lessened, perhaps a great man. He had the kind of large personality that sometimes can tolerably house even a major flaw. In his sixties, he read a novel and drank a bottle of gin every night. Arthritic, it was how he achieved sleep.

*

The erotics of memory.   —Joyce Carol Oates

*

He remembered a great deal, but the memory was uninteresting, tedious, and he was even a little annoyed at its tenacity.

—Anita Brookner

*

The invented person, borrowed from the real—abstracted, isolated —is the person we finally know, or feel we know. I make myself up from everything I am, or could be. For many years I was more desire than fact. When I stop becoming, that's when I worry.

*

Too many poets are insufficiently interested in story. Their poems could be improved if they gave in more to the strictures of ficiton: the establishment of a clear dramatic situation, and a greater awareness that first-person narrators are also characters and must be treated as such by their authors. The true lyric poet, of course, is exempt from this. But many poets wrongly think they are lyric poets.

*

I hate good taste. Those who say they have it exhibit its opposite.

*

As Kafka put it, there is an infinite amount of hope, but not for us. This statement really contains Kafka's hope; it is the source of his radiant serenity.   —Walter Benjamin

*

The world, finally, tries to rob us in lots of ways. I like poems to do a bit of taking back for us.   —Terry Blackhawk

*

Fall seven times, stand up eight.   —Japanese proverb

*

Edward Hopper said that "painting will have to deal more fully and less obliquely with life and nature's phenomena before it can again become great." So will poetry. Yet that won't be enough. It will require compositional skills and angles of vision equal to Hopper's.

*

The tyranny of the actual begins.   —Philip Roth

*

The highway is the road most people travel, often obliviously. I like going off onto the side roads, getting lost a little, finding my way back. This is how to better appreciate the highway. The mysteries of the side roads interest me, but the mysteries of the main road interest me more. I'd like my work to be the eyes and ears of such traveling.

*

Lovers are unreliable witnesses, which is why reliability is not always to be desired.

*

Mickey Rivers, a former Yankee center fielder, when asked if he was worried about being traded, said something I try to remember to live by when things are going bad. "Ain't no sense in worrying about things you got control over, 'cause if you got control over them, ain't no sense worrying. And there ain't no sense worrying about things you got no control over, 'cause if you got no control over them, ain't no sense worrying."

*

Lewis Hyde's book *The Gift* made me, for a while, more generous. For about two weeks, I wanted to give everything away. Barry Lopez's book *Arctic Dreams*, equally moral and powerful, made me want to write graceful yet heavily freighted sentences. I value both books, but I'll return more often to *Arctic Dreams*.

*

I don't think I'd complain if I were overrated.

*

I believe everything you tell me, but I know that it will all turn out differently.   —Henry Miller

*

I don't trust people until I know what they love. If they cannot admit to what they love, or in fact love nothing, I cannot take even their smartest criticisms seriously.

*

Can I change myself with some discoloration, that unclearness I despise in the work of other men? And what should I avoid? Anything contrived. Anything less than vital.   —John Cheever

*

Summertime, the children older now, seventeen and twenty, their noise more quiet than in the past, but noise nonetheless. I realize how comforting those sounds are, the sounds that for years I complained about and worked to. I should admit it, silence has given me more trouble than my children have, though I love silence. Tonight, here in my room, something will come, I'm confident, the old music of my children outside my room; working music.

*

One of the big differences between a genuine sage and a preacher is gaiety.   —Henry Miller

*

R. P. Blackmur on Wallace Stevens: . . . erudite, by which I mean intensely careful of effects.

*

What does it mean if you know that a particular disappointment or sadness in your life cannot, relatively speaking, compete for emotional attention with a normal day for a normal person in the Sudan, in Bosnia? Do you write the poem of disappointment differently?

*

If we've thought or felt it and it continues to nag, hang around, or especially if we fear it, it's perhaps the impulse with which we should begin our next poem.

*

To be of more than one heart.   —Victoria Hearne

*

We need aesthetic intimacy, not aesthetic distance.
                                                 —William Matthews

*

A story about metaphor: you go into a variety store and find that something you desire, but which you can't articulate very well, is unavailable. The clerk, in fact, says nothing like that exists. You tell him it will exist very soon, it even exists now, but certain connections that need to be made have yet to be made. Reserve a place for it, you tell him, always keep a shelf open, the future will be kind to you.

*

Our lives are, as a rule, spent in the gray zone of relative values and dull half-measures.   —Stanislaw Baranczak

*

It is said that when a mole fails to touch anything with the ends of its whiskers, it develops a neurosis.

*

The often debated rift between abstraction and concretion is, I think, nicely complicated by what Joan Miró said in declining an invitation to join a group of abstract artists. "They ask me into their deserted houses as if the marks I put on canvas did not correspond to a concrete representation of my mind, were not part of the real itself."

*

There's not much that feels better than a firm, urgent No to someone else's big, restrictive Yes. If that someone has power over us, and moreover is an upholder of shibboleths, we are likely also to be frightened by our audacity, cast asea by it, no land in sight. If we are to become ourselves, something like that must happen at least once in our lives. It must be more than mere defiance. It must feel costly. We shouldn't know how we'll get home.

*

In his soul a bit of a clerk.   —Philip Roth

*

To properly affirm a shibboleth, e.g. "Love thy neighbor," suggests a passage, a journey from doubt to clarity, and must presume unlovable neighbors along the way. At the far reaches of insight, wisdom may not be far from corniness. Same idea, different kind of arrival. So much, finally, in the tone.

*

Wendy Cannella, a student, in response to Frost's admonition about free verse: "Tear the net down. Turn the court into a dance floor."

*

Most reckless things are beautiful, just as religions are beautiful because of the strong possibility that they are founded on nothing.
                                                        —John Ashbery

*

It's at this point that literature enters the domain of ethics; it is here that the conflict between the natural and the contrived is introduced, and here that it obtains its heroes and martyrs of *the resistance to the facile*; where virtue is manifested, and sometimes hyprocrisy.
                                                —Paul Valéry on revision

SOME THINGS I WANTED TO SAY TO YOU

If the horse you ride
is blind it's good

that it also be slow,
and please stroke it
a hundred more times than you would
the powerful, dazzling one.

To be generous is one thing,
but there's a clerk in some of us,
quick to say yes.
Worry about the command
in the suggestion.
Worry about smiles, and those men
whose business is business.

There are the joys and enigmas
of an evening alone
to appreciate.
There are always the simple events
of your life
that you might try to convert
into legend.

Did you know
that a good dog in your house
can make you more thoughtful,
even more moral?

And sex without conversation,
sex that's exotic or sleepy . . .
oh don't let anybody tell you
there's a wrong way to have it.

Tell your lovers the world
robs us in so many ways
that a caress is your way
of taking something back.
Tell the dogs and the horses
you love them more than cars.
Speak to everything
would be my advice.

Carolyn Forché

This excerpt, from one of four seasonal notebooks kept during 1991, documents a moment in my struggle to conceive a theory of poetry of witness, as nonrepresentational poetic evidence of the experience of extremity. I was, at the time, writing notes toward an introduction to Against Forgetting: Twentieth-Century Poetry of Witness, *which I had spent the previous decade editing, and which W. W. Norton would publish two years later. At this stage, I was particularly disturbed by the implications of deconstructive thought for the literature of the Holocaust/Shoah. I was also puzzling over the refusal of many American poets and literary critics to engage the political except in reductively ideological terms. I was concerned to establish a sphere of the social or public, between the political institutions of the state and the intimate sphere of quotidian domestic life. It was in this "space," I felt, that poems are read, shared, and known.*

There is a kind of writer appearing with greater and greater frequency among us who witnesses the crimes of his own government against himself and his countrymen. He chooses to explore the intimate subject of a human being's relationship to the state. His is the universe of the imprisoned, the tortured, the disfigured, and the doleful authority for the truth of his work is usually his own body.
. . . So let us propose discussion of the idea that a new art, with its

own rules, is being generated in the twentieth century: the *Lieder* of victims of the state.

—E. L. Doctorow, from a preface to *The Crowned Cannibals* by Reza Baraheni

. . . a state is a human community that (successfully) claims the *monopoly of the legitimate use of physical force* within a given territory. . . . The state is considered the sole source of the "right" to use violence. Hence, "politics" for us means striving to share power or striving to influence the distribution of power, either among states or among groups within a state. . . . When a question is said to be a "political" question, when a cabinet minister or an official is said to be a "political" official, or when a decision is said to be "politically" determined, what is always meant is that interests in the distribution, maintenance, or transfer of power are decisive for answering the questions and determining the decision or the official's sphere of activity. . . . The state is a relation of men dominating men, a relation supported by means of legitimate (i.e. considered to be legitimate) violence.

—Max Weber, "Politics as a Vocation"

These pages document an ongoing struggle within myself. They mark my attempt to conceive of a passionate and committed form of disinterest/universality.

*

The assumption behind the critique of politics is that there is some realm which is never articulated—of common sense or the universal—that is ahistorical, pre-political, and pre-social. The derivation of this is the natural law notion that people exist in the state of nature and they come together to form states. The humanism of the last two centuries, the educational humanism of the academy, has based itself and its authority on these eternal verities, specifically through the ideology of Arnoldianism from the late 1860s onwards. It sees its role as providing standards of excellence and eternal truths, which lead the mind out of its particular interests, toward the generalizable interests, which are the interests of the ruling group at any one time. This can be seen in the interpretation of the Aeneid for the last one hundred and fifty years. What was taken in the 1880s as the great epic of empire, teaching Englishmen and Americans how to administer, became in the 1960s the great anti-imperialist epic.

* * *

In the twentieth century the social and the political have become so intertwined that it is very hard to distinguish them. There is poetry in the twentieth century that does not further a specific ideology, but engages the historical as a critique precisely of the incursions of politics into other forms of association. This poetry, while not political in the narrowest sense, is a protest against the violence perpetrated in the name of politics. Frequently, the critique will adopt the languages of religion, or of a humanistic, universalizing Marxism, especially when it is oppositional—that is to say, Marxism that has not come to power, or in the name of abstract notions like "justice." This poetry creates a public sphere in literature against the depredations of the private by the political, and situates itself in the realm of the social. It wants to use the affections of the private sphere as a way of critiquing the depredations of the political.

One would not want simply to relegate the poetry of witness to the public sphere, as it also situates itself in the intimate (private) and political realm. . . . Extremity marks the poetic imagination; one doesn't live through extreme conditions of this kind without being affected by them, and this mark appears in trace in the subsequent works, which can be read in light of what the author endured, whether or not the works explicitly address the experience.

(Lawrence) Langer identifies something he calls "wounded space." Memory is not only a spring, but also a tomb. He speaks at length about memory as excavation of a ruin, which reminds me of Benjamin. For the witness, he says, the Holocaust is "at once a lived event and a died event." Langer makes distinctions between kinds of memory: tainted, anguished, humiliated. He identifies anguished memory as that which eliminates repose. It pits authenticity against logic, and the failure to connect these two undoes every model and code. . . .

*

(Hannah) Arendt is writing from the point of view of the person speaking. She is interested in the person's speaking and his or her integrity. (Ludwig) Wittgenstein is arguing against epistemology. He's not arguing about the person speaking, but those who are listening. He's saying that those listening have no reason to doubt pain, because pain cannot be known by another person; it can be expressed by pointing or groaning, but there are no criteria for knowledge. His argument is not an argument against skepticism, but that there are moments when the skeptical argument has no place. Arendt and (Elaine) Scarry are speaking existentially, and Wittgenstein is speaking as a philosopher trying to argue against the tyranny of epistemology, and the tyranny of certain notions of knowledge and falliblism. Why do I think Wittgenstein is right? All we have is language. And I know that I do not write from thoughts that already exist, but from thoughts that come to existence as they are inscribed. What would it mean to say that you have thoughts before you have language? Freud maintains that the unconscious is pre-linguistic, that there is no language in the unconscious, that it's only when things come to consciousness that they acquire language. So it might be true that we have thoughts that are pre-linguistic—however, *then* we are using the word "thought" for all mental processes, and that might be inaccurate. Conscious thought—how can you think a conscious thought that is not linguistic? Or is not shaped like a language? I don't think you can. So that's why I think that Wittgenstein is right. The emphasis is on looking at the words on the page, rather than trying to re-create a pre-existent thought that served as the motive force for the words on the page. That frees us from the metaphysics of worrying about that which we cannot know, which is what the author intended to do. The author intended to *write*. In other words, the notion of intentionality is dissolved if you emphasize the words on the page.

*

To argue completely against moments of nobility would be to concede everything to the dark time. One can celebrate the power of resistance to degradation without saying that degradation is productive. One sees in the nobility, in the moments of altruism, something that is very beautiful because hard won, without having then to sing paeans to the human spirit. The very human spirit that rises up in the concentration camps is also the human spirit that *created* the camps. Perhaps these separate issues are occluded when we speak about such generalized abstractions as "the human spirit." I think this is what Arendt tried to do in *Eichmann in Jerusalem*. In that book, Arendt's question is, "Why is it that some people become Nazis, and other people hide Jews?" There is nothing specifically altruistic about the human spirit. Rather, the three nations that saved the Jews, or tried to—Bulgarians, the Danes and the Italians—all did so for different reasons. The Danes because the Jews were citizens of

Denmark, and they saw in the Jews fellow citizens. According to Arendt—and if her explanation is an interesting one politically for the Danes, it is somewhat feeble for the Italians (because of their "humanity" and three thousand years of civilization), and she has no idea why the Bulgarians did it. This is not a weakness on Arendt's part. In fact it is one of her strengths that she admits that when these things happen, they usually happen in groups, not in individuals. Arendt sees resistance as *contagious*, as she sees complicity. They are both contagious, and we don't know why.

There *is* a humanity toward which we aspire. Eichmann was unwilling to be *human*, that is to say, to live with other people. He was unwilling to accept alterity, which for Arendt is the definition of the human. Eichmann's pathology was a weak narcissism that couldn't imagine the alterity of others, and that's why he's given over completely to cliché. Arendt's is a very strong form of existentialism. For her, to be "human" means to do two things—there are only two things that humans can do that other animals can't do: one is to persuade, and the other is to act, on the basis of that persuasion, and that for Arendt is the essence of politics. So that to be "human" is to live in non-violent political relations with other people. That is the *telos* of the human. For Terrence (Des Pres), the "human" is a "God-term" which he doesn't define.

*

How can we know another person's pain? I'll return tomorrow with arguments against even thinking about that question. Perhaps the word "know" means something different in the language game of epistemology and in the question of pain, or what happens in other minds. If I understand it correctly, one of the more interesting aspects of Wittgenstein's critique of metaphysics is that he shows that there are different meanings of the word "know," specifically in relation to pain. Stanley Cavell then proposes that, in fact, pain is not something that can be known, but only something that can be ac-*know*ledged. I must do more research on this. The arguments about whether you can know another's experience, or the claim made by witnesses that their experience is unknowable, avoids the issue of why it is we have witness in the first place. The literature of witness is one in which the questions concern authenticity and response, rather than knowledge, which is very different. The point is not whether the other persons *know* what this pain was, in other words "experience" it, but rather that they are forced into a position where they have to respond to it.

There is a problem in the question of testimony with the notion of literary language "expressing" extreme experience, and the distinction between this representation and the experience itself.

It is representation, but it's re-presentation, not re-experience. When you enter into the public sphere of writing, or the social sphere of poetry, what you are doing is demanding a response from the reader as much as attempting to re-create something that happened once.

> Man, pushed to the very limit of his condition, found once more in the written word a last rampart against the loneliness of annihilation. His words, elaborate or awkward, cadenced or disorderly, were inspired only by the will to express, to communicate, and to transmit truth. They were formulated in the worst conditions possible, were spread by impoverished means and dangerous by definition. Those words were opposed to the lie fabricated and maintained by powerful groups which had gigantic technology at their disposal and who were protected by unbounded violence.
> —Michael Borwicz, *Les Ecrits des condamnés à mort sous l'occupation allemande* (1939–1945)

These works *aren't* representational. I'll argue for the examination of witness as a *representational* mode of language as evidence, and as a way of thinking about repetition which is not governed by difference, but is founded upon a genuine sameness, that is, the original event *recurs* in the language present before us. I'm interested in the impress of extremity upon the poetic imagination and the ways in which these events incise consciousness.

> What the poem translates, I propose we call experience, on condition that the word be taken literally—from Latin, *experiri*: the risky crossing . . . , and this is why one can refer, strictly speaking, to a poetic existence, if existence it is that perforates a life and tears it, at times putting us beside ourselves.
> —Philippe Lacoue-Labarthe

This is where I find the trace, and this is where the event recurs. Witnesses beget witnesses. Evidence begets evidence. A poem by Celan is evidence of what happened to him.

> Writing leaves the trace of an original disaster which was not experienced in the first person precisely since it ruined this first person, reduced it to a ghostlike status, to being a "me without me."
> —Claire Nouvet, *An Impossible Response* . . .

One thing remained attainable, close and unlost amidst all the losses: language.

Language was not lost, in spite of all that happened. But it had to go through its own responselessness, go through horrible silences, go through the thousand darknesses of death-bringing speech. It went through and offered no words for what happened: but it went through these events. . . .

I have attempted to write poems in this language, in those years and in the years that followed—in order to speak, in order to orient myself, in order to explore where I was and where I was yet to go, in order to define reality for myself.
> —Paul Celan, Bremen, 1958

*

Perhaps the strength of deconstruction in America has been its demystification of very simplistic notions of representation, but, as Wittgenstein shows us, there are many different kinds of representation, and representation is not a fixed relation between two things that is already established, but one that keeps being re-established in new relations that aren't fixed. So that relation of word to world, to say that language doesn't express the world is, I think, primitive. I think this is using a very limited notion of representation in order to construct its paradoxes. In the end, language expresses everything that can be expressed. One of the great strengths of deconstruction and of modern philosophy and critical theory has been to make richer and more problematic our understanding of what representation *can* be, rather than seeing what representation *is*. I think this is important. The real wisdom of deconstruction is that it shows our notions of representation, and our representation to ourselves are in fact very rich. There are many different notions of how representation works, and many different notions of representation. And what might be necessary first is not to divide them into dichotomous binarisms, representational vs. non-representational, but say if all of this linguistic material is representational, then how does it work? In other words, *thick descriptions* of representations, rather than a realm of the non-representational. Although that is an important critical gesture, it keeps us locked in the binarism. It might be more interesting to say there are many different modes of representation, not all of them have the same relation to the reader, and not all have the same relation to whatever that thing is that we call experience.

*

"The idea of mass graves seems to pertain especially to the twentieth century. There are two thousand five hundred British war cemeteries in France and Belgium. The sophisticated observer of rows of headstones will do well to suspect that very often the bodies below are buried in mass graves, with the headstones . . . in rows to convey the illusion that each soldier has his individual place." (Paul Fussel, *The Great War and Modern Memory*) This is an interesting point, and a painful one. There is a further distinction to be made between false mass graves that still resemble cemeteries, and mass graves that aren't even marked. Dachau. Auschwitz. The killing fields in Cambodia. And places we don't even know about. The point of mass graves is not memorialization. The military's war dead might have been buried together, but they are remembered as individuals. How different that is, say, from the mass graves outside Vilnius. These "non-people" were so completely massified that their individuation was lost completely. Fussell talks about the centrality of the notion of irony to our understanding of war as distinctly modern. It might be modern, but that irony is central as a *post-facto* way of viewing an event. It's only after you've gone through the event, or have some reason for the ironic re-description of the event that you can describe it ironically. Irony is a form of self-reflection, and can be effective if people are using the language that Fussell describes later, in his description of war in the terms set up not by Walter Scott, who thought war was hell, but by those who glorified it. In other words, the mock-Romanticism and the mock-Medievalism of the language of war. The language of going off to war in 1914 needed to be demystified. Irony was an important trope, but I wonder if it is a useful trope against war when war is perpetrated cynically. That is to say, when we know—when large numbers of the intelligentsia, the reading public, are cynical about war—as during the Vietnam War, or more importantly, as during the Gulf War, when many were cynical about why we were doing this. Most knowledgeable people were of the view that the war was being fought for oil, that we weren't concerned with democracy in Kuwait, and a fair degree of cynicism was masked by our sheer excitement over the fact that techno-warfare "worked," and that the army did a "good job." But only the most benighted and the most unhappy, those who were fighting hardest against their cognitive dissonance, thought that the reasons for going to war were innocent. In that case, if one were being ironic, might not one be supporting the very cynicism that caused the war in the first place? That ironic distance is very important if you are going to demystify another language. But here the language was already demystifying itself: James Baker basically admitted that he could not find a good legitimation for this war when he first proposed that it would save American jobs, then changed tack to issue dire warnings about the Iraqi nuclear threat. We had to fall back on the notion of supporting our troops, rather than believing that we were fighting a just war. Even the political right acknowledged that it was probably an important war to fight, but not necessarily a just one, and not necessarily a moral one. If a war is fought cynically, then irony will not fight against the war, that in fact something else will have to, and that might be authenticity on one side, and a sense of cosmopolitanism. . . .

*

One of the dangers of irony, and ambiguity is merely another side of irony, is that you reinforce the status quo by stating that the situation is "ambiguous"—or you carve out a personal space of resistance through irony. In certain circumstances, a person's capacity for irony is very important, but I'm not sure it is sufficient. Most truth is ambiguous in that it requires very thick descriptions, but that does not mean that we must always take a distanced relation to circumstances in the hope that at some other time, or, metaphysically, in some other state of being, we might understand the truth a little better. "Right now it's too ambiguous. We can't make a move." The danger of that is obviously that you give the world over to those who have power, and you don't use the tremendous pathos and power of commitment and notions of truth, nor deploy the power that inheres in them against the power of violence, which is both the limit and the end of politics.

Fussell writes "simple antithesis everywhere, that is the atmosphere in which most poems of the Great War take place, and that is the reason for the failure of most of them as durable art." Understandably, he attacks melodramatic dichotomies. However, I wonder if perhaps—and this is where he gets more Johnsonian than he does new critical, that his notion of "durable" is a way of forgetting what Fussell wants us to remember: that war is specific, that it is horrible, that it happens to individuals. He's brilliant on the battle of Passiondael, whose name sounds like Waterloo, when in fact it wasn't a battle in the old fashioned sense at all, and it wasn't localized. If you could walk from the North Sea to the Swiss border and never come above ground, the notion of localization is no longer germane, because you're not moving with small mobile armies, but with large armies that are spread all over the map and fighting each other constantly. The notion of "durable art" might in fact miss the point of what is going on in this art. What he means by durable art is art that is ambiguous, that relishes ambiguity. I don't understand why that has to be the only durable form—he's using a Johnsonian notion and new critical criteria as a way of side-stepping the commitments of the art he's describing. His grand narrative of modernity is that the Great War marked our first fall into binary ideology, and what it did was solidify the notions of binary thought. The problem is that literary discourse, which is always seen as ironically more sophisticated and more naive than political discourse, falls into a form of petty adolescence or childhood when it tries to go cross into politics. Again, this is Fussell the New Critical ironist speaking. The difference between dialectics and binary forms of thought: dialectics are a way of thinking about a number of things at the same time. It's a mode of thought that allows you to *think* numerousness and heterogeneity. Binary thought, however, is one that keeps opposite poles opposite.

A way of understanding deconstruction and why deconstruction was so popular in the United States is that in many ways it was an introduction (especially in Paul de Man) to dialectical thought. Fussell quotes Louis Simpson and he wants to refute him. Simpson maintains that language basically can't touch the body, the sheer physicality of a soldier's life can't be rendered into words. The reason is that soldiers have discovered that no one is really interested in the bad news they have to report. What listener wants to be torn and shaken when he doesn't have to be? We have made unspeakable mean indescribable. It really means "nasty." I think this is where Fussell's moralism and his hard empiricism are in fact accurate. To say that things are indescribable, that they leave language, is in fact to fall into the metaphysics that allows such things to happen again and again. They are not beyond language. They are not beyond communication. They are not beyond expression. To say that they are is to turn them into an event that doesn't happen and a death which doesn't touch us. It's this aspect of Heideggerian thought which is the most dangerous.

*

Brooks and Warren's book on literature came out in '39—but it wasn't until *after* the war that new criticism really became institutionalized in the American academy. It was a perfect ideology for the cold war, because it stressed ambiguity, irony, and distance. It was a way of "freeing" oneself from ideology, which had become, after the war, understandably suspect. The ideologies of which they were suspect were essentially communism and fascism, and that is why the strength of new criticism and the particular domestications of deconstructionism can be found in the United States. De Man's deconstruction is a critique of the fascist temptation. When they discovered that he had been a minor collaborator during the Second World War, rather than claiming that this showed that deconstruction was tainted from the start, perhaps it showed that deconstruction was a very strong response. Look at the major deconstructionists: Derrida, a French Algerian Jew; Geoffrey Hartman, who was forced to flee Germany because he was a Jew, and de Man. There's a reason why they all came together on this, because they had all suffered, in one way or another, from excess of ideology.

*

What I find significant about Berel Lang's work is his warning against writing about the subject of the Holocaust, or, as he'll later clarify, of the *Shoah*—unless one can add to the documentary knowledge something concrete, unless one discovers something new. And he talks about mediation of language and the position of the writer with respect to the material, and why one can't write about that event without taking many things into account. Then he talks about the distinction he makes between writing about the event and writing oneself, the writer writing him or herself in the present, through the event, and he likens that to the re-telling of the story of Exodus. This is precisely his answer to what the justification for writing about the Shoah is, the Haggadic stress on the eternal presence of God's actions for the Jewish people, that is to say, thus Adonai, the Lord, did for me when he brought me forth from Egypt—which is stressed several times in the Haggadah. So that in fact one writes oneself into it by placing oneself in relation to it, rather than it in relation to some great objectivity. One of the arguments in my book (*Against Forgetting: Twentieth Century Poetry of Witness*) is going to be against the notion of an enlightenment objectivity and an Archimedean stance outside of systems and outside of history. Lang seems to want to assert the *situatedness* of all knowledge, all responses and all events. The reason is that the moment of genocide is one that stresses specificity but also a certain kind of universality: "We are all humans, except for the Jews."

*

We were aware that the visible earth is made of ashes, and that ashes signify something. . . . And we see now that the abyss of history is deep enough to hold us all. We are aware that a civilization has the same fragility as a life. . . . Everything has not been lost, but everything has sensed that it might perish.
                    —Paul Valéry, "The Crisis Of The Mind," 1919

Alice Fulton

Working notebooks are reassuring because it's easier to start from something rather than nothing. In notebooks, writers feel free to be awkward or polished, silky or sullen. To try opinions without commitment: without anyone watching. Notebooks are dedicated to a perpetual sketchiness, and that's their charm. I keep many simultaneously. The ones I value most serve primarily as a "life list" of language. Because such collections aren't very readable, I've chosen other entries for inclusion here. This selection represents a small gleaning from a large volume of rough notes generated between August 1991 and July 1994. During that time, I was working on my fourth book, Sensual Math. *At two points in 1993, I made lists of notions or tropes I had developed or wanted to develop in the book. The lists were long. I've italicized them under the heading* Book Shapes *and pieced them throughout the entries here, an organization that probably gives a false impression of control. The process of thinking was much messier than my editing would lead you to believe. I didn't, for instance, come up with themes and research them. Rather than tell me what I should be thinking about, the* Book Shapes *more often told me what I had been thinking about. I compiled them retrospectively. While working on this selection, I wondered whether my interests would interest anyone else. I still don't know. The published notebooks of other poets have given me pleasure, and that's all I have to go on. Reading them, I've been surprised by moments of accord. Is it possible that a notebook—with its weird passions and intimate crankiness—*

might make us more sympathetic to another's sensibility? That would be something.

Book Shapes, 1993: Emergence. Coming out. Darwin. Evolution. Novation. Critique the infatuation with newness—that something is good because new, or that newness exists. The element of mimicry in all innovation or creation.

＊

Newness is not a truth or an actual, so much as a feeling. We pretend something is new because we wish it to be. Newness is exciting. It is an emotion.

＊

from talks with John Holland: people assume that Einstein's theory would have been discovered by someone eventually—but this isn't quite the case. The info would have taken a different form—it would not necessarily be applied to time and space. Form is not ineluctable.

＊

" . . . we read well, and with pleasure, what we already know how to read; and what we know how to read is to a large extent dependent upon what we have already read (works from which we've developed our expectations and learned our interpretive strategies)." Annette Kolodny

＊

The truly new always looks truly wrong.

＊

"Even a new rolling pin has an embarrassing element." Dickinson, Letter #311

＊

Imitating introduces innovations. An imitation is often a new thing despite itself (if only because of its different context).

＊

Memory is imitation, or a model. All thought is a copy of something, re-arranged, recombined in new ways. Thinking—is duplication.

*

from talks with John Holland: It's a mistake to equate language with thought. Language is so late in the process of evolution. There's something below words & language, bubbling, that might be akin to recombination.

There is a deep need for symmetry. Animals have it too. If you fold something over, you get likeness. While with boundaries, Other/Self (Immune system), you get difference. Symmetry is not surprising, not predictive. While the Other—is surprising.

Evolution & thinking are the same process.

*

... "the pursuit of the 'new' is the preoccupation of high modernism; if anything, the postmodern casts doubt upon the possibility of a 'new' image that is not in some way already implicated in the 'old.'" *Feminists Theorize the Political*, Judith Butler

*

"neo" means old, a revival

*

So many poems move on by saying "Once"—this or that happened. It's the twice & thrice of happening that amazes. Most everything happens "once." But to happen twice or more means pattern, spells, magic: superstitions & science arise from things that happen more than once. Reproducible results.

*

Book Shapes: Resemblance. Clones. Impersonation. Lies. Masks. Imitation. Simulants. Synthetics. Coverings. Veil. Tags. Identity. Costume.

*

Why do we value what is real? Rather than imitation? Real in what sense?

*

4/26/92: I just read the section from *Mimicry in Plants and Animals* (Wolfgang Wickler) that John wants us both to work from. I am blank of ideas, of connectives at this point. . . . I might be able to do something with deception. . . . "Many living things survive by pretending to look or behave like something else. . . . Such deception, or mimicry, is . . . practiced by plants, as with the orchid that resembles a female bee so that a male bee will alight on it and effect pollination. The fact that one organism can enjoy a selection advantage by developing some of the identifying characteristics of another species provides scientists with a classic test-case for evolution."

*

Bee orchids: The orchid's mimicry of the female bee makes male bees want to have sex with the orchid (they can't tell it's a "dummy"). Copulation leads to, results in, the flowers' pollination. The flower's continuance or well-being, its future, is assured by pollination. Like women impersonating "cultural" ideas of the female.

*

"She was a female impersonator who happened to be a woman." Phyllis Rose on Josephine Baker

*

"Women consider it a masculine trait simply to be yourself. But they end up being caricatures of themselves, which makes them easy to mimic." Lynne Carter, female impersonator, quoted by Marjorie Garber, *Vested Interests*

*

The orchid as crossdresser! It dresses itself up as a female bee, in the costume of a female bee.

The role of "crossdressing" in evolution, in botany, science.

I think many "normal" women are crossdressers in the sense that they put on a female costume that represents them as Woman (our culture's notion), when under the costume they are female, not this "dummy" Woman. Orchid in drag; female in drag when she dresses up as dummy luscious *she*.

T.V.s, crossdressers, blur the boundaries of Otherness. Are we afraid of that blurring because . . . it threatens? . . . Yes. But by blurring the boundary between orchid & bee, the orchid survives more efficiently! By incorporating, into its corpus or body, the Other, it evolves.

*

"Treason doth never prosper, what's the reason?
For if it prosper, none dare call it treason."

—Harington, *Epigrams*

*

"Most people spend so much time looking natural, when somebody like me takes less time to look artificial." Dolly Parton

*

"Whereas Modernist poetics was overwhelmingly committed, at least in theory, to the 'natural look,' . . . we are now witnessing a return to *artifice*, but a 'radical artifice,' to use Lanham's phrase, characterized by its opposition, not only to 'the language really spoken by men' but also to what is loosely called Formalist (whether new or old) verse, with its elaborate poetic diction and self-conscious return to 'established' forms and genres. Artifice, in this sense, is less a matter of . . . elaboration and elegant subterfuge, than of the recognition that a poem or a painting or performance text is a *made thing*—contrived, constructed, chosen—and that its reading is also a construction on the part of its audience." *Radical Artifice*, Marjorie Perloff

*

Book Shapes: androgyny. gender. blurred lines or boundaries. otherness. Give. Crossover—genetic & gender. Crossdressing. Permeability. Quality of through. See-through or wearing away. Against autonomy, self-reliance. The subject is stretched to include the other.

Immersion, as opposed to difference or delineation. No lines or borders in immersion. The sign of immersion == is a hinge, a close joining. Against transparency. The sign throws you back to the seam, stitching. Notice the way it hangs, hinges, is made. Bride. Bridge. The Church is the Bride of Christ. Two yin lines in a hexagram ==

*

"Communion extends beyond border: it is with one's enemies also."
John Cage.

*

"During meiosis, parts of each chromosome strand in a pair 'cross over' to the other chromosome, in sort of a swapping arrangement."
Artificial Life by Steven Levy

*

Thou art That (immersion)

*

"with no distinction between contemplator and contemplated." *Being Peace*, Thich Nhat Hanh

*

Book Shapes: The quality of betweenness: what comes between two quantities, objects, people. Or the nature of being between categories. Being in the Midwest. Being neither a "language" poet nor quite in the mainstream. Being neither a gendered female nor a male. The horizon is a between. The priming on a canvas is. Bring in electrons as emblem for betweenness?

*

"the blue note is that vocal sound which floats *between* the major and the minor. The more such notes—often adding the seventh and fifth notes of the scale—the 'meaner' the blues." Sheila Davis

*

Interference *between* measurements is a key element in Heisenberg's principle.

*

Kepler confirmed by triangulations that the orbit of Mars was an oval: rather he finally concluded that the true orbit lay halfway *between* the circle and the oval. . . .

*

" . . . in our description of nature the purpose is not to disclose the real essence of (physical objects) but only to track down, so far as it is possible, relations *between* the manifold aspects of our experience."
Niels Bohr, my italics

*

"Cherish Power—dear. Remember that stands in the Bible *between* the Kingdom and the Glory, because it is wilder than either of them." Dickinson's letter 631, my italics

*

the space in the middle == Fauve, feral. The explosive slantwise force.

*

fuzzy logic: wants to capture qualities such as "warm" or "fast" within a mathematical framework. It allows people to specify the degree to which something occurs—how hot it is outside or how fast a motor should turn—without setting a particular threshold value for crisply separating "warm" from "hot" or "moderate" from "fast." The boundaries between categories become, well, fuzzy. Conventional logic is based on the idea that a statement . . . is either true or false. Fuzzy logic deals with the degree of truth, expressed "as an assigned value between zero and one." The choice is no longer just zero or one. Non-duality is a continuum rather than an either/or.

*

Book Shapes: Thirdness rather than binary thought.

*

non-dual rather than one. Non-duality means not two, but it also means not one. "Because if there is one, there are two. If you want to avoid two, you have to avoid one also." *Being Peace,* Thich Nhat Hanh

*

from talks with John Holland: How do you determine or define a line? (I mean a line drawn, as in geometry.) It isn't enough to think of it as this entity with nothing underneath it. An infinity of points? How are the points related to each other? There are different kinds of infinities. (This is set theory.) There are countable infinities. The number of points in a line are called uncountable. You can't assign an integer to each point in the line without having stuff left over. If you put down two points in a line, you can always find a point between those two points. That's very different from a countable infinity. *Between* any points in a line you can stuff all the integers and you'd still have leftover points. Any piece of a line is a continuum. It is gaps—a line isn't solid. The process of taking away proves that something is left. The set that's left has the same order of infinity as the line itself.

Between the countable infinities & the infinity that corresponds to the line there is another infinity that's different from either. Continuum hypotheses says that there is no third infinity. It's either one or the other. If math is going to be self-consistent, you have to answer the foundational question: is there a third infinity?

*

"third"—describes "a space of possibility . . . challenges the possibility of harmonic and stable binary symmetry." *Third* questions the idea of one: of identity, self-sufficiency, self-knowledge. Third World, Third actor, and the Lacanian Symbolic. The Third Coast, where I live! "Emergence" of the Third World broke down binary U.S./Soviet power relations. Sophocles added a third speaker to the protagonist and antagonist of Greek classical drama, "enabling a freer, more dynamic dramaturgy." quotes from *Vested Interests*, Marjorie Garber

*

Book Shapes: Authority! Do more with authority. . . . Authority has connotations of the real, genuine. Of good taste. Dismantle it. Ask what authority do I bow to, do I honor? Humor is disruptive of authority.

*

12/1/91: On the plane, Hank (reading Cris's chapter on Marianne Moore) said, very seriously, "What is the poetic term for a question mark appearing at the end of a line and having resonance with an elephant's trunk?"

*

Comedy could be a "rifting" or disruptive force, one that calls identity into question, subverts categorization. There's *jouissance* in toying with what myth purports as true: the archetype crumbles, sways drunkenly at least.

*

"The roots of the travesty of myth are very old . . . in the folklore of primitive peoples . . . serious myths coexist with comic ones, where the deities are at once venerated and ridiculed. This 'ritual laughter' in later times disappears from the sacred sphere." Mary E. Barnard, *The Myth of Apollo and Daphne*

*

" . . . carnival laughter, laughter that mocks and derides, but that is also a triumphant laughter, effecting a secret liberation . . . from social constraints, from law and order." ibid.

*

Charles Peirce's speculations—that " 'natural law' is not law at all but merely a set of habits fixed more firmly than any habits we know. . . ." If this is so, the snowflake (possibly) was not always inanimate. It surrendered (possibly) at some time, its life, which had achieved a perfect organization. Joseph Wood Krutch suggests that ants might be on their way back to the inanimate. Meanwhile, computers are on their way to being animate.

*

"Natural" is a habit.

*

"Consciousness exists in nature, just as light and electricity do." Nick Herbert, physicist

*

Nature is a psychopath.

*

Why is Woman Seen as Closer to Nature? Pregnancy. Childbirth & rearing. Woman's body places her in social roles that are considered to be lower than man's.

*

Book Shapes: Daphne: culture/nature contest.

*

Daphne rebelled against the identification of women with nature. This reading of the myth is bigger than seeing it as a rape narrative.

She wasn't running from rape but from marriage/childbirth: woman's identification with nature.

*

A myth is a cultural script.

*

"The culture/nature distinction is itself a product of culture. . . ." Sherry Ortner, *Women, Culture, and Society*

*

" . . . the adherents of rape culture see female sexuality as a property which only men can own, which women often hoard, which can thus justifiably be wrested from us, and which women themselves merely hold in trust for a lawful owner. . . . The most deep-rooted upheaval of rape culture would revise the idea of female sexuality as an object, as property, and as an inner space." Sharon Marcus, *Feminists Theorize the Political*

*

On Mary Somerville—"The Queen of Nineteenth Century Science:" " . . . unlike so many other women scientists she never deviated—at least in public—from the preoccupations and conduct considered socially acceptable for women and perhaps this in part was the key to her success." *Hypatia's Heritage*, Margaret Alic

*

"Women scientists . . ." Women poets. "Man" is never an adjective.

*

The unseemly has been the enemy of women's progress.

*

Thoughts in preparation for Robert Turney's "The Fear of Women:" Unlike men, women are afraid that men will be afraid of them. Why are women afraid of women? Contagion. Why are men afraid? Women's power to refuse. . . .

*

1/15/93: Hank said that last night after the upsetting stuff, trying to get to sleep next to me was like lying beside a jostled beehive. There was all this swarming at the head of the bed. And he could tell when I finally got to sleep. It was like the sun going down, when the bees slow down and just start to crawl.

*

"Through a kind of artificial mythopoeia, the writers invent new variants for the tale, altering the ancient model, sometimes radically. In Renaissance theories of imitation, this transformative process is compared to bees gathering pollen from flowers and converting it into honey—an image that originates with the ancients and that becomes a commonplace in discussions of imitation." Mary E. Barnard, *The Myth of Apollo and Daphne*

*

"The fugue . . . appeals to musicians who know how to listen, to those who are able to single out a voice and detach it from the others, even when that voice happens not to be the subject. For the subject by its melodic character, its rhythmic contours, its continual reappearance, can be discerned, indeed, even by the inexperienced." Wanda Landowska

*

In poetry today, all the poems about museums & paintings are about art as commodity: the collected and marketable art. Poets never write about unknown artists. . . .

*

"My stake as a marginalized Other . . . should make quite clear my empathetic relationship with quantum subjects, such as photons and electrons. . . . Quanta are my soul sisters. We have multiple identities. We can't be explained away by categories which are taken to be 'objective,' 'natural,' 'universal'—existing outside of language, gender, sexuality, humanity, space-time (culture-history)." Karen Barad, physicist: "Meeting the Universe Halfway," *Feminism, Science, and the Philosophy of Science: A Dialogue*. The quotation is from an earlier, unpublished version of the essay.

*

" . . . most of the mass in the universe exists not in luminous stars or glowing gas clouds but in an invisible form . . . dark matter." *Scientific American?*

*

from *Smithsonian:* "There is more dark matter in the Universe than just that found in halos. . . . Each search makes assumptions about what dark matter is, then builds an apparatus to detect it. . . . Visible matter, which we always considered the very fabric of the Universe itself—the stuff we have spent millennia trying to understand—turns out to be something of a cosmic afterthought."

*

I want to find synonyms that can replace the use of "black" or "dark" as negatives: how about klan, hearse, pogrom . . .

*

from *The Encyclopedia of Ignorance:* Nothingness is a structure.

*

" . . . the postmodernist seeks to reveal the systems of power in the world that legitimize certain representations and not others." Anne Herrmann, *The Dialogic and Difference.*

*

David Porter asks Dickinson to provide "legitimate" representations, those that have defined a major poet in the dominant literary Western culture. But her work, her life, her entire way of being a poet legitimizes not "certain representations" but uncertain ones, "others." It brings background to the fore. Questions finish, polish, regularity of meter. It is an unnatural sounding poetry, deviant.

*

from conversation with Hank: Ambiguities in the sketch can be made more ambiguous in the painting. Painting can yield a more complicated sense of space. Central idea—no point of purchase—no firm objective reality in the space created. Both in paintings and in the world. They represent that shifting—continual—in the world. In that sense, the abstractions are representational. Color adds fun. Natural world color is changing & textured in contrast to advertising color, pop culture color, which is constant & flat, more mechanistic. Natural forms have more texture. His paintings—try to represent motion in a static form—an oxymoron.

*

Book Shapes: The grotesque. Hybrid forms. Recombinant monsters: Ninja turtles, the Fly, Mr. Ed, Daphne. gargoyles. strings. take. spiral. Impersonation. Wedding. finding a language. Inclusions. Oblique. Aberration.

*

"Daphne's transformation defies categorization and definition altogether. Hybrid Daphne is simply a 'non-thing' devoid of logical structure and order as we know it, an ambivalent and anomalous form that has ceased to be human and is not yet fully laurel. No words adequately describe it; it is as if language itself were paralyzed. . . . Daphne's grotesque transformation conforms to Wolfgang Kayser's notion of the grotesque as an intrusion of a strange, incongruous phenomenon into the rational order of nature, the subversion of the familiar world by the uncanny & the absurd. . . ." Mary E. Barnard, *The Myth of Apollo and Daphne*

*

The bee orchid is a hybrid or grotesque: Daphne's transformation into the laurel, human/plant, is like the bee orchid's metamorphosis to insect/plant.

*

"Every period in the history of the grotesque gives rise to angry voices that, for one reason or another, speak against its bizarre, strange presence." Mary E. Barnard

*

"Enclosed please find five colors of makeup; she insists upon a clown face even though she has fairy wings. Try to talk her out of it." *Two to Four from 9 to 5.*

*

Book Shapes: Handwriting: the human hand, its eccentricity, is the ultimate in taste, rarity. No two alike. Seams. Process.

*

" . . . this spirit of play is omnipresent in medieval grotesque art: in the tiny monsters of the anonymous craftsmen of the misericords, in the enigmatic gargoyles, and *above all, in the marginal drolleries of myriad manuscripts.*" Mary Barnard, my italics.

*

" . . . consider such earlier nontransparent page design as that of the medieval scribe . . ." transparent typography has once again "given way to 'the word as such.' " *Radical Artifice*, Marjorie Perloff

*

The hand in art. Oils can be worked. Stay malleable.

*

handwriting around the edge like tatting, like lace made by hand.

*

handwriting as a kind of interference: "noise is not only incidental but essential to communication" (and she cites "waverings in the graphic forms, failures in the drawing, spelling errors . . .") "If, for example, a letter is written in careless or illegible script, there is interference in the reading process, which is to say that noise slows down communication." *Radical Artifice*, Marjorie Perloff

*

"Noise, as unanticipated excess, as sirens' song. . . ." ibid. Yes—a temptation, the temptation of gossip. What I learned from handwriting in "Point of Purchase": it has the allure of gossip, the informal, illicit. It upstages the printed word. . . . It is personal, idiosyncratic. Type is monochromatic. Handwriting in conjunction with type is irresistible, seductive. But . . . handwriting without type is tiring!

*

"Krafft-Ebing—she had never heard of that author before. All the same she opened the battered old book, then she looked more closely, for there on its margins were notes in her father's small, scholarly hand and she saw that her own name appeared in those notes. She began to read, sitting down rather abruptly. . . ." Radclyffe Hall, *The Well of Loneliness*

*

Jamie Hillegas, a Huron High student, killed himself last winter, "apparently despondent over not winning immediate admission to Harvard or Yale." A friend placed red roses on his grave along with a copy of the program for Huron's Senior Honors Night. There was no mention of Hillegas in the printed program. But in ten places—under the listing of students receiving local and national recognition—the name "Jamie Hillegas" had been written by hand. A note on the cover, in the same handwriting, read "Revised for our dear friend Jamie." *The Ann Arbor News*

*

"In the conventional printed book, after all, the written surface is, so Lanham reminds us 'not to be read aesthetically; that would only interfere with purely literate transparency.' On the contrary, a page of print should stand to the thought conveyed 'as a fine crystal goblet stands to the wine it contains . . .' Such 'unintermediated thought,' such 'unselfconscious transparency' has become, says Lanham, 'a stylistic, one could almost say a cultural, ideal for Western civilization.' "

Radical Artifice, Marjorie Perloff

*

"We are always looking first AT (the text) and then THROUGH IT, and this oscillation creates a different implied ideal of decorum, both stylistic and behavioral." ibid.

*

Book Shapes: Emotion. Embarrassment. Face. Facade. Ripping the veil, covering. Transparency is a surface, a style or rhetoric in itself. Transparency is only apparent.

*

Emotion is the best mnemonic device.

*

"Appearance, which is constantly on the point of passing itself off as reality, must constantly reveal its profound unreality."—Sartre. This reminds me of the poem's surface—

*

"obverse"—meaning on the face of it—is an interesting way to describe the surface of the poem. It also means "counterpart" or "complement."

*

James Boyd White, writing of Herbert's very noticeable rhyme scheme at the line endings of "Paradise" says "when meaning of this kind appears in the text it seems to come from somewhere else, not from the speaker or poet, as the light comes from outside the window and shines through it: it is an act of grace." This view is directly opposite to the stance of most readers of contemporary poetry, who feel that such effects come too noticeably *from the poet*; they make the poet's hand or manipulation of language, too visible. And they upset the fiction of transparency.

*

In people, life, I think heart—the inner kindness—is most important. The surface (clothes, etc.) unimportant. But in poems, I think the surface is part of the subject or inner life. The surface is a depth in itself. The world of contemporary poetry reverses these judgments: people judge poets by their looks, style, clothes. And they judge the poems with no regard for the surface; they want only the meaning (which in their view is available only when the surface disappears, does not get in the way, is transparent).

*

"Her style may loudly call attention to itself, but it does not usually do so as a construction to be admired in its own right. . . . Dickinson's conspicuously deviant style is part of a larger rhetoric of stimulus. It is meant to cherish a power that extends considerably beyond the author's direct control." Gary Stonum, *The Dickinson Sublime*

*

"Difficulty of surface enables interpretation by preventing a too simple or merely assumed understanding of the topic at hand." Cristanne Miller, *Questions of Authority: The Example of Marianne Moore*

*

—it came to me that the reason to make things less plain in a poem is that only by getting the reader to participate in making the meaning does it become a poem.

*

Hank: If the image lacks complexity, it's too easy to be grounded somewhere in it.

*

People dislike the complexity of critical (literary) theory more than they do the complexity of science.

*

"Your Thorns are the best part of you. . . ." Marianne Moore

*

"I am tired of bursting apart (or perhaps 'of being everywhere at once'), of breaking into bits like Osiris. Each book of poems is a book of partings and severings, with Thomas's finger in the wound between one poem and the next." Marina Tsvetaeva, translated by Joy Dworkin

*

" 'Self-pity' is just sadness, I think, in the perjorative." Renata Adler, *Speedboat*

*

"And staples, in the Song . . ." Dickinson, poem 512 ==

*

All Solomon's sea of brasse and world of stone
Is not so deare to thee as one good grone.
                    —George Herbert

*

detective or mystery convention is of course the exposition scene at the end, in which the detective tells a gathered group, often including the culprit, what happened. If addressed to the criminal, it's in the second person, informing the criminal of her/his own biography. The same convention is used in contemporary poetry—informing some "you" of her/his own life. No wonder it sounds accusatory. 8/22/92

*

7/29/93: I'm tired of the kneejerk epiphanies of contemporary poets. There's too much praise, too little effort to change. Poets praise & think their work is done.

*

"Yet whatsoe'er is by vain criticks thought./Praising is harder much than finding Fault. . . ." Sheffield

*

the difference between emotion & delight. Emotion is a physical sensation—delight is cerebral. Joy can literally make the heart beat faster. Delight does not make the heart beat faster.

*

Hank is reading an article in *Barrons* about some anthropologists who decided to study a group of pension fund managers. Hank says they're just like poets.

*

H. said he saw two *doves* at the feeder, trying to peck each others' eyes out.

*

Book Shapes: The unwanting. Enough. The line infinite & closed. Surfeit rather than desire. To have rather than yearn or lose.

*

On Dickinson's poems: "To read through them all is always to risk the vertigo characterizing the reader's sublime, a bewilderment in the face of some vast surfeit of meaning." Gary Stonum, *The Dickinson Sublime*

*

Write about the pleasures of attainment, having, holding. A poetry that doesn't desire but delivers. Satiation being part of what it offers. Rather than absence, value presence. A poem praising the boundless intensity of attainment (rather than longing). The actual satisfaction of desire dwarfs the infinite . . . ?

*

"Text of bliss: . . . the text that discomforts (perhaps to the point of a certain boredom), unsettles the reader's historical, cultural, psychological assumptions, the consistency of his tastes, values, memories, brings to a crisis his relation with language." Roland Barthes, *The Pleasure of the Text* (1975)

*

"If a reader is tired from my work—that means he read well, and read something good. The fatigue of a reader is not devastating but creative. Co-creative. It does honor to both the reader and to me." Marina Tsvetaeva, "A Poet on Criticism," 1926, translated by Joy Dworkin

*

Moby Dick " . . . seems to provide an *exhaustive* repertoire to all possible methods for thinking about the whole. . . ." Robert Weisbuch, *Atlantic Double-Cross*, my italics

*

"for the saint and the poet alike . . . make excess ever more excessive." Yeats

*

Book Shapes: America. Prestige, value, taste: How good taste is a power structure that . . . excludes, makes others into Others, *makes others feel small.*

*

I started crossing my sevens for clarity—now I want to unlearn the habit, gesture: finicking, unAmerican, ornamental as it is.

*

Why do scientists like diagrams and humanities people dislike them?

*

Science involves taste. It has an aesthetic dimension. Scientists start with an idea, an intuition, that two things are connected. Then they have to find the proof. They have to say, if my idea is true, then I'll find this new thing or these new effects.

*

shopping is the chief use of the American imagination. . . . It's our primary creative act.

*

"Whitman's good accumulates, Wordsworth's good purifies." Robert Weisbuch, *Atlantic Double-Cross*

*

We had a wilderness, a frontier. Our impulse has been to make it a plenum or crowd.

*

from conversation with Hank: As to advertising, pop culture, it's hard not to inadvertently glorify the object by the fact of your attention. Your attention to it is a form of homage.

*

"The first time I visited Buddhist communities in this country I asked a friend, 'please show me your Buddha, your American Buddha.' The question surprised my friend, because he thought that the Buddha is universal. In fact, the Chinese have a Chinese Buddha, Tibetans have a Tibetan Buddha, and also the teaching is different." *Being Peace*, Thich Nhat Hanh

*

" . . . white Americans have supposed 'Europe' and 'civilization' to be synonymous—which they are not—and have been distrustful of other standards and other sources of vitality, especially those produced in America itself. . . ." James Baldwin, *The Fire Next Time*

*

"It's a complex fate, being an American, and one of the responsibilities it entails is fighting against a superstitious valuation of Europe." Henry James

*

the cafes in Ann Arbor that pride themselves on being "European" —what an affectation! *Which* country exactly?

*

Book Shapes: Opening. Breaking. Flaws. On the value of mistakes. The value of the rough edge, of eccentricity. Showing process. Seamy side. Stitches, sewing. Inclusions—flaws that give value . . .

*

"Truth comes out of error more readily than out of confusion."
Francis Bacon (because error is formal, identifiable as wrong. When
we have something ruled out, we can consider its opposite, for
example.)

*

"Most natural emeralds are heavily flawed. These flaws are generally
so profuse that they take on an acceptance of their own. It's not
unusual to refer to an included area as a 'garden' of included 'flowers.'" *Beyond the Glitter*

*

It was defects in the early universe that induced matter to clump
together & produce the present pattern of galaxy distribution. This
is a speculation. (gleaned from *Scientific American*, 3/92)

*

" . . . a variety of topological defect, called texture, . . . could initiate
the formation of large-scale structure while avoiding the obvious inadequacies of the other kinds of defects." This physicist is talking of
the *inadequacies* of defects. Some defects are more adequate than
others.

*

6/18/92—Just heard a story on NPR about dancer/choreographer
Michael Clark (he's Scottish). His work "changes direction" in mid-
leap—an arabesque veering off into an entirely different direction.
Physically demanding dance. He's cast his 63-year-old mother, top-
less, in his production of "The Rites of Spring." She plays the sage.
His "Modern Masterpiece" uses music of The Sex Pistols alongside
classical stuff. Clark's dancers—you can hear them gasp for breath
above the music. To make us aware of the effort. (To let the noticeable effort or superstructure be a part of the poem intentionally:
handwriting was a step in this direction.) Clark said he loves the moment when a dancer *almost* falls. That is his favorite moment in
dance. The loss (briefly) of equilibrium, or the hint of disequilibrium
as a gain.

*

from talks with John Holland: There's an emphasis on equilibrium in mathematics. Steady state. Come to rest. There are powerful tools to handle it. But there's no good way to talk about evolution in terms of equilibrium. Equilibrium is essentially dead. Uninteresting at best. Open systems (humans) can't be described well mathematically.

*

Book Shapes: the again, the used—with patina, nap, tarnish. To read again is to read better.

*

Character, Sonya's, reaction to Shostakovich's "Concerto for Piano and Trumpet" in the novel *Imaginary Crimes* by Sheila Ballantyne: "The sounds that leaped into the room were bombastic, agitated and grim; I felt their discord in waves, like small shocks. . . .

I can't explain why I didn't turn it off and put the record back; there was a perverse, inexplicable satisfaction in letting it go on. I played it a second time, awed to be a firsthand witness to such corruption. By the third play, I began to notice harmonic sequences of rare, majestic beauty, and dark, elegant passages born of a staggering melancholy. It was hard to believe that less than an hour before I'd found it revolting. It now seemed a rich and complex statement, a message from an underground voice who spoke in code in order to be heard. . . . The bombast was a front; underneath was delicacy, knowledge, unspeakable longing. I didn't know it then, but what had started as an act of rebellion was becoming a form of love."

*

"The Buddhist way of understanding is always letting go of our views and knowledge in order to transcend." *Being Peace*, Thich Nhat Hanh

Donald Hall

Reading, I make notes on margins; watching basketball, I daydream about linebreaks, reach for a blank book, and take a note. The house is cluttered with blank books, none filled and all jagged with half lines of poetry or fragmented notions. From time to time I finger through them, wondering, What did I mean by that? But sometimes I take up another blank book to carry a notion further.

For the most part, the letters I write to friends substitute for journals and notebooks. I improvise a suggestion in an argument with one friend, then continue it in an argument with another. Or these remarks are not arguments but elucidations of opinion by analogy in search of principle or generalization. Daydreaming about these propositions, while I am not writing a letter, I reach for a blank book.

Reading the prose of poets, I find help in their essays, but often I prefer their notebooks, letters, or table talk. In their most casual, or maybe responsive, sentences I find the most utility. Poems are the main work, and notations to the main work turn up at the peripheries: in letters, in notebooks, on margins.

August

Eric Gill: "Work is sacred, leisure is secular." Georgia O'Keeffe: "The days you work are the best days." Matisse: "Work is paradise." Rodin:

"To work is to live without dying." And then Flaubert, to keep us honest: "It passes the time."

*

I get so pissed-off at the plain-talk people—who claim that Whitman wrote street talk and that William Carlos Williams let it all hang out—that I forget the beautiful *art* of simplicity. When I read a stretch of short, simple, powerful things by Jack Gilbert, I remember how utterly moving plainness can be: "Divorce":

Woke up suddenly thinking I heard crying.
Rushed through the dark house.
Stopped, remembering. Stood looking
out at the bright moonlight on concrete.

Everything is there: exact adequacy, intelligence that withholds comment, and the luck (or vision) of the natural symbol. There is also that invaluable thing—with luck you hit on it five times in fifty years of writing—when you say something that everyone has experienced (waking up feeling, not knowing why) which is not common literary property.

*

If you find yourself telling an anecdote or a fantasy, to illustrate something, more than seven times in your life, try writing it out and see what happens. Like photography draining color from the landscape. T called to say that J died Monday evening. She was euphoric; the dreaded thing was over. He died quietly drifting in and out of sleep for two days. Until the Thursday or Friday before, he spent at least eight hours a day sitting up in his chair, downstairs, trying to read. The hospital bed was upstairs, and T slept in the same room. No IVs. The Doctor said: If he complains terribly we will do it. There had been no eating or drinking, I suppose, as the tumor filled his throat. Did he have a tracheotomy? I don't know. A day or two before he died T interviewed a nurse; she didn't know if she could handle it alone. J said, "No," emphatically, and followed: "We've been through this before." T laughed as she told me, "Not exactly through dying." (Through many things, I suppose, without the help of others.) An hour or two before he died he said it wasn't so bad. "Amen," he said, "amen"; then: "It's coming. It's coming."

T told me all this on the telephone, as she must have been doing for two days straight. The years of his dying—except for the beginning, the announcement—have been good for them; more open affection from J, more connection to world and family. The last four months, when he knew it had come back, were especially good; a honeymoon, she said. Just the two of them. Children and grandchildren visited but mostly they were alone.

They did his dying as well as they did their living—mostly. Models: J's combination of gentleness with a resolute aversion to compromise—his courage in effect: skeptical, loving, in love with poetry, without ambition, with insufficient self-regard, brave without bravado. T's relentless ongoing scrupulous examination of *everything*, inside and outside.

*

Reading Ruth Stone's poems, wonderful with that ending zag which is unpredictable, exact, repeated, yet it never becomes mannered.

*

A disaster of a reading! All day I heard how G read to an audience of *two hundred* the night before. "Don't tell me about it." In an auditorium seating five hundred we pulled maybe eighty. M led off and read badly, passive and throwaway, scattery, without concentration. So I read badly too. Flat, flat. I couldn't have picked a worse bunch to read new poems to. They sat there like dandelions on a lawn. So I went to the Tried and True, and I still felt flat. I tried harder. I strained—and everything came apart. I gave up, and played the tape: angry, contemptuous, miserable.

Afterwards they told me I was great. With one of them—maybe the second or the third—I argued, which is stupid; it begs for praise. Imagine the reasonable discussion: "You were great." "Actually I was ghastly." "Ah, yes, I see. You have a point. I must have been mistaken."

Some who praised seemed sincere. So? They could have lousy taste in poetry readings or stars in their eyes. And of course I could be wrong—just reacting to empty seats, like old Robert Frost.

*

September

L preaching again. Although he is rational or humanist, he becomes a vehicle for spiritual energy, maybe because he loves ritual and the centuries cast themselves through its shape. He has a clear vision of Jesus, historically clear, uncluttered by decorative plaques or pious archaism. Something speaks through him that is holy whether he is conscious of it or not.

*

Poetry fails, in each poem, to be as good as poetry ought to be—or as I somehow think it somewhere is, somewhere I'm not looking. Every flesh is flawed and poems are flesh.

*

The last few days I've dredged through old boxes of photographs, finding things for the Gale book. Depressing—and tomorrow is the service for T. I feel volatile, continually nauseated. I fear coming apart—and more than that I fear the lunch before: strangers, small talk, anxiety. Less and less do I want to be with people, especially strangers; or with more than two people at once, even friends. In the photographs there are so many who visited us here ten years ago, whom I photographed—and I forget their names. Then there are all the dead cats and all the dead people: Reuel, Caroline. Maybe the gallery of aging bothers me more than the dead. My own, my children's.

Looking for pictures I found dozens of letters and postcards to my grandparents, and my grandmother's annotations, and the Sunday school program, 1931, when I first went to Sunday school, with the crayoning I did there, and my mother's postcard to my grandmother after I got home telling how I talked all the time about New Hampshire. I was brought up to love New Hampshire! There's a postcard I wrote to my grandparents about Fluffy and another, 1944, about the death of my blind chick. Typed letters from Exeter talk about track, busyness, poems in magazines.

*

Somebody writing about Garrison Keillor's essays: " . . . they are a throwback to a time when America was genuinely innocent."

When was that? Everyone confidently refers to a time when this country still had its cherry. The time when America was innocent is always twenty to fifty years ago. Lately it's mostly before 1945—before victory, before Hiroshima. But sometimes it's before Kennedy was killed, before Chicago in 1968, before Watergate. I'm old enough to remember people saying that it was before the Depression, before Prohibition, before the Great War. There are always fine reasons, always fatuous. Reading history when I was a kid I thought variously that it was before the Spanish war, before the gilded age, before Grant and Reconstruction, before the Civil War, before the Fugitive Slave Law, before the Mexican War. . . .

But go read Henry Adams about Jefferson's lies and Madison's chicanery. What innocence? We imported black captives, Yankee ships and Virginian customers, through the horror of the middle passage to work and die raising tobacco; then we turned Virginia and Maryland into breeding farms exporting forty thousand black slaves every year to work in the deep South. Some Eden. No nation was ever innocent.

When we think that our country was innocent in the past, we are thinking of latency when we were five years old. As ever, the personal is laundered into the historical.

*

October

In *Publisher's Weekly* a week later someone claims that the 1939 World's Fair, New York version, is memorable because "of American innocence, now gone the way of the passenger pigeon. It was the last flowering of our optimism. . . ." Hah! That World's Fair was whistling in the dark against Depression on the one side, with its threat of revolution, and on the other World War II with Fascism howling out of Europe. Innocence! In 1939 only the wretchedness of a terrible war—which many of us optimists thought that Germany would win—began to raise wages and provide jobs. Innocence and optimism and bullshit.

*

Granted that most writers are bi-polar—established by statistics, confirmed by reading biography—this characteristic blood-chemistry is compounded by the volatility of reputation, or even by the melodrama of the daily mail. Independent (largely) of the writer's bipolarity are the extraordinary ups and downs of book reviews, like the good luck or bad of the NYTBR assignment. And in the mail a young editor of an old house in New York introduces herself and wants to reprint two out of print books in a new series. In the same mail an old friend screams that my new work is total disaster. The telephone rings and I have won a prize I never thought about, $10,000. A week later the young editor has eloped to Syracuse and abandoned her projects. Next day I am included in a new anthology, seven poems, and my name goes unmentioned in a history of my own generation.

One *wishes* one never thought of such matters. However, one is equipped with two lungs, one liver, one heart, and two kidneys. Needless to say a single disappointment (insult, bad luck, snub) is equal in intensity to five hundred triumphs.

Bi-polarity happens indoors and out. The genuine problem of blood-chemistry—blessing and terror—is multiplied by unexpected shifts of circumstance. I *think* that the outdoor swings are less common for tenured Professors of Economics or people with longterm jobs with big companies, businessmen or lineworkers. The self-employed real estate agent, or the small contractor, goes through a volatility like the writer's. A taste for volatility, for the dangerous and exciting roller coaster, may explain why some of us work alone. (Even tenured professor-writers work alone *as* writers—and ride the Wham-O Train.) But all writers suffer this soar-plunge whether or not they have a taste for it. It's part of the job description.

*

Multiplying mutability by bi-polarity accounts for the compulsiveness of writers, a proneness to pencils sharpened in a row, to schedules, to lists and numbers. We hear so often: "I get up at four and work until noon." "I do five hundred words a day." Rituals are magic, and every writer plays magic games with paper, pads, pencils, pens, or computers; with magic chairs and with magic coffee cups. Control of time by schedules and lists supports the manic-depressive beset by mutability, by instant heaven and hell in every mail and every shrill of the telephone: Routine, routine, you can *count* on it. We graph our moods against the repeated grid of The Day.

*

Last night I read my poems at a small town library near by. When I did it ten years ago, ten or twenty neighbors showed up, mostly elderly and female. They were still there last night but another hundred and thirty added themselves and the reading moved to the Town Hall. Many of the audience had never heard of New Hampshire ten years ago. Lots of older people (my age) but some younger ones also. I got some star stuff: "I only found you two years ago!" "I couldn't believe it when I read it in the paper. . . ."

Of course I want it: *I also don't want it.* It's disturbing in this place because it is alienating. And the change is upsetting: Ten years ago, people talked not about me but about the things I was writing about; now the writer is more important than the place. Vatiphages have arrived and settled in like tent caterpillars. Of course as people they are all right; they like it here and they want to read their neighbor. But I feel them *deferring* to me, like people at universities. They're not my cousins: of course I am more like them than I am like my cousins.

*

November

Reading an awful essay about the kitsch of the suburbs. A row of sitting ducks. Vulgarity is everywhere and this essay has been written for sixty years. Mencken did it with a sense of where he was attacking from, not only to proclaim himself superior. This fellow puts forward a familiar notion: The past (which means his own youth) was rough, raw, sexy, poor, and (therefore) virtuous; he's another smart aleck showing he is better than the people he lives among. Eighty percent of human endeavor exists in order to prove that we are better than somebody else.

I do it too. I've done it all my life. And "everybody does it" is no comfort. Who wants to be everybody? When I harangue about the McPoem or the bodilessness of critics and teachers, I praise myself. Depressing! When I was a teacher I proved myself better than businessmen and now that I free-lance (which is being a small business) I rail about academics. I've always screamed about the suburbs because I was raised in the suburbs and you always remain what you were raised as. Therefore I'm like the woman who belittles the fem-

inine in order to separate herself and kowtow to men—or in order
to be what she cannot be.

The alternative to self-deceit is silence.

*

Is there something inherently wrong with suburbs? I still think so; or
want to think so. Conservative attempts to praise the suburbs have
not convinced anybody, least of all suburbanites—all of whom want
Country Dwellings preferably in a condo on a golf course between a
lake and a ski slope. What's *wrong* with suburbs? I think it's *crowds
of the same in motion.* A crowd is something that wants to resemble
itself or to repeat itself or that emphasizes what it has in common.
The suburbs are numerousness compounded by mobility. A popula-
tion that stays in the same place develops quirks over the generations.
But suburbs are interchangeable like the parts of the mass production
that created industrialism and therefore the suburbs we know—like
fast food, the same burger from coast to coast. When executives or
deconstructionists get relocated every few years they are interchangeable parts. So are the schools their children move into and out of.
We can move from Tacoma to Tucson to Providence to Toledo and
always live in the same house on the same block with the same neighbors. Houses built in bunches stay priced the same and decay together. The neighborhood stays the same, thinly, as people move out
when they get richer, poorer, older, or transferred to Cincinnati. It
is natural that the interchangeable neighbors exchange with each
other on the level, always superficial, where they resemble each other:
cars, food, furniture. Products, not heart-things or soul-things. The
suburbs become engines of surfaces that replicate each other.

*

Just lately, in her eighty-fifth year, my mother tells one story over
and over again: The man who always took out her storm windows
and put them back was kind and courtly to her. "Tell me what I can
do." She liked him; she often spoke of him. This October as he took
out the storms they were talking together about my father; my
mother said that he had died just after his fifty-second birthday. The
man kept shaking his head. "That's my age," he said, "and that's too
young to die." He looked fine; he felt fine. The next Thursday she
read his obituary.

Never feel pity for anybody else; it's your turn next.

*

The pleasure of writing is that the mind does not wander, any more than it does in orgasm,—and writing takes longer than orgasm. I can't stand movies because I cannot play close continual attention. While I watch baseball I read a volume of letters between pitches. Even reading a good book—which is the third best thing—my mind sometimes wanders; or I watch myself reading. When I write I *never* watch myself writing; I only *am* the struggle to find or make the words. I am fundamentally boring with a boring mind until, I hope, the word with its sounds and associations becomes a texture in front of me for working over, for shaping, for cutting, and for flying on.

It's the medium not the matter which affords this concentration. If I am working on a headnote for an anthology I am wholly engulfed by concentration on the rhythm and phrase, syntax and pitch, though I write nothing more than "John McPhee (b. 1930) writes. . . ." It is the grain of the wood, not the image of the Madonna, that concentrates the mind.

*

The poetry's in the redundancy. Reduction to message is reduction to concept, the abstract fallacy. Essence of Vanilla! So redundancy is never redundant (the nominalist's self-contradiction) but minutely varied in ways both visual and audible—the thousand tongues of style.

*

Chief among the activities that bore me—because I cannot give sufficient attention and my mind wanders and I want to be doing something else—is talking with other human beings. When my friend sits across the room from me I become impatient. I complained to A about this reclusiveness, and he imagined a scene I had already thought of. As I am sitting in the living room talking to my friend Z, with whom I enjoy a correspondence, after twenty or thirty minutes I become bored and restless. I want to go off into my study, close the door, and be alone—where I would be perfectly happy to write a letter to Z.

*

Writing Style

Work is style, and there is style without thought; not in theory, only in fact. When I take a sentence in my hand, raise it to the light, rub my hand across it, disjoin it, put it back together again with a comma added, raising the pitch in the front part; when I rub the grain of it, comb the fur of it, reassemble the bones of it, I am making something that carries with it the sound of a voice, the firmness of a hand. Maybe little more.

On the other hand there is no thought without style. Unless language taps chisel into stone, nothing is being thought. By itself the stone is only the blunt opacity of an area for thinking in; the stylus does the thinking—by cutting, by making clean corners, by incising. When we believe in translation into concepts, philosophy or poetry, we do not really think. Of course, when you use the stylus you are not necessarily thinking. But *unless* you use the stylus you are *certainly* not thinking. It is not always necessary to think. When it is necessary to think, poetry, because it is the most controlled stylus—because it makes more facets to control—is the ideal instrument of thought.

I understand that this notion is not generally accepted. "Poetry is for decoration and prose is for thought." Piss on that. Some philosophers know better, like Cavell not to mention Wittgenstein or Heraclitus. The stylus cuts word into stone, therefore the apothegm and the fragment. Emerson carved in stone; they were small stones and hard to build with but they were carved stones as Nietzsche understood.

*

In making sports analogies to the arts, the mucker knows no limits. Therefore let us dismiss poets of impeccable technique and nothing else: "Good field no hit."

*

Vatiphagy again. There's a knock on the front door, which my daughter answers, startled because the front door opens only once every forty years, for a coffin. She interrupts me at my desk to tell me that someone wants to see "Donald Hall." The quotation marks which she distributes allow me to understand that the object which it is desired to see is some sort of institution, possibly architectural, surely out of the way; or perhaps a rare bird, appropriate for a life list. When I meet the woman at the door I note that another sits in the car, the shy one, as the bold one tells me with triumph that they have spent the entire day looking for me; she expects felicitations on their accomplishment. I do not ask them in. I allow myself to be led to the car, to meet the shy one, and I nod my head and smile falsely for a minute before I pull myself away (work ended for the day) and as I leave them I am congratulated: "How wonderful that you have this place, with all your solitude and seclusion."

*

November

Remember when I had a poem in *Poetry* and a month later received an envelope forwarded from Chicago, "personal and confidential," with a sheet of paper inside. A tiny unsigned note praised a poem— and when I unfolded the note a twenty dollar bill fell out.

*

Dream of Little Joe Jesus.

*

Work and the materials of work. In March of 1986 we left here for seven weeks to travel in China and Japan reading poems and lecturing. I knew that I would stop working, the longest patch in the ten years since we moved from Michigan to New Hampshire. I thought it would be good for me to break my routines, and that I would build energy for work when I returned. (It worked that way; when I got back, after two days of feeling awkward at the desk, unused muscles, I let loose in a tidal wave of joyous work.) For weeks we traveled, talked, banqueted, and read. The trip was exhausting, exciting, consuming. Toward the end I felt restless with the desire to be home and to write, but the circumstances seemed too jumpy for work. Over seven weeks I wrote nothing but a hundred and two postcards.

Our last stop was in Sapporo, on the northernmost Japanese island of Hokkaido: birch trees, snow, Holstein cattle; amazingly like New Hampshire. After a day of public talk, we visited the Hokkaido historical museum where the director showed us around and took us on a tour of a reconstructed village, a Japanese nineteenth-century Williamsburg, and then bought us lunch. As we finished our noodles, the director shyly and apologetically reached into his pocket for a sheet of paper with two lines of typed English on it. He needed to write a caption in English, for a photograph, and would we mind terribly glancing at it to see if he had made any errors? His English was fine and in his two sentences he had merely omitted an article. I marked the page. Then I noticed that the second sentence trailed off, that if I reversed the order of clauses, its order would be more vigorous. I fiddled with it. Then I noticed that I could collapse the two sentences together into one complex sentence, using only two-thirds of the words he had used, making a sentence that mounted vigorously, with the lowered pitch of a parenthetical clause, to a firm conclusion. As I messed with the director's manuscript and prose style—ignorant of his subject, with no interest in his subject—my heart pounded with joy.

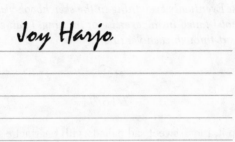

Joy Harjo

My earliest poems were derived directly from journal work. I would write wildly and intuitively in my journal to rev up to the higher frequency of a poem. I'd revise and play out possibilities in the journal, then transfer to a typewriter to revise and see the final poem. Now I do most of my journaling and writing on the computer, though I keep a journal and pen by my bed for dreams. I've included a few dreams here, but most I keep to myself, especially the very powerful, for I don't wish them to lose power by revealing them to possible misuse.

I sometimes read back through a journal to find scraps of meaning I am missing from some larger piece, when I need something personally historical, or to find a quote or something else I've stuck in the pages: newspaper articles, images, or lists. It's like fishing. Sometimes I see something that totally surprises. Often I write in my journal while I am still quite asleep. These entries are the most surprising, and often include information and leaps of logic I don't figure out until something happens a few years later.

I wish I could include songs. Last night I dreamed a rewrite of a song my band and I have written to go with the poem "She Had Some Horses." We added another movement that enlarged the overall meaning. By the time I awoke to deadlines and the need to bake bread for a lunch for visiting relatives, I had forgotten it. Maybe the skill to notate in shorthand what I hear in dream music will come.

My journal is like the sketch book I used to carry around when

I painted. I sketched gestures, ideas for larger drawings and paintings. Eventually everything in the sketchbook was used, whether or not I failed in the exercise of imaging. I gained knowledge of my art through each venture.

7/16/94

I can't help it, I love sweet sad ballads with heartache saxophone: Art Pepper, John Coltrane, especially Coltrane. The music breaks away at any crust of unlove to the longing for that home far from the density of years of soap opera on earth.

*

1/3/94

the explosion at genesis creates stones who tell the stories of how we lived. I consider the radius of intimacy and imagine you showering in the artificial light of the motel room, before dawn when most earthly spirits are returning from memory. . . . it was a tender arc marked by absolute grace and a little rain.

There is no love beyond faithful love. Le Ly Hayslip's mother, from *When Heaven and Earth Change Places*

*

10/19/93

The heart has four winds. I heard them last night as my son, his daughter Haleigh and I drove from a birthday dinner. It was raining and dark, difficult to differentiate between shadow and pavement. I remembered weather in the womb. . . . And then the four winds as they created the child, talked to her, shaped the elegant and tiny bones. All humans come out of the dark this way, into the dark. Each human knows a woman intimately. The four winds of the mother's heart directs the fate of the child. Perhaps the path forms the physical heart, consequently.

Remembering and imagination enter and leave from the same area of the soul.

It was hot and wet. To feel was another dimension not available to me, another field in the weave of magnetic waves—yet, approaching me were spirits who rose in waves from the brackish sweet smell of the newly dead whose corpses littered the killing ground. I'm sorry, I said, though I no longer had a mouth or a tongue. Though I no longer had words with which to approach the altar of the living.

There's a lullabye. Made to calm the ruler of sharp things.

*

undated from this general time

When you grow up you either make uneasy peace with the density of destiny, and entertain the possibility of a reckless, cruel god, or watch television with the rest of the escapees.

See those sensitive hills? They need to be talked to, sung to. . . .

*

7/8/90 Tucson

We descend into the damp city. I anticipate the wet flowering of the desert. And it will remind me of the warm pools of moisture under your body after we have made love, when we are at the mercy of a tenderness beyond this world.

*

6/3/91 Honolulu

Full of beans, rice, sweets and a crimson tea. A light mist outside, all seven windows open and trees brushing the second story. Talked of massacres, genocide at dinner last night with Haunani-Kay and her companion David—how those words don't translate, nor do body counts. What's missing are names, terms of endearment, and stories. There's always been a problem negotiating from the language of commerce to the spiritual realm. . . . The smells here are so old, sweet and familiar.

*

6/4/91

Some spirits go willingly (at death). In the tragedy of massacre the shock of rolling thoughtlessness can trap one in the house of disbelief. The body is a house of memory that decay cannot loosen.

*

11/10/91

"Blazing above Powell Observatory near Louisburg, Kansas, the aurora borealis filled the sky Friday evening. The northern lights, not usually seen this far south, painted the sky with shimmering curtains of reds, greens, blues and whites. Chances for more displays are good tonight and later this week. Get away from city lights and look north any time after dark." The *Kansas City Star*, Front page.

*

6/20/91

The first thought is of the angel of death, who can take everything but the heart rooted to acts of imagination. What is imagined and what is not?

In the first dream her spirit had knocked on the door of my truck. She was living in the Fifth World, or are we in it?

I don't think worlds are as easily defineable as that . . . they exist simultaneously. The people are always emerging. They are always falling through the hole in the sky.

I think death has been overrated. I heard too many fire and brimstone stories from the stiff pews of Christians. I saw too many cheap Hollywood movies featuring winners and losers, though no one ever won. No Indians survived. In Ecuador the tribes from the southern hemisphere thought we'd all been killed by John Wayne. Now *there's* an angel of death.

And what of my friend who this afternoon weeded her garden, wielding a cigarette in one hand as she coughed with the cancer eating her, a friend on each side holding her up? She wants to leave with a little grace, yet doesn't want to leave at all. What do we know about anything?

We cannot escape memory, but carry it in us like a huge organ with lungs sucking air for survival. It is an organ like the skin, covering everything, but from the inside.

Was there ever mercy? Is Mercy an errant angel so horrified by cruel acts of humans she cannot bear to look on us? Mercy, come find us in the labyrinth of cruelty.

I don't know what to tell you, beloved.

*

2/10/92 Bonn

In Beethoven's house . . . there is no evidence of Beethoven's mother in this place. Who was she? There would be no Beethoven without her.

*

10/20/92

I felt the immensity of my anger for the first time. I felt totally present as yellow sharpened itself against the blue sky.

*

3/9/93

Each path reeked of afterbirth, rain and mice. . . . Humans only think we can bend time into increments of money.

*

3/25/93

As soon as I stepped from the automatic glass doors of the hotel a dragonfly alit on my arm. I once knew that language.

*

8/10/93

(*From these notes came the poem "The Naming," for my granddaughter Haleigh Sara, who was born in Green Bay, Wisconsin. The poem with story follows.*)

The most honorable wars weren't fought with swords of the yelling of fools. The greatest thinkers (each representing their tribe) sat on opposite hills and had a contest to outimagine the other. You can manipulate an enemy's weakness so the enemy destroys himself/herself with foolishness. *PERIGORD – CASTle(s) – 1974*

Names are the least idle of sounds. The night after she was born I spent the night in a hotel near the lake left over from the ice age. A conference of tribes gathered in the ballroom a few floors below.

I think of names that have profoundly changed the direction of disaster. Of the raw whirling wind outlining femaleness emerging from the underworld. It blesses the frog taking refuge under the squash flower cloud, the stubborn weeds leaning in the direction of the wind.

Clouds scheme and provoke a glitter of electricity.

*

THE NAMING
For Haleigh Sara Bush

I think of names that have profoundly changed the direction of disaster. Of the raw whirling wind outlining femaleness emerging from the underworld.

It blesses the frog taking refuge under the squash-flower cloud, the stubborn weeds leaning in the direction of wind bringing rain.

My grandmother is the color of night as she tells me to move away from the window when it is storming. *The lightning will take you.*

I thought it was my long dark hair appearing as lightning. The lightning appears to be relatives.

Truth can appear as disaster in a land of things unspoken. It can be reached with white arrows, each outlining the meaning of delicate struggle.

And can happen on a night like this when the arrow light is bitten by sweet wind.

My grandmother took leave years ago by way of her aggravated heart. I haven't seen her since, but her warnings against drownings, lightning or anything else protending death by sudden means still cling to my ears.

I take those risks against the current of warnings as if she had invented negative space of wind around the curve of earth.

That night after my granddaughter-born-for-my-son climbed from the underworld we could smell ozone over the lake made of a few centuries of rain.

I went hunting for the right name and found the spirit of the ice age making plans in the bottom of the lake. Eventually the spirit will become rain, remake the shoreline with pines and laughter.

In the rain I saw the child who was carried by lightning to the other side of the storm. I saw my grandmother who never had any peace in this life blessed with animals and songs.

Oh daughter-born-of-my-son, of my grandmother, of my mother; I name you all these things:

The bag of white arrows is heavy with rain.

The earth is wet with happiness.

*

I never liked my mother's mother, Leona May Baker. When we would visit her and my grandfather in their two-room house in northwestern Arkansas where they were sharecroppers, she would awaken me long before dawn. I would be irritable with lack of sleep as she would sit by my bed and catalogue the gruesome details of every death of every relative and friend as well as each event of personal disaster within her known landscape.

My grandmother, who was half Cherokee and Irish, was orphaned at a very young age and raised by full-blood Cherokees in Jay, Oklahoma. She gave birth to six sons and one daughter—my mother. Each birth added to the burden of life. Once she took out a gun and shot at all of them as they ran through the trees to get away from her. My mother recalls the sounds of bullets flying by her head. My grandmother disliked my mother.

With the impending birth of my son's daughter I was prompted to find out more about this grandmother who I had never made peace with. My mother told me of her incredible gift of storytelling, how she would keep the children entranced for weeks by tales she would invent—they had no books, television or radio. And then she told me this story:

My grandfather Desmond Baker left to work on the railroad when they were especially destitute. While he was away my grandmother had an affair. When he returned nine months later she was near full term with a baby who wasn't his. He beat her until she went into labor and gave birth to the murdered child.

Shortly after the killing my grandparents attempted double suicide. They stood on the tracks while a train bore down on them as all the children watched in horror. At the last possible second my grandfather pushed my grandmother off to safety and leaped behind her.

I began to have compassion for this woman who was weighted down with seven children and no opportunities. Maybe her affair was the lightness she needed to stay alive.

When my granddaughter Haleigh was born I felt the spirit of this grandmother in the hospital room. Her presence was a blessing.

I welcomed her.

- The spirit who came to take care of my heart
- The eating and sculpting with shit episode
- Relentless toilet training
- Polio scare and hospital:
    separation
    spinal tap

- Father in jail
- Father chopping the Christmas tree top off with an ax in the living room
- My brother's birth
- My mother's scarlet fever. I am sent far away to relatives I dislike. They take my stuffed black cat away from me and try to replace it with a doll. I am bereft.
- The "following sound" revelation, set off by a trumpet jazz solo on the radio as I am just learning language.
- Difficult birth and separation
- Sun mote language
- Sexual play retribution in public
- Stomach aches, throwing up and castor-oil
- I begin hiding from my father
- Carried home from parents' parties wrapped in my father's brown leather jacket, smells of her perfume White Shoulders
- The babysitter scene, a house at night filled with strange and frightened children cared for by an elderly man and woman. I am terrified. They put me to bed in a crib. My friend Ronnie, whose parents beat him for wetting his pants, comforts me.

*

3/23/94

My father, too, continued to drink. His white co-workers called him "chief." He just drank off the sting. . . . My parents both liked to dance and party and some of my favorite memories the few years just before the birth of my sister was being a child running with other children at these parties. And carried to the car after I'd fallen asleep, wrapped in the leather bomber jacket that had been my father's but taken over by my mother. It smelled of White Shoulders and tobacco. The smell was home to me, and it was comforting to be carried in, tucked into my Army cot to sleep. I could feel the tenderness well up in my parents as they looked at me, as I feigned sleep. . . . His violence became a thick monster whirling through the rooms of the house. I saw this thing once as it pounded on the front door on Saturday afternoon. My mother grabbed up my little brother and me and we hid in the back bedroom.

*

4/8/94

Certain numbers chase you through life. The house I was raised in until I was eight was number 419. (Later we moved into a house that had so many traumatic experiences I could not find it when I went back a few years ago, though I knew the street and the number. It was there, though I could not see it. My mother now rented it out.) Nearly forty years later I was picked up at the airport in Albuquerque, from Tucson, by an old friend for a reading to be held at the law school the next afternoon. It was a perfect spring night and my blood went excited at the familiar smell of the land to which I returned as a relative. My blood also felt the halo of impact preceding a life changing event. When I read the address to the house to which I'd been invited for a little wine and talk before retiring, I knew something would change. The house number was distinctly 419. . . . I soon lived in that house. It became the home I had been approaching for many years.

W. H. Auden " . . . poetry makes nothing happen; it survives."

*

3/24/94 (in between Albuquerque and Chicago)

What was certain was a sensitivity that crackled and burned. I could hear words and the roots of words veering from the base of silence. I wonder where my father is now in the stream of all things that once had a place here? Does he think of me or of the tragedy of connection? Did he ever experience beauty from the inside out? There's a dinosaur under the house, and other bones of those who once walked the surface of the planet, like my father. I've considered this planet as a prison, a school for the hard headed. . . . What comes back to me is the result of my actions for instance—fury begets fury. The form may change. Hatred is self-hatred, though it may mask as xenophobia or other forms of fear and aggression.

*

1/26/94

In this dream Rainy, Sue and I walk under a huge overpass to watch the planes taking off and landing at an airport about the size of LAX. We are so close it is frightening. One plane falters, then goes down.

It is absolutely terrifying, particularly to listen as the breaking apart metal monster slides across the grass towards us. We run hard away from it, in anticipation of the explosion. I've dreamed many variations of this scene. It's always just as horrifying.

*

2/7/94

Sandra Cisneros is holding a turtle. I am aware that turtles can snap, bite hard, but this turtle reaches out his head to nudge me. The turtle then turns into a baby boy in a high chair. Or he appears to be a baby boy in a high chair. He's pissed because he's a fully conscious human in a baby's body. I tell him he can pass as a dwarf once he can walk.

*

7/26/94

To be born into a family of mixed nations, involving alliances and enmities from time immemorial, in a land of refugees from persecution in Europe, the Americas, Asia and anywhere else there are evil governments and religious fundamentalists who mete out destiny, or of forced slavery over an ocean turned red from the blood of those who didn't survive, or moved from homelands against the will of the tribes—the land on which all are to be settled amicably into a "melting pot"—is to be disturbed and shaped by the spirits of ancestors who fight it out among themselves in the world intersecting the physical, who cannot rest because the direct track to the original heart has been lost, (and it's easy to get distracted by neon, fast food and the appearance of nude bodies on billboards), as well as fiercely loved and guarded by those who see themselves in you, a promise for continuance when continuance is a myth buried in libraries and in stories told under the stars in sacred languages that have been kept burning by sheer will, sheer love.

*

sometime earlier

I was the first born, arrived with great difficulty to this tempestuous love, this shakey sea. I was born during a new moon, a moon that represents new beginnings, the direction East. East is the harbor for those spirits who point us on our journey. East is the direction of our tribal homelands, the place of forced exile not but a few generations ago—in the southeast of this continent, made of nearly tropical foliage, water, and thick with animal power. My birth contradicted the prediction of destruction, the myth of the vanishing Indian that was bought and sold by the American public, for if we disappeared guilt would vanish, and the right to the land by strangers would be sealed. Though we lost over half the tribe during the forced walk from a land that had nurtured our people through millennia, we didn't die. I was the next loop in the spiral of memory.

Anselm Hollo

One of the pleasures of "notebook" writing is, of course, that the writer is free to make indefensible utterances—and it is then up to her or him, or to authorized literary executors, to censor them (or not). You can say anything. It's all right. The notebook is also a commonplace book, a collection of quotes that seem possibly useful, or curious, or so incredibly stupid that they're worth preserving; these include "quotes" from oneself. That's the notebook as sottisier. Since the advent of the personal computer, I compose much of my writing, including poems, on the screen, but I still prefer the notebook to any portable version of my trusty old Mac. From time to time, I go through notebook jottings to find, now and again, the beginnings of a poem, or at least a line or two. The poem at the end of my entry, here, which is part of a fourteen-sonnet sequence, demonstrates obvious (and some not-so-obvious) gleanings from preceding notebook entries. I love reading poets' notebooks. Poets are curious critters, and it is a pleasure to relax with the jottings and musings of other practitioners.

1979–1993

"Lampshades! Lampshades!
All sizes! All colors!

Blue for comfort! Red for passion!
Get yourselves a lampshade, Comrades!"
                                —Mayakovsky, "The Bedbug"

Mina Loy the greater poet designed lampshades
(he writes these essays in his head)

*

A great deal of *evasive* action in the "language-oriented" écriture: it's
like trying to tell someone something without 'really' telling them
. . . tease tease . . .

*

Nobel Prize to be divided in 3 equal parts between:
        h.c. artmann (Austria)
        Paavo Haavikko (Finland)
        Ernesto Cardenal (Nicaragua)
                    (conveyed to PEN 1-24-80)

*

If you could find a large enough ocean to hold it,
Saturn would *float*

                                            (radio info)

*

music: people who really understand it must have a hard time in this
(human, social) world—seeing, feeling, as they must, how terribly
skewed that world is—in terms of over-all construction

*

    "aesthetics
    is for the artist
    as ornithology
    is for the birds"
                —Barnett Newman

*

re: "line breaks":
"She was speaking quietly but fast, and pausing for breath in the
wrong places, the way politicians do when they fear interruption"
                        —Gavin Lyall ("The Crocus List")

*

My tribe of poets isn't really "out for scars"
they'd much rather stay in their rooms
giggling over their notebooks

*

"Satire
is an overloading of meaning
that so burdens the reader's belief
that it collapses,
exploding meaning
and hopefully leading it
in a direction opposite to
its stated intent"
                              —Daniel Gercke (*Colorado Daily*, 2-26-86)

*

give me phrase or give me fable

*

Uninspired
today
my 'inspiration' is like Kit Robinson's cats
First
they moved into the kitchen wall
Then
they were gone

*

guy looks like a giant molar with arms & legs

*

Je ne l'ai pas connu
Peter Whigham
but he sure was one hell of a translator
& not a mean poet
like his greatest past voice Catullus
perhaps even too kind
he came my way once

bewildered-bearded
silent & manic like so many of us

*

Ah, real estate ahoy! it is Columbus Day
the globe is still a globe, the paleface still holds sway
the buck's a buck, a slave's a slave—
etc.

*

"Anthologies are to poets as the zoo is to animals"

—David Antin

*

permanent diaspora—the ideal state
(my sympathies always with the Gypsies
rather than the Zionists or now Palestinians, etc.)

*

writers of small language groups—their admirable stubbornness in clinging to the 'absoluteness' of their particular language—*their* words—by extension, that's of course true of everybody—

*

"[critics] will always choose poetry which labors to be 'poetic,' whether by remembered forms or by a nostalgic, privately pained tilt of the head and vocal chords . . ."

—Marvin Bell

*

re: translation as dealing-with-another-language—it can make you 'say' things you'd never 'say' in your 'own' language—i.e., not 'speech' in the sense that Robert Grenier dislikes it—more in the sense that he *writes* it

*

what's feeble in (some) 'language-oriented' stuff is when it becomes these *bleak little exercises*

(or else when it expresses nothing as much as the need to exercise *control* over the work, *total*, if possible)

*

Ezra Pound's complicated love life
drove him to Economics?

*

Harper's Index—greatest American 'serial poem' of the Eighties

*

EP
just a cracker who fell in love with books

*

All poetry is 'hermetic,' 'cryptic,' heretical use of words—not to
sell, not to instruct in skills designed to produce & sell—so, in that
sense, l'art is always pour l'art: the un-paraphrasable is what we
want

*

when "straight talk" was shown to be crooked
& "sincerity" merely as in "yours sincerely"
we got $l=a=n=g=u=a=g=e$

*

"Dolphins (as we speak)
are carrying on 2
conversations simultaneously

& within the clicks of one
lie the squeaks of the other

they are alive in their little wandering pool"
          —Ted Berrigan & Anne Waldman ("Memorial Day")

*

Le style pompier—the poetry of pompous statement—what *everybody*, from post-WW 2 Vienna School to the $l=a=n=g$s has been
trying to get away from: yet these 'elevated diction' folks (mostly
white Southern, in these States) keep cropping up . . .

*

"We're all toast, anyway"
—dude at Brigham Young University, to Jane, re: radiation hazards

*

Translations—often, perhaps always? at least partial mis-hearings—
what happens to every poem when someone else reads it

*

the "Mac" put Tzara's instructions for Dada poem in "scrapbook"
(can't recall telling it to do so)

*

"post-national"
(je suis)
but also "lower-case american"

*

"I cut the orange in two, and couldn't make the two parts equal. To
which was I unjust? I'm going to eat them both!"
—Alberto Caeiro (Fernando Pessoa)

*

attention exactly *between* the words

*

"No provision for transvestites in Geneva Convention"
"OK—put 'em in a separate tent"
—News, Panama, January '90

*

The "joys of opacity"—still a post-romantic yearning for
"l'innommable"—but Samuel Beckett (now gone) did it better: he's
never "opaque"—& he's still the champ

*

'history' understood as "tales of the tribe"—nothing but an incite-
ment to endless *revenge*—maybe only those who are truly 'mixed' &
'exiled' can step outside it: I come from at least 5 pairs of "arch
enemies"—Finn/Swede, Finn/Russ, German/Pole, Pole/Russ,

Russ/Germ—etc. etc., the gods know how it multiples back & back . . .

*

troubadour tradition: *oppositional* to patriarchal 'mainstream' (even if 'sexist' 'pedestalist' etc.)

*

getting old when you start noticing how almost impossibly hard the young find it to be anywhere "on time"

*

few notes, many poems
(the ideal state of affairs)

*

the unbelievable badness of the well-intentioned

*

"He could play a tomato can and make it sound good"
—Red Rodney, on Charlie Parker

*

"signage"—buzzword at librarians' conference—means "to put up signs," like "No Eating"

*

"what happened between the time he wrote those *nice* poems . . . and . . ."

*

It's a *pulse* I'm after, one set up by cadenced phrases. Sometimes it goes on for a bit, sometimes it's over almost as soon as it began (Anton Webern's tiny pieces)—but then it changes, and changes again. Ted Berrigan used to say poets had a little guy in an office tucked away in their heads who "took care of things like meter."

*

What do generations whose earliest moments have been recorded on film or videotape learn from those images and sounds when they review them later in life? What if one recorded every waking (possibly even sleeping) moment of one's life, up to, say, thirty-five—then spent one's remaining years watching the tape?

*

A night ride down a wide avenue, black, a-glitter with rain: *der Kurfürstendamm*. . . . Each mental replay a re-*make*, its materials fragmentary, in far from archival condition. A walk past the *Reichskanzlei* and its stone-faced sentries. "Who's riding so late through night-wind wild / It is the father with his child." But my father was back in Helsinki. This was 1939, Berlin, with my mother.

*

Meet large bearded patriarch in rocking chair, thumb on right hand sliced off at first joint in long-ago woodworking accident. My father's mother is an even fuzzier snapshot: small busy woman, black shawl with fringes. . . . Just before the second great slaughter of my century.

*

To improve our chances of survival we packed our bags and steamed across a gulf to another city, where we stayed long enough for me to learn to read in *their* language: until then, I had spoken only our main conversational lingo. Sister Irina grew tired of reading and translating speech-balloons in my favorite comics *Felix the Cat, Mandrake the Magician, Nancy & Sluggo, The Phantom*, on the back pages of the strange city's dailies. She obtained an ABC book and taught me to read in *their* language. When we returned to our city, my father taught me our country's dominant language in a couple of months, to prepare me for Miz O's elementary school just around the corner from where we lived. Home was the second floor of a large building in the Old Town of our city: twelve-foot ceilings, tall tile stoves to burn wood fetched up from the cellar and stored in a big box in the kitchen.

*

On translation: The Latin *shrug* does *not* involve a raising of shoulders / contraction of shoulderblades. It is, instead, an oblique glance skyward, plus a tilt of chin, accompanied by palms outspread between waist and shoulder level: Hence, "shrug" (noun or verb) is not really translatable into Spanish. (Informant: Argentinian poet Mario Trejo.)

*

A most succinct formulation of true 20th century aesthetic (and art-
ist/critic relationship):

> I
> put it down. You
> got to pick it up.

—Thelonious Sphere Monk, quoted by David Meltzer on p. 79 of
The Name: Selected Poetry 1973–1983, Black Sparrow, 1983.

*

now doomed to write
elegies
until the end?

*

"If novels and poems fail to interest the Agora today, by the year
2091 such artifacts will not exist at all except as objects of monkish
interest. This is neither a good nor a bad thing. It is simply not a
famous thing." —Gore Vidal, *Screening History* (*New York Times
Book Review*, 30 August 1992)

*

translating the fragments of Hipponax: a "strange transmission"—or
just the urge to get involved with some really *rowdy* dead guy?

*

Contemporary Canadians (thinking, here, of Gerry Gilbert, the late
bp Nichol, others) seem both saner and more comprehensive in their
work than most present U.S. poets (exceptions excepted)—they are
not afraid to include much of what seems "dull," quotidian,
"trivial"—they're more Greek—less Roman, less into Bread & Circuses, "special effects," or a striving for same. No more "substantial"
than a good tune. I love it. & I really mean that.

*

What I'm most allergic to in poetry is the flowery earnestness that
tries to convey an oh-aren't-we-all-in-this-together sort of feeling;
that's worse, even, than vehement righteousness—because the

latter, at least, is inherently funny in its indignation, anger being comical.

Another variety of earnestness implies that the author is an adept in some secret school of wisdom; it doesn't grate on me as much, but it does tend to put me to sleep.

Just think about it for a moment: Ezra Pound is funny, William Carlos Williams, Allen Ginsberg, Robert Creeley, Gregory Corso, Frank O'Hara are—not necessarily all the time, but frequently enough to make one put up with all their other delusions and pretensions.

*

"As we grow older, our nervous systems decelerate and our sense of *personal* time dawdles correspondingly. But *civil* time, of course, tramps on remorselessly, its divisions constant and inexorable. This is why our lives seem to pass more quickly as we age."
—William Boyd, *Brazzaville Beach*, p. 149

*

Pol Pot's "cultural revolutionists" *ate* their victims: the ultimate transgression, similar to practices of "black magic" drug smuggler (perverted) *santería* types; same desperate bag. . . . The simulacrum of 'immortality' that kind of temporal power creates. The old Marquis nods and smiles: "Told you so. . . ."

*

"I'm going to sit down and enjoy a really *empty* experience."

*

"the sonnet . . . is not a form at all but a state of mind. It is the extremely familiar dialogue upon which much writing is founded: a statement then a rejoinder of a sort, perhaps a reply, perhaps a variant of the original—but a comeback of one sort or another."
—William Carlos Williams to James Laughlin
(in *Selected Letters*, New York: W. W. Norton, 1989)

*

"And what was it *like*, that *world* of yours?"

*

both fortunate & un-
—to have lived these past thirty years
when so many delightful poets
have been writing so many terrific poems:
there was so much to read
there wasn't much time left to write

*

Thinking of the *bambini* . . . all the little rituals . . . past, lost, over
in any case; but now we can't even wax sentimental over them.

*

treading
            the fine line
                        between farce & pathos

*

why oh why did I spend eleven dollars on this tome in which two
dead men *gibber* at each other? [Olson-Dahlberg correspondence]

*

"It is well known how Mary Magdalene came to Provençe to live after
the Crucifixion, but less known that at Maximilien near Marseilles the
tip of her nose used to be on view: no more than that because she had
been cremated, but the tip of her nose remained imperishable because
there Christ had kissed her."   —E. S. Bates, *Touring in 1600*

*

"Myth—the practice of memory."
            —Joanne Kyger, at Naropa panel discussion, summer '93

*

"Almost any noun
is better alone than chaperoned
if it's the right noun, and very few
can stand two
adjectives. 'Unsettled dream' is
stronger than
'unsettled white dream'."
            —Ezra Pound to Parker Tyler, May '35 in: Charles Boultenhouse,
            Parker Tyler's Own Scandal, Film Culture #77, Fall '92

*

"We are but older children, dear,
Who fret to find our bedtime near"

—Lewis Carroll, to Alice

*

Benjamin Péret knew how to make a poem move *and* stand absolutely still at the same time.

*

when frozen water falls from the sky
we think of those who've said goodbye

*

"Confusion of voices as from several transmitters"

—EP, Canto 72

*

who reads 100 poems writes like 100 poets
who reads 1,000 poems writes like herself
—Ancient Chinese poet (?) via Gerry Gilbert via Joel Oppenheimer,
in J.O.'s *Poetry, the Ecology of the Soul*, p. 27

*

"Sometimes the only person who has devoted fifteen minutes of mental receptivity and appreciation to a book, aside from its author and (with luck) its publisher, is the cataloguer at the library who described it for the O.C.L.C. database."
—Nicholson Baker, *Discards*, in *The New Yorker*, April 4 '94

*

In Utopia, Home and Exile are simultaneous. I don't think artists really, actively, exist anywhere else but there. Was Emily Dickison "at home"? Sure, but she was/is also totally elsewhere, and it's in that "elsewhere" we meet her, not in some dreary New England town.

*

"Yours is not to complete
the work, but neither are you
free to abstain from it."
                    —Rabbi Tarphon, Pirkei Avot (2:21), via Joel Lewis

SONNET IV FROM NOT A FORM AT ALL BUT A STATE OF MIND

it is well known that Mary Magdalen came to Provençe
to live after the crucifixion
but less known that at Maximilien near Marseilles
the tip of her nose used to be on view

no more than that   because she had been cremated
but the tip of her nose remained imperishable
because there   the christ had kissed her
& who is going to pay   any attention to anything

when we aren't here anymore   "& what was it *like*   that
world of yours?"   so much depends
on Fire Engine Number 5   myth is the practice of memory
dit Joanne Kyger

Johannes Kelpius first american composer
founded a commune called "the woman in the wilderness"

Garrett Hongo

*These journal pages emerged out of a time when I was "between books"—*Yellow Light *and* The River of Heaven. *I began it while working on a Ph.D. in critical theory, then kept it through my first academic jobs—first as a visitor at USC and then at UC Irvine, next as an assistant professor at Missouri. I felt even more then that I was an outsider than I do now. My constant company of white professors and students assumed that cultural identities were all fixed and solved, or that they were at the very least not a concern of anyone "serious." I wasn't having the kind of close conversations with people about politics, literature, and ethnicity that I craved. This social and professional life offended me, yet I could not complain. By then, I had decided against a simple cultural nationalism—writing my first book of poems persuaded me out of that—yet I wished not to work towards any kind of "assimilationist" or "closet-ethnic" aesthetic either. I wanted to be rooted, I wanted to think my way towards a considered aesthetic and political position regarding my passion to create compatible poetic, regional, and ethnic identities. These journal pages helped me do that. I put together much of the aesthetic that resulted in* The River of Heaven— *a book poised between Hawaii and Los Angeles, attempting to occupy the silence between cultural centrism and the realities of diaspora. Yeats's* Autobiography *and Allan Seager's biography of Theodore Roethke,* The Glass House, *were inspirations regarding these kinds of regional and ethnic self-creations. My own journal, then, became an opportunity for fulminating these*

102

kinds of issues. It was an affair with my own emotions and intellect and a resolute pursuit of an unsanctioned, hidden history. Like poetry, it was a secret place of the heart, a smithy of my soul.

1982

October 1: Balboa. There's something like an "imaginative will"—a desire to exercise the mind, to use the imagination, a wish to conjure worlds of one's imagining simply to enjoy the task of that imagining. It's fun to tell stories, so we tell them. Wolf tickets sold not for profit but for the gain of the feelings they inspire.

*

This is what the theorists mean, when they talk about the "repose of the imagination." The self-contemplative ideal that Flaubert is sometimes said to have invented, that Stephen Daedalus endorses and improves upon in A *Portrait of the Artist as a Young Man.*

This is why so many of us prefer to live in these worlds of our own design—the idea of the poetic retreat, "Peter Quince at the Klavier," Kamo-no-Chōmei in his hut ten-foot square, Kenkō in his idleness, and Bashō in his unreal dwelling. I'm told that Pope had a fabulous garden to which he'd retire to write his caustic verse epistles. Whether he really did or not I'm not sure, being no scholar, but I am sure that he had a bower of sorts within the territory of his own poems. It was probably more pleasant for him than in society.

The Chinese have a word for poet that means "sorcerer" or "magician," but it also means "hermit." The notion contains within it an idea of the poet as alchemist of the human spirit, poetry as a kind of spiritual pharmaceutical.

But society still remains and so does the world. What can poems do for them? I'm fairly Confucian about this question and believe that if poems can order our thinking and inspire noble emotions within us, then in doing these things, they indiretly help the world. Poems inspire *jen,* a kind of metaphysical propriety and liberation within us that we need to keep going, maintain a generous-minded social equilibrium that can carry us through most of what's mental and trivial in our daily routines. Like the song says, "You gotta have heart!" and good poems, like good songs, restore that in us. *Kokoro*, the Japanese say, the life spirit. Love.

*

But love is as hard here
it has to be carved into a tree.

—Lance Patigian

*

October 8:   The world's body has been denied us. I want it back. And I use the erotic resonance of that metaphor purposefully because it is precisely that strong physical relationship with the world that modern, particularly modern urban, life seems to deny us. Poetry is my way of re-establishing that relationship, recapturing that lost love. It's a hermeneutic desire.

For Japanese Americans, the past is a corpse, a dead and foul thing we have all either avoided or been shielded from. Because of the circumstances of our history and its conjunction with a perhaps necessarily stoic psychological culture, the past has been something to be ashamed of and overcome, forgotten. I want to go into this territory of our dead, make them speak and reveal to me their emotional lives still unaccounted for. I'd like to spend my time listening to these ghosts, learning what I can of the circumstances of their lives—the immigration and early settlement. WWII and Relocation, the postwar return—and tell about them in a book of poems.

I propose to enter these lives through the study of documents and oral histories.

It's my way of bringing back what John Crowe Ransom called "the world's body."

*

October 17:   What the Derrideans seem to want is the freedom to read a text in the same way as a poet "reads" the world—for the play of signifiers it "engenders" in their own texts.

*

1984

June 23:   Eugene. Seems to me the most beautiful, sentimental, and extravagant of all arts must be the hand-gestures of the hula. . . .

*

The "Romantic Image" is simply a tool for emotional concentration and the release of emotion and a more complex imagery towards the making of a symbolic pattern that *has* emotion in it (i.e., that inspires and not merely "stands for" emotion). Yeats made it a craft and a discipline because of his needs and his background—his aesthetic roots in Pre-Raphaelite painting and an ideal of craftsmanship that must have been born partly out of a nativist pride, partly out of an atavistic affection for things Greek—" of hammered gold and gold enameling. . . ."

*

The trick is to make the memory, (or) the *imagined* experience, stronger than anything else in one's consciousness, to make the "pretend game" the one that counts, that is the death trap. Tricks of the mystics and the contemplatives should prove handy: simplify one's life; spend lots of time in solitude; avoid chaotic, undisciplined experiences until one is prepared to encounter them; quell the violent passions (jealousy, envy, malice). I'd add one dictum probably not present in any handbook for contemplatives—cultivate a refined sensuousness. Lots of the great and the near-great did this—one has only to think of Monet's gardens at Giverny, Neruda's study full of varicolored, beach-scavenged bottles, ships-in-bottles, conch shells, and that sea-siren Madonna he scrounged and subsequently enshrined near his desk. Wordsworth had the entire Wye Valley, Frost his New Hampshire farm, Jeffers Tor House, Yeats his tower in Coole Park or Ballylee.

One of my most profound regrets is that I don't have a proper portrait of my father. I wonder—could I get a snapshot somehow and ask Wakako to paint one for my study?

Or could I imagine one myself? Paint it, "with poetry" as it were?

I remember a service picture, not a formal one, but a studio group portrait of three G.I.s in uniform, one of them my father. I seem to remember they had leis and big grins on, a stripe or two each, and service decorations. And except for being sepia-toned, the print was untinted.

What was lost?—those sparkling moments of clear emotion and generousness in the past, heirlooms of consciousness.

Returning vets, conquering heroes, 18 or 19 years old . . .

*

Worry is a mental erosion, a disease like leprosy upon consciousness, contagious and ultimately, to the imagination, fatal.

*

1985

January 14:　Columbia. Reading Robert Morgan's poems, I realize that my instincts are quite conservative in terms of poetic value—
    richness of diction and imagery
    strong, straight } crafted narrative
    a vanished thing set down in
        language the goal—this
            seems Frostian somehow,
                perhaps Yankee,
        though I can call up similarities to Japanese & Chinese
           poetry—
                Tsuravuki's *Preface*
                T'ao Ch'ien's poems for wine &
                friendship

My early teachers were conservative too in terms of their literary values—Bert Meyers, Stanley Crouch, and John Haines. They wanted a fairly straightforward and simplified diction, an elegance or stateliness of *tone,* and startling or even sometimes dazzling imagery and metaphor. Ideas were restricted to the aesthetic or the chthonic, a certain kind of primitivism the force behind much of this, with radical politics thrown in as spice, conscience, and Utopian dream.

Coherence, literary and political and emotional, was above all the guiding principle—a hatred of cultural and spiritual atavism.

Derrida in his critique of Kant and Hegel attacks this as a desire for religion, their philosophies a kind of secular theology smuggling back deism in what purports to be a rational philosophy, irrational desire masquerading in the rhetorical robes of dialectical reason.

Poetry, for my teachers, conducted no such masquerade. Rather, it declared itself as heir to the role religion might have served in more coherent societies, ritual might have performed in primitive cultures.

*

June 27:   Volcano. I guess it's true—my problem is a chronic one, that consciously and unconsciously I *make myself cultureless because of an internalized oppression.* I try to fit in with my surroundings to the point that I repress the better nature within, eliminate the Hawaiian, ghetto L.A., and Japanese roots.

There is nobility in these ways, there is a good and strong side to these impulses I should try to learn to tap into and restore so that I can maintain myself better as a healthy and creative psyche.

Here in Volcano, I feel like I've found the real thing again, found my *own way* and I'm not so worried about being competitive so long as I can always come from myself, so long as the poems can come from that better part of me so I breathe easy when I write, reach out to all the best parts of memory and imagination.

*

July 6:   Kawela. C. says that what I *wish* I could be is a "folk" artist the way Lau is or say, someone actually genuine. But the reality is I can't be that since I don't come out of an intact, received tradition but needed to construct my own art, amalgamating elements and influences eclectically, choosing and absorbing from pop culture, high art and literature, and a smattering of learning in Oriental studies. Not even the folklorist that Yeats or Synge were, the scholar that Snyder and Merwin are, I've had to freeboot, wildcat, and jerry-rig my practice together as Simon Rodia did his towers, Mingus did his music.

*

Writerly riches are like vast landholdings—rent comes in from everywhere and you can inhabit what parcels you choose, when you

choose. If you have a village, a kingdom, that you write from and
about, you are wealthy to the point of embarrassment. *Material*. Rich
in material. Faulkner, Garcia Marquez, Hardy.

[I write this 500 yds. from where my Kubota grandfather died in a
state nursing home on Kamehameha Highway. I write this 2 miles
from the sugar mill, surrounded by canefields where two generations
of my family worked as laborers, where they owned nothing, not even
the shacks they lived in.]

*

August 6: Eugene. Poetry is a funny, appealing life. What it does I
think is allow me to try to live as rich an emotional life as I can, mark
passing events with a few words of the proper solemnity, speak as if
I were writing letters to home to someone like my wife. Poetry ritu-
alizes the emotions, makes, in the words of Grotowski, a kind of poor
theater out of them, gives them a small public spectacle so that they
can appear and be honored.

O-BON: *DANCE FOR THE DEAD*

I have no memories or photograph of my father
coming home from war, thin as a caneworker,
a splinter of flesh in his olive greens
and khakis and spit-shined G.I. shoes;

Or of my grandfather in his flower-print shirt,
humming his bar-tunes, tying the bandana
to his head to hold the sweat back from his face
as he bent to weed and hoe the garden that Sunday
while swarms of planes maneuvered overhead.

I have no memories of the radio that day
or the clatter of marchetes in the Filipino camp,
the long wail of news from over the mountains,
or the glimmerings and sheaths of fear in the village.

I have no story to tell about lacquer shrines
or filial ashes, about a small brass bell,
and incense smoldering in jade bowls, about the silvered,

black face of Miroku gleaming with detachment,
anthurium crowns in the stoneware vase
the hearts and wheels of fire behind her.

And though I've mapped and studied the strike march
from the North Shore to town in 1921, though I've
sung psalms at festival and dipped the bamboo cup
in the stone bowl on the Day of the Dead,
though I've pitched coins and took my turn
at the *taiko* drum, and folded paper fortunes
and strung them on the graveyard's *hala* tree;

Though I've made a life and raised my house
oceans east of my birth, though I've craned
my neck and cocked my ear for the sound of flute
and *shamisen* jangling its tune of woe—

The music nonetheless echoes in its slotted box,
the cold sea chafes the land and swirls over gravestones,
and wind sighs its passionless song through ironwood trees.

More than memory or the image of the slant of grey rain
pounding the thatch coats and peaked hats
of townsmen racing across the blond arch of a bridge,
more than the past and its aches and brocade
of tales and ritual, its dry mouth of repetition,

I want the cold stone in my hand to pound the earth,
I want the splash of cool or steaming water to wash my feet,
I want the dead beside me when I dance, to help me
flesh the notes of my song, to tell me it's all right.

Donald Justice

A notebook is for jotting down unfinished ideas. These ideas seldom go any further, perhaps for the best. There seems to be even a kind of idea we could think of as a notebook idea, pure and simple. Such ideas may in fact have their own charm, their own seductiveness, just as the fragments of unfinished poems sometimes do. If the ideas are any good in themselves, they would have some value for others; if not, not.

HE [seizing her hands]: My, how cold your hands are!
SHE: I've been turning the ice-cream freezer.

*

MOZART: Tears are the dominant my death resolves,
          Death being tonic for the Christian.
              [After reading the Turner biography]

*

O attic solitudes! O clouds
All afternoon becalmed and ~~pure~~   near

*

Faust: A Skit
Narcissus: A Dialogue

*

1974

July 7: Idea for play. Death of a Poet. Lorca in California. Time: 1999. Reagan has been governor for generations. Orange groves, guitars, motorcycles.

"Like a moonscape paved": how California looks now.

Full of broad half-deserted freeways, up and down which bands of helmeted motorcyclists cruise.

Of Los Angeles, crumbled by a succession of earthquakes: "Oh, yes, we could rebuild it, but what would be the use?"

"Was it not a judgment of God? Were not the sins manifest, and the sinners very great?"

Squatters on the ruins—families live in tents on the hill bearing the name Hollywood—and of them this observation: "Who knows? They may be the pioneers of the future. The Ninety-Niners."

Name of political party or movement? "Don't you think Fascism is a pretty used-up term?"

*

SONG OF THE STATE TROOPERS

Blue are the cycles.
Dark blue the helmets.
The blue sleeves shine
With the rainbows of oil-slicks,
And why they don't cry is
Their hearts are leather,
Their skulls are hard plastic.

They come up the roads.
By night they come,
Hunched over headlamps,
Leaving behind them
A silence of rubber
And small fears like beach-sand

Ground underheel.
Look, concealed by their helmets
A vague outline
Of pistols is forming.
They go by—let them pass!

O town of the moonflower,
Preserve of the orange
And the burst guava,
Let them pass!

Song of the Hours

Three cyclists pass under
Christina's window.
How far out she leans!
But tonight she ignores
The flowering goggles.
Tonight she sees nothing
Of fumes, of bandanas.
And the breeze of eight-thirty
Comes fumbling the curtain,
Clumsy, uncertain.
     [PAUSE: *guitar chord.*]
O, the scent of the lemons!

Two hikers pass under
Christina's window.
How far out she leans!
But tonight she ignores
The bronze of their torsos.
Tonight she hears nothing
Of radios, of sirens.
And the breeze of nine-thirty
Encircles her waist.
How cool it is, how chaste!
     [PAUSE: *guitar chord.*]
O, the bitter groves!

A young man stands under
Christina's window.

How far out she leans!
But tonight she ignores
The shadow in shadow.
She sees and hears nothing
But the night, the dark night.
And the breeze of ten-thirty
Comes up from the south,
Hot breath on her mouth.
    [PAUSE: *guitar chord*.]
O, the teeth of their branches!

*

F. S. FLINT: I have never yet heard verse read in any way pleasing
to me except perhaps Miss Florence Farr's speaking to Psaltery of
W. B. Yeats's verse.

*

1980

December 12:

I think I could forgive you almost everything,
If you were here.
That way you had of speaking just too softly,
An act of aggression, really—
Now I would bend to catch your words
Without objecting or complaining.

And I can hear your voice repeating again the names of the heroes,
For there were always heroes—
Hemingway, Franz Kline, Bird, Ché—
And your voice naming them over is that of a king's
Elevating commoners,
Or that of an old astronomer naming stars.

There is a light that reaches us only after a long time.

Dust, dust, and a few lines mortal and evanescent.

*

DAUGHTER: You're smiling, Father.
ST. JOHN: What, me?

ST. JOHN: But one doesn't have to know much theology to become
an atheist.

Awful writer! He makes his characters speak bad English,
and they are no more aware of it than he is, poor fellows.

Appearances go quite deep enough for me. Get appearances right and the rest follows. Distrust the profound

Like James, I adore adverbs. Immensely.

I never lose my temper unless someone does something to
annoy me!

We are old, yes, when we begin to tell ourselves that we
are not.

*

ST. JOHN: Look at the abyss long enough and it looks right back at
you. *It's* not afraid.
FRIEND: That's Nietzsche, isn't it!
ST. JOHN [grudgingly]: It may be.

*

1983

October 13: Once you turned off Ocean Drive you felt the difference. The sun was no less dazzling down those side streets, but it
was no longer welcomed. Old people sat behind drawn Venetian
blinds, diminutive fans turning. In the heat of the afternoon nothing
moved. Cats slept in the shade of shrubs and occasional great tree
roots. Once I stopped to watch a train of ants maneuvering torpidly
across the pink stucco of a storefront, spelling out in insect hiero-
glyphics some cryptic message. Probably a warning about the future.

The moon shining on the sidewalk looked like snow.

* * *

It was a chilly morning for Miami Beach, and Levin wore an old yellow cardigan for warmth. Every half hour or so he would unbutton another button. The sweater had begun the day buttoned all the way up; now only one or two buttons remained to be loosened.

I stood behind the desk and lighted a king-sized Pall Mall. The classic brands were just then coming back after the war.

Everything looked worn-out and old, but to me it all seemed new and strange.

A short flagstone path halted at a plaster birdbath, dry now but still green with an ancient slime. Beside it there was an unoccupied stone bench. I say unoccupied because in all the months I worked at the hotel I never saw anyone sitting there. Once I did see an abandoned newspaper lying on it.

The only younger people we had all season were the two criminals.

Levin waited. At last he said, "I had a letter from my daughter. She has decided against coming down this winter."

*

RILKE [Good Friday, 1913]: What, oh what would have to happen to me so that I might feel it?

*

1984

February 15: In early middle age Eugene takes on a pupil different from the others—more talented. Other pupils strange in all the usual ways—wild eyes, wild habits, etc.—but the new pupil is strange in being so ordinary, except for his exceptional musical gifts. He seems as much interested in going into the family business (laundries?) as into music. And this bourgeois youth is so much more talented than the others that Eugene is both baffled and amused. Finally, the young man turns down a first-rate scholarship—and after a while Eugene sees him no more—or only perhaps at an occasional concert or recital, with his family—eventually with wife and child. The former pupil seems quite happy, free of any regret. But Eugene himself cannot escape a feeling of deep regret whenever he encounters his former pupil.

*

A room at the back of the house I was born in—the sleeping porch, with its tarpaulin blinds. Out behind, with blinds rolled up, a huge Australian pine, some oleanders, a sandy yard. Boarders slept in that room, sometimes a boarding uncle. I accompanied my mother into the room when she cleaned it. A mysterious semi-darkness in there with the blinds down. Once an open suitcase, partially packed or partially unpacked, lying on the bed.

*

Illustrations in the book of French fairy tales (Art Nouveau?) given me by next-door neighbor, a Mrs. Roland—her husband a policeman on the vice squad—would ride his motorcycle home and lean it casually in the portecochère. A gift of Bacardi from the Rolands (Prohibition still in effect)—contents poured out in back yard, the bottle used as doorstop. His suicide, involved in some scandal.

*

Crossing the river from Georgia into Alabama—the summer my feet became the same size as my father's and I could wear his shoes (huaraches). The very thin sales-tax coin, almost weightless, representing one mill (I believe). *Oklahoma Kid* (Cagney and Bogart) on a Saturday night in the makeshift movie-house, probably in Dothan, the sepia tones of the print blended with the dust and heat and sweat of the night. Wooden benches.

*

Florida (à la Henry James):

Here was the Infinite Previous—an age
When nothing yet was set down on the page,
A plate too primitive for all our inks,
A Nile before the Pharaoh or the Sphinx.

*

Orpheus in Hell

It was a tropical landscape, much like Florida's, which he knew.
Childhood came blazing back at him. They glided across a black
And apathetic river which reflected nothing back,

Only his own face sinking gradually from view.
As in a fading photograph. There was no other cloud.
The trees applauded inwardly. Nothing was loud.
. . .
He played a little on the King's piano, played Chopin.
. . .
And everything became familiar as he sang.
. . .
It was not possible to say just when he had begun
Departing, only that he was gone.
And that the landscape had continued on in him.

First person?

*

A copy of Chekhov's stories lying open on a table. I realized all at
once how glad I was that this man had lived. And that I did right to
be glad.

Of what writers now could that honestly and simply he said? Take,
for instance, Norman Mailer. Please.

*

What does music mean? Stravinsky, who must be listened to, believed
it meant nothing but itself. Obvious truth—for music does certainly
mean itself if it is music. Can it mean anything beyond itself? Not
the vulgar imitative stuff like the sheep bleating in Strauss. Not even
the more refined imitation in baroque music when, following the
verbal text, the voice-leading rises in hope or descends in despair.

That music which is most immediately rewarding—perhaps permanently so as well—often seems to behave *as if* it were referring to
something, perhaps not presently known but ultimately knowable, if
only . . . This has something to do with the ineffableness most people
do actually feel in the presence of the greatest music.

Once in a while the listener does catch a hint of the Unexpressed.
A possible example: the little triplet figure in bars 9 and 10 of Chopin's Nocturne in F Major, opus 15, number 1, and then repeated
toward the end of the piece as the main theme returns.

What it would seem to be imitating, if anything, may be some brief utterance of, say, a languishing and rather pathetic ingenue, as she questions or perhaps resigns herself to fate. A poignant and brief sight—trivial and familiar enough. But then, in addition, just underneath this pseudo-reference there seems to lurk another feeling, more hidden, not probably quite conscious on the composer's part. I want to suggest that in this little triplet figure we can catch—or almost catch—a premonition of the composer's early death; and I believe that a fleeting half awareness of this possibility contributes to the poignancy of the little moment. No doubt this notion will strike most readers as quite mad, at least when put as baldly as this. And yet . . . why not? I have absolutely no wish to deny that the figure remains a triplet in notation and that the *musical* idea must have been primarily to effect a small and pleasing variation on the opening theme. The composer did often ornament the original statement of his themes, and with much more elaborate figures than this. Indeed, it is part of his signature, which here emerges as only a very modest flourish. That is, the music remains music and goes on meaning itself without interruption. And yet . . .

Even Stravinsky allows for some translation of musical notation into statement or feeling, as when he distinguishes between Brahms's *lyrical* triplets and Mahler's *rhetorical* triplets. This much at least may be true: Chopin's triplets here are very lyrical, we may even say *poetical*, in that sense of the poetic we mean to invoke when speaking of anything but poetry itself and which has nothing to do with poetry.

*

AUDEN [in a letter to a friend]: I've decided to go out in the New Year, as soon as the book is finished, to join the International Brigade in Spain. I so dislike everyday political activities that I don't do them, but here is something I can do as a citizen and not as a writer, and as I have no dependants [sic] I feel I ought to go; but, O, I do hope there are not too many surrealists there.

Ah, ces banales
Musicales.

Of course they are absurd,
These little Bohemias of the suburbs.
And yet . . . and yet . . .

Wallflowers becalmed
Among the palms.

Society being merely prelude
To the final bliss of solitude.

A violin soaring upwards through Tschaikovsky,
Slightly off-key.

And cloudy afternoons
And organ-grinder (?) tunes.

How often, these Sunday afternoons,
One feels the desire for something different, less jejune.
Something both savage and ~~tragic,~~ let us say . . . /   genuine.

And there are times
Not all the gathered gloom of the sunken world
Can match the awful significance of one shaken curl.

It is this that ties the tongue in knots
And cannot be depended on or quite forgot.

Hearts in prison,
Slow-moving seasons.

Brisk strolls around the edges of a park—
Against the wind, bent, pursued by darkness.

The street lamp's halo:
A sudden glancing blow of yellow.

*

Iris, and Jimmy the Greek, and beautiful Nancy Banks
Of Cleveland, hand in hand with Pony, her dark child—

Where are they now?
                    But we were talking jazz—
And Lady Day on a barstool once in the White Rose:
And that has got me brooding on the rose.

*

MEZEY: It's a funny country, America. Success is even more dangerous than failure.

*

O for a draft of Hemingway prose! His prose is "poetic"—and all this
overwriting, mine included, is not. Of course Hemingway's is a type
of overwriting too. One reason the old Constance Garnett translations remain the secret favorite of many, including me, is just that
they *have* no style. Is that not, after all, the ideal condition?

*

Why must I like it when they tell me my stories are "well written"?
Of course they are! Would that this were not what they found to say
about them, all the same. This ugly little piece of jargon seems to
have become a code word for dull. Worse of course would be to hear
that they were "well crafted."

*

E. R. BURROUGHS: I am a very old man; how old I do not know.

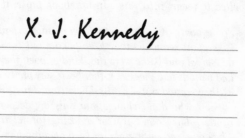
X. J. Kennedy

Somerset Maugham once advised every writer to keep a notebook. Although he considered it unlikely that any of the writer's jottings would ever end up in a finished work, he believed that the mere habit of notebook keeping might make the writer more observant. In various notebooks—not the one excerpted here—I've taken Maugham's advice to heart. I've kept notebooks called NAMES, IDEAS FOR STORIES, and GOOD LINES OVERHEARD, and, indeed, they have helped me pay attention to memorable names, stories, and good lines. But the POETRY notebook, while it hasn't helped my powers of observation worth a hoot, has been for the last forty years a place to vent steam in private, a seedbed for critical articles, and a parking lot for notions to retain.

As a rule, its contents don't aspire to become poems. Poems for me don't have any prose preexistence. They start right out trying to be poems. In their early, unlicked state, they are usually lousy, but they provide something to work on. So it was with some surprise that I recall one poem (or is it merely light verse?) that began as a notebook entry:

THE DEVIL'S ADVICE TO POETS

Molt that skin! lift that face!—you'll go far.
Grow like Proteus yet more bizarre.
   In perpetual throes
   Majors metamorphose—
Only minors remain who they are.

This epigram was simply an old notebook thought that I felt impelled to recast into verse. In notebook prose, it read like this:

> *Some poets, it's true, need to grow and expand continually. Like giant sequoias, they keep poking out fresh rings. Gerard de Nerval and Rilke were that kind of poet: they changed, they had periods like Picasso. Other poets stay pretty much the same as they started out—Emily Dickinson, Frost, Richard Wilbur —poets who don't change, but only dig deeper into their territories. They don't try for amazing formal transformations. They don't attempt epics, or keep opening new passages to India (which usually lead a reader to a winter bolted into polar ice)—they just settle into doing whatever they can, striving to do it better. I find this attitude likeable.*

In versifying this thought, I added the Devil. He would encourage all poets to be developers and Passage-to-India discoverers, even though such expansiveness may not be their natural bent. A lot of poets take this diabolic counsel to heart. They're always desperately trying on new identities in front of the critics, putting out press releases to herald their latest new directions. And the critics praise their bravery, their zeal to develop and change.

But maybe I'm just trying to excuse myself for having stayed pretty much the same. In the years since my first book, in 1961, I haven't learned a thing, haven't tried new tricks. I've only kept writing the same old kinds of stuff—ballads and other story poems, epigrams, epitaphs, songs, lyrics, children's verse, light verse. Probably I haven't grown, but merely wilted around the edges, while doing my damnedest to ignore the Devil's advice.

1972–1978

Don't delay forever in writing your ambitious masterpiece. Recall that comic strip artist who drew "Happy Hooligan," the character with the tin can for a hat. By the time the poor fish had made enough money to quit drawing the strip, his hand was deformed, and all his attempts at Mona Lisas came out wearing tin cans like Happy Hooligan. I believe he committed suicide.

*

Sometimes I wake in the middle of the night with good lines in my head. To go back to sleep, or get up and write them down? Recall what William Saroyan said: that if he'd got out of bed and written down all the good stuff he'd been too lazy to save, he would have been the greatest American writer. There's some use in keeping pencil and paper at bedside—and a small flashlight as a courtesy, if you don't sleep alone.

*

To hell with poetry that has no more interest than the mere miserable prose meaning of it.

*

People who distrust poetry but adore ideas always make much of the late poems of Stevens. Not that they're bad poetry, but they do attract a certain stripe of critic: brilliant, unplayful, and totally deaf to words.

*

John Brinnin quotes a wonderful remark by William Carlos Williams: "I didn't go in for long lines because of my nervous nature."

*

Kingsley Amis has pointed out that light verse is a parasite that feeds on serious poetry, can't live without it. So is open form poetry, which without traditional poetry would have no frame of reference. For their own survival, open form poets ought to pay us old formal geezers to keep writing. They need us as America needs England. (I'm thinking of Karl Shapiro's poem praising the English: "Establish them, that values may go on.")

*

Dylan Thomas has an appallingly ingenious poem of a hundred lines that rimes the first and last lines, then rimes lines 2 and 99, and so on down to a riming couplet in the middle: lines 50 and 51. Mike Fixler [Milton scholar teaching at Tufts] knows a name for this game and claims it's ancient. He says that Lamentations, the most heart-rending book in the Old Testament, is written in Hebrew as an alphabetical acrostic! Let them mull that who charge poets who write in strait forms with being insincere.

*

The world is full of poets with languid wrenches who don't bother to take the last six turns on their bolts.

*

The kind of reader I write for must be fast getting scarce: the reader who notices rhythms. Lately B.B., an intelligent bookstore proprietor, asked me where I'd got the form of the little short "Japanese Beetles"—he couldn't figure out whether they were inspired by haiku or tanka. He'd counted syllables and was puzzled to find ten to a line. So eye-minded was he, he'd never realized the things were in pentameter.

*

Some critical fallacies that now prevail:

1. That confessional poets tell the truth about themselves. Hell, I'll bet the truth would be too piddling—they'd never admit how petty their foibles are, how humiliating. Of all the confessional poets who have confessed, does any deserve absolution?

2. That poets who have broken with traditional form are brave, daring, and original, while by implication those who continue to rime and scan are craven, lockstep imitators.

3. That the arrangement of poems in a book has sublime importance. Me, when I read a book, I don't give a hoot about how the poems are arranged; all that counts is: are there a few good poems in it? Auden once twitted this fallacy by arranging his *Collected Poems* by titles, in alphabetical order.

4. That beats placed with random irregularity can produce a *rhythm* (nervous, staccato, and therefore true to the pace of contemporary life). No rhythm can be produced except by repeating something.

5. That poetry should be obliged to mirror current events. (Guess that wipes out most of Herrick, Dickinson, John Clare, Roethke, etc.)

6. That a major poet is one who writes a new book every year.

*

Josh (age 8): "How do lullabies work on babies? Do they bore them to sleep?"

*

Woe's me—born just a little too late for the crest of formal poetry that rose in the 1950s, so that my stuff didn't begin to appear till the great stampede out of traditional form was on. So I came to the poetry scene like some guest who shows up just when the party is ending, the punchbowl drained, the streamers all tromped to the floor.

*

1984–1991

A gent in Houston, Loren D. Stark, sends an ad for a fascinating product that hits me as insane: *The Poets' Rhythm Dictionary*, designed to help poets find a word with the right rhythm. The first part of the book consists of 25,000 words in alphabetical order with "the correct rhythm symbol" marked on each word. I gather this would tell you nothing you couldn't find out from the diacritical marks in any dictionary. The second part of the book "lists the words under the correct symbol heading." O wow—if it has a heading for an iamb, what a hell of a lot of words must there be under it.

Now why is this notion so fug-headed? Intriguing to think why. I reckon (1) words in English do not have absolutely fixed rhythms when laid against a meter, else scansion would not be so subjective and controversial. (2) And who thinks first of rhythm? You say what you want to say. Say anything strong and say it well, and the rhythm takes care of itself.

*

In Tucson, I met with students in a workshop taught by Jane Miller. One student had titled a poem, "South Africa: For Nelson Mandela's 70th Birthday" and Miller objected to this title as too obvious. "Titles should be oblique," she declared. "They shouldn't tell us what the poem is *about*." I didn't see why they shouldn't. I like titles as obvious as billboards, myself—signs that point to the center of the poem.

Especially if a poem is rich and complicated, hard for a reader to enter. Then, the reader casts about for any sign: which way to go in?

Jane Miller was a forthright, lively gadfly, and I liked her a lot. She took me to task for never writing in *open* form. Why didn't I try writing something that went against my nature, the way she and her students do when they write experimentally in meter? I said I couldn't do that. I like to stick to my nature. Pitiful though it may be, it's all I've got. (U. of Arizona, Nov. 15, 1988.)

*

Has Wilbur's aim been low? Some—like Randall Jarrell, though he later changed his mind—say that Wilbur never takes large enough chances. His best works are short, and we, with our fondness for imposing edifices, prefer prodigious attempts, even failures like Thomas Wolfe's hippopotamine novels, which he himself couldn't complete, or like Hart Crane's grand and partially maudlin "Bridge." But the history of Wilbur's work is a history of successes—not vast, but modest successes, and they add up.

Has any historian of poetry ever realized that in poetry the successes are all that count? Most literary historians and seekers of dissertation topics look for epics—poems of colossal sweep, works of huge length and devouring ambition—and find Wilbur disappointing. He's been content, it seems, to let poems happen to him, content to render them in words as concise and inevitable as he can. For this reason, some critics will not grant him the epithet "great poet," a label that requires of its wearer efforts quite extraneous to the writing of poetry—efforts such as clasping the whole of America to one's beefy chest. Seen in this light, Emily Dickinson, that designer of brief lyrics, may not be so great a poet as Walt Whitman, not so ambitious and reportorial and encompassing. Yet when you compare her quality control with Walt's, she is certainly a hell of a lot more capable of writing poems.

*

A competent formal poet thinks in cadences. Rhythm and sense arise at the same time.

*

Warren Hope writing on James Reeves (in *Drastic Measures* Spring '88) says, "He once told me that he disliked great poets, preferring good poets on the ground that they are, 'Oh, so much *better*.' Greatness seemed to him a matter of mere size, goodness a matter of morality, of quality."

Half true. Great poets are also good poets (Dante, Yeats, Rilke, Milton), but there's sense in Reeves's remarks. Would-be great poets (Olson, Robert Duncan, Zukofsky) are only occasionally good, but indeed wonderful are those minor poets by whom we cherish only a handful of poems (Edward Thomas, Marvell, Clare, Louise Bogan, Stickney, Henry Reed &c).

Most of the factors that cause a poet to get into a history of poetry are quite irrelevant to poetry: things like significance, ideas, scope, the reflecting of cultural trends and forces, ambition and size of output, influences and personal associations with other poets, and so forth—none of which has much to do with poetry. All a poem is is an emotionally disturbing structure made of words.

*

Not sure, here in 1988, that we're enjoying a renaissance of rime and meter, as some claim. Magazines these days print a large number of formal poems embodying weak, moot feelings, cast into stanzes that look piled up laboriously. Today I browsed through proofs of an anthology of poems by high-school-age poets being published by Dick Lourie's leftwing Hanging Loose Press—they wanted a blurb out of me, of all people!—and raw stuff though it was, it was more fun and had more life to it than most formal poems I've seen lately.

*

A long poem—how well is it put together? Easy to tell. A simple test: Do you need to turn the page to know you've come to its end?

*

Bob Phillips, reviewing the *Selected Letters of John Crowe Ransom* in the NYTBR, quotes a choice Ransom remark: "Criticism is quite presumptuous, and I give it more and more reluctantly; I don't think it's quite a good man's business to do too much of it because it results in one of two ways: He commits gross injustices, or he is drawn too much out of his bias and nature by the effort of understanding and sympathy."

Those two faults dwell in practically all the reviews I've written. At a stroke. Ransom here explains my own customary unwillingness to review and my torments in the act of reviewing. I always feel that to write about someone's poetry is going to turn me into a wrongheaded bastard, or else into a silly grinner at anything mildly respectable. The only kind of poetry worth writing about is the kind naturally in tune with your own, which you approach with some zest, understanding, impassioned admiration, and a fair sense of its faults.

*

Three cheers for any poet who handles words with the intent joy of a little kid playing with blocks.

*

So many poets nowadays give us moral browbeatings. They imply that they confide things so intimate, so essential (to them, at least), that if we don't listen respectfully we are boors. Such poets often tell us about their childhoods and their spouses and their families. They're forever baring the secrets of the marriage bed, their awful or joyful confrontations with their children and their parents. Transfixed by looks of pain that seem to say, "Here's my heart, you bastard—you wouldn't dare stomp on it, would you?"—and we politely squirm, unable to run away. And yet we have every right to stomp on the unwanted gift of that heart, just as persons who receive, unasked for in the mail, junky crucifixes from monastic orders have a right to pitch them away.

*

1992–1994

A formal poem written without the energy to sustain it is a mausoleum built for a flea.

*

A poetic form in the abstract is the most boring thing I know. The form of a sonnet, say, divorced from any particular sonnet. And yet dictionaries of poetic forms seem to multiply nowadays, and teachers of writing make students write poems to fulfill an assigned form. I can't imagine such an approach. Poems for me never begin with the abstract idea of a form. You can't *set* yourself to write a sonnet or a villanelle. Any sonnet that makes good is a sonnet-sized explosion in heart, mind, and gut, and it sneaks up and takes you by surprise.

*

A line with which to decline an invitation to write a poem in praise of somebody or something that somebody wants praised (e.g., an anthology of poems about JFK, about Marilyn Monroe, etc.): Billions for defense, but not one poem in tribute.

*

I've revised old stuff so much, I ought to do a *Poems New and Corrected*.

*

TV producers haven't ever figured out what to do with poetry. They can't abide mere wordage without inventing some distracting picture to go with it. They dread the thought of an hour-long camera-fix on a talking head. And indeed such a thing would be intolerably long for viewers accustomed to rapid-fire fifteen-second takes.

Now, I suspect that a televised poetry reading could be effective, but only for patient viewers already hooked on poetry. And it would need to be delivered by a poet of Thespian talents. Most viewers would need special training in order to get through such a thing. A single head talking away for an hour can be fascinating, but only if the listener is predisposed to sit still that long, and the head is a fascinating talker. How well the film *My Dinner with André* succeeded, static as it was. And I recall fondly the spellbinding appearances of Frank O'Connor years ago on CBS Sunday morning TV. All he did was sit and tell stories.

*

To be universally acclaimed in your own day is often to be forgotten in the next.

*

There ought to be a way for hungry poets and artists to draw on the profits from their work after they're dead. We need a bank machine connected to the future, into which poor suffering nuts like Poe or

Van Gogh could insert a plastic card and share in their movie roy-
alties, or some of the millions from the sale of "Sunflowers." Maybe,
even without time travel, the UN could take on this project. They
might set up a commission to estimate the probable future worth
of work, and start paying off while the artists and writers are still
alive.

*

Dorothy has discovered a wonderful German word: *Schlimmbesse-
rung:* an intended improvement that only makes things worse. What
poets do who revise too extensively.

*

Trying to understand the effect of my mixed Irish, Cornish, and
German bloods, I had an epiphany. It struck when I heard this line
from Bob Newhart, in a stand-up comedy routine, speaking of his
Irish-German ancestry: "It makes me a meticulous drunk." Right
on—my verse is Celticly wild, Teutonicly fussy.

*

Damned if we haven't gone and raised a generation deaf to the music
of poetry. The poor fish can't see anything in a poem but its literal
meaning. That's the impression I got from an attack on Mother
Goose (*Boston Globe,* Nov. 15, 1993), in which the writer viewed with
high dudgeon the notion of telling kids about the Old Woman Who
Lived in a Shoe and beats her children, or about the ladybug whose
children will burn. The metrical frame and rime-scheme of the
poems—which declare, "This is a game, for Chrissake, this is fool-
ing"—didn't even register. Some schools have abandoned Mother
Goose altogether, because it's easier to ignore so politically incorrect
a writer than to try to edit her. So most kids nowadays grow up
ignorant of those great, tough-skinned little capsules of outrageous
nonsense and metrical power.

I suppose that this deafness was inevitable, not only from the rise of
PC but from the decline of attention to print, the runaway expansion
of TV-watching, and the polarization of society that puts expensively
printed and illustrated kids' books beyond the reach of many people.

*

Words fall apart, as Eliot reminds us, and poems become sand that the wind drives away. Still, there's something to say for even a brokendown Ozymandian torso, which at least has *some* shape left to it.

*

James Fenton really sticks his neck out, in "Some Mistakes People Make About Poetry" (*N.Y. Review of Books*, Mar 25, 1993): "It would be very odd to go to a concert hall and discover that the pianist on offer *wasn't any good at all*, in the sense that he couldn't actually play the piano. But in poetry this is an experience we have learned to take in our stride."

*

The dumbest thing I've done lately was to declare, in a blurb for Bob Phillips' new book, that Bob is the only poet in America who doesn't bore me. No doubt every poet in America who sees that, except Bob, will hate my guts.

*

I've tried too hard to intensify a poem with words that call attention to themselves. As a result the poem departs too far from speech and looks labored, consciously fabricated. So I've been going through my recent work, turning show-off words into ordinary ones that could actually come out of a human mouth. Not that an occasional show-off word isn't terrific, but ah, you can't show off all the time, or the reader won't ever sit up and pay particular attention to anything.

*

In his *Atlantic* article "Can Poetry Matter?" Dana Gioia calculates that the nation's 200 graduate writing programs will produce 20,000 accredited poets in the next decade. And yet surely the country can absorb 2,000 more poets a year, if it can absorb 20,000 more chiropractors annually, or 250,000 more doorbell-ringing Jehovah's Witnesses.

*

I like to hear poetry read in a small room by a voice without amplification. Reading poems through a microphone is like making love with a condom on. It prevents dangerous contact, but it makes the act less interesting.

*

Anthologies tend to represent poets in too much depth. Few poets alive have had more than three memorable poems in them. But anthologists are always trying to show the configuration of history, trying to include Significant poets (with a capital S), and so they end up with twenty or thirty big bales of wheat full of dull chaff. I'd love to see an anthologist forget history and Significance and just pick good poems. A marvelous anthology of American poetry since 1900 might need no more organization than the Greek Anthology, a loose sheaf of miscellaneous poems that happened to survive. How many contemporary poets have written only one or two good poems, and those poems absolute knockouts! Such an anthology might include a couple of hundred poets. One or two fine poems apice by, say, Norma Farber, Ernest Kroll, Luke Zilles, Marcia Stubbs, Mildred Weston, Roy Helton, Elinor Wylie, and others whose triumphs are few but sensational—better than Wallace Stevens' average. Not that Stevens wouldn't still deserve more space, of course.

One of the most readable anthologies ever assembled is Philip Larkin's much maligned *Oxford Book of 20th Century English Verse.* Though Larkin was forced to yield to orders from his editor, for the most part he doesn't represent poets in proportion to their imagined stature in literary history. Usually he includes poems he likes, some by poets you never heard of before. It's a quirky choice, and in some cases he short-changes poets he doesn't dig. He represents Geoffrey Hill by a single poem, though Hill deserves a dozen. But for all its faults, of all the anthologies I know, Larkin's lets in the least chaff and has the highest proportion of wonderful stuff you won't find anywhere else.

*

The creative writing industry, in which teaching poets beget more teaching poets, took off like a successful chain letter. But as it would seem from a recent bulletin from the Associated Writing Programs, the end is near. Unless the government steps in and funds a huge program to make work for poets, or unless the poets retrain themselves for non-teaching jobs, there'll be hundreds unemployed. The MFA business has proved to be a vast chain letter scheme in which the first participants collected, while the latecomers got left holding the bag.

*

Writing with a computer, you write in one endless unbroken line. A certain mental outlook sets in, that isn't conducive to strict arrangements of words in finite lines. It tends to make you feel that all words are created equal, and they go on nonstop.

The result of this mind-set, I'd expect, will be that in time any verse written in individual lines will come to seem odd and antiquated. The prose poem has nowhere to go but up. Already, in our non-reading culture, the only poetry that seems natural and acceptable to most MTV-watching young people is such fragmentary poetry as finds its way into popular song.

Paradoxically, the technology of computers, videos, film, and sound recording isn't helping audiences to enjoy poetry of greater formal sophistication. Instead, all this technology is fast returning poetry—such poetry as reaches the public at large through the mass media—to its original condition, that of song.

This transformation isn't necessarily anything to deplore.

Yusef Komunyakaa

For or me, there has to be an absolute flexibility in maintaining a notebook. My notebooks are really scrapbooks—pieced together with fragments, phrases, sentences, paragraphs, long and short passages, magazine and newspaper clippings, postcards, etc. Thus, I attempt to avoid any kind of rote structure. Sometimes the passages are logical and controlled, and other times they are abbreviated and somewhat improvisational sounding. Later, however, these items seem to dictate their own coherence. Some are like jumpstarts for the imagination; others function more like jumpcuts—little bridges that spring up between ideas and feelings. Connectors. Accidental linkages. Surprises. It is often a ledger of emotional pressure points, and I can return to moments in the recent past that link me to the present and the impending future. I can see and feel the evolution of an image. As I view the germination of images and poems, I am a few steps closer to understanding the chemistry of the imagination—how each word takes on a life of its own. There is that rare poem spun whole from an image buried in the yellowing pages of a haphazard notebook, and I call such a poem a gift.

Lokman (c. 1100 B.C.) Aesop (c. 560 B.C.) How could these two have been the same man? True, they spoke a similar wit; but maybe this came about only because of the similarity of background and situation. Both were black slaves, and they relied on wit and satire to keep sane. Perhaps so. They were more than stand-up comedians of antiquity; each was a first-rate fabulist and thinker. There are thousands of African parables with this same caliber of wit. Is there something here beneath this simple deduction?

A basic humanism.

"Prometheus, in making man, did not use water to mix the clay; he used tears."   —Aesop

" . . . The wise and prudent man will draw a useful lesson even from poison itself, whilst the precepts of the wisest man mean nothing to the thoughtless."   —Lokman

> I call Gold,
> Gold is silent.
> I call Cloth,
> Cloth is silent.
> It is people that matter.
>
> —a saying of the Akan people of Ghana

*

(Two corps girls, resplendent in their white tutus for *Etudes*, stand in front of the stagehands' room, giggling as they read a poster which has been tapped to the wall: "Each one of us is a mixture of qualities, some of which are good and some perhaps not so good. In considering our fellow man we should remember his good qualities and refrain from making harsh judgements just because he happens to be a dirty, rotten no-good son of a bitch.")
—Franklin Stevens, *Dance As Life*

*

Centro Internationale Poesia della Metamorfosi
Comune di Fano
Provincia di Pesaro e Urbino
Regione Marche
Convergno Internazionale
LA POESIA
AMERICANA
I nuovi itinerari
Fano 9, 10, 11 giugno 1988
Palazzo S. Michele – Chiostro delle Benedettine

They want me to talk about jazz and poetry, Vietnam, and contemporary African American poetry. I'm dealing with jetlag, the rich food, and this constant celebration in the air. In fact, at this moment, I'd rather be thinking of Fellini ("Il Mago"); I'm still unable to believe that the Vatican could have branded his *La Dolce Vita* as "obscene" in 1959. Anita Ekberg obscene? War, fascism, hatred, the ability to balance one's heart with gold and pillage—well, now, those are things that I call obscene. Perception has everything to do with the lens we peer through. What we bring to a place or thing. I can almost see James Wright walking the streets of Fano, among these ancient bricks mottled by sea salt. We'll visit Urbino tomorrow. I have no idea what the others are thinking about the infamous ancient city, if they can already see the fields of poppies on the hillsides—*Citta ideale*/Ideal City—I only know that there's an unusual equation in my mind. Urbino: Florence: Africa. After all, it is what we bring to something that curves the equation, right? That "Moor," Alessandro de' Medici, was of course the first Duke of Florence—rumored to be the son of Pope Clement VII himself. After his dramatic demise (the Michaele-Lorenzaccio plot), Alessandro the Moor's body was secretly stashed in the tomb of his nominal father, the Duke of Urbino, under Michelangelo's *Il Penseroso*. But what a huge life this man, whose mother had been a slave, lived in such a short time.

"I did in fact keep a house-dog—a beautiful, large, shaggy brute that Duke Alessandro had given me. It was a first-rate hunting dog, and when I was out shooting it used to bring me back any bird or animal that I hit, but it was also a splendid house-guard. As it happened, at that time, as was only fitting at the age of twenty-nine, I had taken a charming and very beautiful young girl as my maid-servant; I used her as a model, and also enjoyed her in bed to satisfy my youthful desires. Because of this, I had my room at quite a distance from where the workmen slept, and also some way from the shop. I kept the young girl in a tiny ramshackle bedroom adjoining mine. I used to enjoy her very often, and although I am the lightest sleeper in the world, after sexual pleasure I sometimes used to sleep very heavily and deeply."   —Benvenuto Cellini, *Autobiography*

This is how poems happen for me. Bits and pieces, glimpses and strokes, hints and imagistic nudges, and at some almost-accidental moment it all flies together—not to make sense but to induce a feeling. I call these *gifts*. "Florentine Mosaic" is just such a gift that has been forming itself inside my head.

*

"Never again shall the Cock Man come to report sunrise."
—from the story of Yang Kuei-fei,
concubine of the Emperor Ming-huang (713–55)

*

"Prince Myshkin, the central character in Dostoievsky's *The Idiot* and a victim of epilepsy, is trying to express the emotions that come over him just before his attacks start. Dostoievsky wrote from first-hand experience. He suffered from the disease himself and knew that inspiration may be a prelude to convulsions as well as to prophesies, poetry or great novels."   —John Pfeiffer, *The Human Brain*

*

I see something or think something that sparks something else, and then things gel. Germinate. Become. For example: one moment I'm gazing at Beauford DeLaney's *Portrait of Marian Anderson* and the next moment I feel them both here in the room, all golden and uncompromising. What did Arturo Toscanini say of her?: "What I heard today, one is privileged to hear only once in a hundred years." That's right. The Finnish National Opera, The Salzberg Musical Festival, Carnegie Hall, Paris' Grand Opera, Buckingham Palace, etc. But do we overlook the fact that the Daughters of the American Revolution refused to let her appear in Constitution Hall in 1939, when she hadn't been discriminated against even in Nazi Germany? Some of us poets have been challenged to face the beautiful and the ugly—to make art out of what we see, hear, think, and feel.

"Few artists, I hasten to add, have ever impressed me as being more sane than Beauford DeLaney. Beauford's sanity is something to dwell on: it occupies a niche of its own. There are some utterly sane individuals who create the impression that stark lunacy might be a highly desirable state; there are others who make sanity look like a counterfeit check, with God the loser."
—Henry Miller, *The Amazing and Invariable Beauford DeLaney*

In the early 1970s, those years I entertained the idea of becoming a psychiatrist, I believed that racism was a mental illness. Perhaps this idea had a lot to do with a kind of elemental hope. A faith in knowledge and one's capacity to change. If it was an illness, it could be

cured, right? I remember compiling hundreds of notes on this topic
—a treatise. Sex. Environment. Cultural and social indoctrination.
Fear. Envy. Nonverbal gestures that pass down racism to the cradle.
Language. Literature. I wish I could find those notes.

*

Equus is one of my favorite plays. The terror that enters the psyche
when passion is denied or undermined. The holiness of passion: an
approximation of the Godhead. When opposites merge—the creative
act—the myth made flesh. Image. Centaur. Possibility.

*

"When in nineteen-thirty-seven, Etta Moten, sweetheart of our Art
Study group, kept her promise, as if clocked, to honor my house at
our first annual tea, my pride tipped the sky, but when she, Parisian-
poised and as smart as a chrome-toned page from Harper's Bazaar,
gave my shocked guests this hideous African nude, I could have
cried."   —from "The Convert," Margaret Danner

As I leaned over the "Hen-Shaped Coffin" by sculptor Kane Kwei at
the University Art Museum at Berkeley, almost hurting to pry open
the colorful burial vessel and gaze inside, I realized that I was envious
of such a people who had so intricately woven art into the social
patterns and rituals of their daily lives. Here was a piece of art defined
by an active duality: it's aesthetically challenging and functional—
not merely circumscribed by a glass case in a museum. Not only is
there this decorative coffin, made of wood and painted with enamels,
but also other shapes: an airplane and onion, also created by Kwei,
numerous paintings and fantastic sculptures of wood and metal.
What really brings this exhibit into focus, creating a necessary tension, is the coexistence of the traditional with the contemporary.
Herewith also exists the fuel for controversy. Many of the pieces are
skillfully fashioned with superb technique and care, but is something
missing? The mystery that attracted Picasso and other cubists to
those traditional Iberian masks, has that quality been acculturated
out of the art through the dynamics of assimilation, technique, and
subject matter? Have the values and principles shaping the pieces
been undermined? Are these still authentic works of art defined by
ancient rituals and customs, or are they pieces designed for commercial venues? Or, are some of us diehard idealists who romanticize
the past and refuse to celebrate the changes that these artists have

witnessed in their daily lives? I would like to think that artistic expression is not static, but organic; that art is defined by time and
flexible nuances. It is this spirit of inclusion that drew me deeper and
deeper into the exhibition. The artists are "doing their thing." They
are from various groups ("approximately 55 paintings, sculptures,
photographs, and mixed-media works by artists from throughout sub-
Saharan Africa—Zaire, Nigeria, Ghana, Senegal, Mali, Sierra Leone,
Mozambique, Gabon, and the Coast") but the underlying matrix of
colors and symbolism helps the viewer to see the chemistry between
artists and their imagistic ideas. In the urge to exhibit the reflections
of diversity, what truly arises out of this daring collection of new
functional, traditional, international, and urban art, is the unfractured
unity of an encompassing artistic tradition. Out of the various themes
in "Africa Explores: 20th Century African Art," two that readily surface are the mermaid/merman and twin motifs.

The mermaid images, on the subject of Mami Wata and Papi Wata,
are rather narcissistic, depicting figures who gaze into hand-held mirrors or recline in self-conscious poses. It isn't just the slight differences in skin tones and physical characteristics that suggest the
otherworldliness of these water-bound figures; something deeper and
more profound illustrates their separateness from the African terrain
and psyche: they are foreigners because the carriage of their bodies
betray them. In other words, they are still seeking pleasure and status
through their exaggerated otherness. The figures evolving out of the
twin cult, however, seem to celebrate a reverence for the similar. The
images evolve out of each other as vivid reflections. It is this same
imagistic continuity one finds in pieces such as "Slaves Yoked Together" and "Figures Carrying Water" by Mode Muntu: the figures
mirror each other, but seem linked or solidified by a silent, unbroken
rhythm—a cadence created through subtle colors. One might think
that to speak of rhythm as a reference to African artistic expression
is to resort to a worn-out phrase. The two moving sculptures, "Festival Boat" and "Decorated Bed for a Christian Wake," however, are
definitely defined by rhythmic complexity. The parts move in a kind
of humorous syncopation—a planned and calibrated tonal extension
of the structure based on contrapuntal patterns. A surreal humor lives
within numerous places in this exhibit. One painting that comes to
mind is "The Battle With Mosquitoes" where three characters are
using unorthodox methods (slingshot, etc.) for exterminating mosquitoes. The vivid colors and active symmetry of this piece evolve

into a dance for the viewer—a ballet of wit. Written text is also incorporated into this painting. Actually, European painters and poets influenced by dadaism easily come to mind. In certain pieces these African artists have incorporated texts excerpted from poetry, parables, folk sayings, and new proclamations. In some pieces it seems natural; in a few others, however, the text is mere extemporaneous embellishment, deflecting the visual energy and continuity of the pieces. This exhibit isn't a marriage of the sacred and the profane. As a whole, with new styles modifying the traditional and the traditional modifying new styles, the exhibit is a pleasurable and surprising success. The politics and rituals are so crystallized by flawless technique and imagination, these artists could venture almost in any direction and still return home honorable.

*

At fourteen, I read the Bible through twice, and then abandoned it because there seemed to have been too many contradictions. Six years later I read it through again, and this time came away convinced that Jesus Christ was a socialist and that is what got him nailed to the cross. True, admittedly, I didn't become a model Christian, but I learned a great deal about imagery and metaphor. The Old Testament is pure surrealism.

*

The Blues has been called The Devil's Music. Maybe it has to do with two words: Possession and obsession. Most artists are obsessed by the creative act, and this is looked upon as negative or abnormal —unless it is linked to money in some way. Then it is viewed as industrious. But possession is a curse, don't care how you turn the key in the lock. Controlled by something (an evil spirit or passion). Mad. Crazed. God forbid if we should lose *control*. Robert Johnson's music possessed him through passion, and perhaps this is why he said he'd made a pact with the devil at a crossroad one night in Mississippi. He surrendered himself to folklore and myth so that these black Calvinists didn't question what he was doing. After all, he was possessed and didn't have any control over the blues (at least, that's what they wanted to think). They chose to see him at the mercy of his art; in fact, music was Robert Johnson's only true salvation.

*

"Lifelines" is a limited-edition portfolio of poems and graphics published by San Francisco's Central City Hospitality House—works by the poor and homeless in the Tenderloin. This is raw inspiration doing what art is supposed to do.

*

You may bury my body oooooo down by the highway side
So my old evil spirit can get a Greyhound Bus and ride
—Robert Johnson, "Me and the Devil Blues"

*

Where Romare Bearden has been rather forthright about the direct influence of quiltmaking on his art, one wonders if quilts—especially the quilts of the poor where pieces of cloth or patches were arranged—haven't influenced the whole concept of modern abstract art. Fine arts. Handicrafts. Low and high cultures. Maybe it is texture and materials that make distinctive differences here. But shouldn't basic concepts matter? Poor black Southern women have always had a tradition of sewing quilts inside quilts as a way of preserving something precious. Don't be surprised if there aren't some bright masterpieces tucked away in semi-dark rooms in numerous dead-end towns. I believe that Romare Bearden would have known what I'm thinking about.

"You do something and then you improvise."

—Romare Bearden

Improvise is an important word/concept to me. I have a habit of underlining it in books; as if I need clues scattered about. *Improvise.*

" . . . he used to sing, improvising all the time, among the very best voices. His singing was so lovely that Michelangelo Buonarroti, that superb sculptor and painter, used to rush along for the pleasure of hearing him whenever he knew where he was performing. A goldsmith called Piloto who was a very talented artist, and I myself, used to accompany him. This, then, was how Luigi Pulci and I came to know each other."   —Benvenuto Cellini, *Autobiography*

*

Since early 1984, the central tone of each of my collections has been dictated by a "first" poem. In *Dien Cai Dau* it was "Somewhere Near

Phu Bai"; of course, in *Magic City*, "Venus's-fly-traps" embodied the tonal impulse for the collection. The other curious thing is that I'm usually working on three or four collections simultaneously—going back and forth between worlds the same way that I do in my everyday life. I enjoy simplicity and complexity side-by-side.

*

I continue to return to Blake's engravings, particularly this one called *Negro Hung Alive by the Ribs to a Gallows*. At first, I was angry at the image; now I realize that Blake was a visionary with a heart— one sees or feels the empathy beneath the ink. Here's an artist who stepped out of his times. Yes, indeed, some are blessed to be out of step!

He also captures Captain Stedman's tyranny and morbid memory— Europe's imperialism.

*

"There are few race-transcending prophets on the current black in-tellectual scene. James Bladwin was one. He was self-taught and self-styled, hence beholden to no white academic patronage system."
—Cornel West, *Race Matters*

"True black writers speak *as* blacks, *about* blacks, *to* blacks."
—Gwendolyn Brooks, *Jump Bad*

I feel that Gwendolyn Brooks has been undermined by lesser talents who happened to have been popular during the 1960s and 1970s. She was an outsider to them and had to compromise for acceptance (not honor or love). In fact, I think that Gwen had often seen herself as an outsider in her own community. It all has to do with surface appearances—and that's still true. Many of those younger poets around her were stylers in dress and poetry—without any artistic endurance. They were "slam poets" of that era, and Gwen had too much hard-earned discipline for them to cope with. But they knew her one weakness: She desired their love and acceptance. They co-erced her into becoming a turncoat against who she really was; thus, her art and creative spirit seem to have suffered greatly. They are the ones who should have been learning from her, but she gave in to their arrogance and bravado. Of course, we are the losers in this literary brouhaha.

*

I hope that I can continue to seek out challenges to expand my imagination. Here's something to remember: as the image of Aurora's son, the dark-skinned prince Memnon of Ethiopia, who was killed at Troy fighting for the Trojans (sounds like those street gangs in Boston and L.A. and only God knows where else) takes shape in my imagination, I realize that the classics were often more inclusive and true to history than the work by us present-day poets and writers.

A REED BOAT

The boat's tarrred and shellacked to a water-repellent finish, just sway-dancing with the current's ebb, light as a woman in love. It pushes off again, cutting through lotus blossoms, sediment, guilt, unforgivable darkness. Anything with half a root or heart could grow in this lagoon.

There's a pull against what's hidden from day, all that hurts. At dawn the gatherer's shadow backstrokes across water, choreographed for an instrument played for gods and monsters in the murky kingdom below. Blossoms lean into his fast hands, as if snapping themselves in half, giving in to some law.

Slow, rhetorical light cuts between night and day, like nude bathers embracing. The boat nudges deeper, with the ease of silverfish. I know by his fluid movements, there isn't the shadow of a bomber on the water anymore, gliding like a dream of death. Mystery grows out of decay of dead things—each blossom a kiss from the unknown.

When I stand on the steps of Hanoi's West Lake Guest House, feeling that I am watched as I gaze at the boatman, it's hard to act like we're the only two left in the world. He balances on his boat of Ra, turning left and right, reaching through and beyond, as if the day is a woman he could pull into his arms.

—from *Debriefing Ghosts*

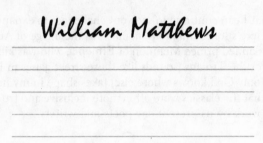

William Matthews

Entries from two different periods several years apart have been combined below. I heard them in the same key, and so rather than simply append the later to the earlier, I folded, as cookbooks say, one into the other.

Why do I record these scraps? So that, later, when I've forgotten what impulse led me to record them (much of what I keep is written by others—I keep a commonplace book and journal simultaneously) or write them, I can pick them up and see them as if they were freshly found rather than long hoarded.

"If we could know ourselves, it would be a violation of ourselves."

—Edwin Muir

*

"*Tsar* and *Kaiser* are both cognates for *Caesar*," the Latin teacher tells students triumphantly. See how the past survives, the teacher thinks. A mob's a mob the world around, thinks a student. We humans are perhaps at our worst when we think we've got something figured out.

*

"To eavesdrop is an ordeal." —Elizabeth Bowen

An oxymoron: "Dead language."

144

* * *

A language is communal and historical. It's a river that sweeps the present downstream, out to sea. Parts of any language die all the time. "He was gay," my grandmother says, who wonders why her Lesbian granddaughter had so few "beaux." My grandmother means he was mirthful. The language has beached her and swirled ahead. The world—she's 98—has done the same.

No doubt some languages have died, but we don't know which ones they were.

When we say "dead languages," we means "the classics"—Greek, Latin, and, for the arcane and scholarly, Sanskrit—which a few of us have assiduously kept alive, the way a few in any generation make geneological charts.

They may be in zoos, but they're alive.

Still, it may be that what we most value in them is in fact "dead," as fossils are. That "senile" and "Senate" have the same root, "sad" and "sated," and likewise "wife" and "gift."

*

From a student paper on whether entertainers have an obligation to act as role models: "The reason young people don't respect their parents is they're not well known."

*

Sebastian has sent me a tape from a new release of Bob Dylan bootlegs, so I spend a happy forty-five minutes comparing the versions of "Idiot Wind" I already have with one new to me. I envy the purely private fun it must be to turn one's work inside out, mock it, vamp it, make it both new and continuous with its former versions. A poem in a book is finished; the type is "set."

I realize that I approach my *Selected Poems* with a grave digger's melancholy but none of the grave digger's nasty humor. The task feels like exhumation.

It has, I know, nothing to do with whether they're good or not, but I'd like the poems I'll select more if I could treat them the way Dylan does his earlier recordings. Do I stand by them? Of course, even when that pose casts me as a gawky kid with a prom date. What did she see in him, or he in her?

*

As the Kunitz poem has it, "I only rented this dust." So then comes the moment you have to turn it in. They've already made an imprint of your credit card when you took the dust off the lot. "How much dust," you ask politely, "do I owe you for the use of this dust?"

*

I may well have on tape every recorded note played by Lester Young. The particles of musical information on each of those tapes are a sort of organized dust.

*

"I need a rhythm section like old people need soft shoes," said Lester. They wheel it through the gates of the fort. Beautiful carving, beautiful wood. The Trojan Slipper.

*

So Lester needed a capable rhythm section. One night he got a drummer he'd worked with before, unhappily. They were sitting around after the first set, and the drummer, who sensed that things weren't going well, was making cheerful patter. "Hey," he asked Lester, "when was the last time we worked together?"

Lester sighed, then said, "Tonight."

*

Musicians' joke:

Q: What class of people likes to hang around with musicians?

A: Drummers.

*

Half-rhymes: by rote, by heart. Dint, ain't. Tell, all. Finish, Spanish. Worst, Proust. Latin, pattern.

*

In a bad end-rhymed poem, you can have 80% of the available fun by reading only the far right-hand strand of the poem, the beach where the vowels break, and where the plot, the argument, the "paraphrasable content" (but not the poem), the matter (but not the energy), are in swarm, like the bees in this morning's *Times*. The street (E. 82nd?) had to be closed off. Why were they there? "Apparently the queen had become attached to a white Honda."

In a good end-rhymed poem the bees are everywhere, but the rhymes help you know where you are. First *you* means the poet, and then the reader. There is no third person in this grammar.

*

Soul: A reader? My kingdom for a reader.

Body: The reader can't come to the phone just now, but how about a mirror?

*

Ali, after his loss to Holmes: "I had the world, and let me tell you, it wasn't nothing."

*

Body: Why no poems in these notebooks, not even scraps or smithereens? What's the project, after all?

Soul: I'm going to ignore the moronic japery about the project. As for poems, there will be wine from these grapes.

*

Some employees of the Federal Reserve Bank wear magnesium shoes to protect their toes against dropped gold ingots.

*

Bread Loaf lecture coming up. . . . How many odd rhetorical forms and feints I've devised over the years to avoid writing a conventional essay, in which, like a sheepdog, the author jollies along a flock of argument.

It's always a writer who thinks of himself as a realist, in the relationship he covets between his work and the texture of experience, who will say to me, quizzically, after I've read the piece, "It was fascinating, but what exactly did it mean?"

There's a rage for meaning, to be sure. Freud's work, in which every retrievable scrap of dream and slip of the tongue are wrung like precious sponges for meaning, may be the great, mad, tragic text on rage for meaning. What did he find? A blurry snapshot. So who benefits? We do, for we have his writings, a great emotional document.

*

"Most of my life has been spent not understanding, and I can assure you, it was not easy."   —Rilke

*

You can abandon your own poem at any point, not so much because it's done, but because 700 calories, or 7,000, of additional energy spent on it wouldn't produce, you judge, proportionate improvement. On to the next, you decide; they're your poems and it's your energy. And you're not done, either.

But Martial's been done since AD 104. What right do you have to abandon that epigram that even Dudley Fitts, or Rolfe Humphries, or James Michie, or Fiona Pitt-Keithley, didn't quite get right, or so you suspect the more strongly the longer you too fail to get it right?

You have every right. You're just a minnow and Martial's a mullet, but he's dead and you're not.

*

Translation's a problem in English. In the first sentence of this year's Bread Loaf anti-lecture I use the word "gaud," but in my Southwestern Ohio dialect it will sound like "god," or, worse, "God," and in order to read it aloud without wrongly causing puzzlement or hurt I'll need to frontload, as the mutual fund sales-people say, the talk with an explanation.

*

"It's all material, I know . . . ," I heard a writer begin a sentence that listed a deluge of grief and death and betrayal that would make Job burst like a boil. Living in the material world . . .

It's pain. The meaning of pain is pain.

*

"Regret is the fruit of pity."

—Genghis Khan

*

How private is a journal if some entries get published? Who's this written for? What does it mean to sing in the shower? If a shower falls over on a desert island . . . ?

*

If you write it, it's not private. Scholars and, of course, lawyers believe this. I once heard a lawyer, not mine, say, "It's our position that this piece of paper doesn't exist."

*

This is my curse. *Pompous*, I pray
That you believe the things you say
And that you live them day by day.

—JV Cunningham

*

Epitaph: Was I right or what?

*

Sibelius, asked the meaning of his fourth symphony: "Play the record again."

*

"I think your poem doesn't take enough risks," one kind of workshop student will say. But nobody ought to be allowed to visit that kind of moral blackmail on a fellow student. The teacher should require the assailant to say exactly what kinds of risk, and exactly where in the poem they should be taken, and exactly where his or her gall and boorishness came from.

*

To get out of her house for a while, my grandmother asked me to take her for a drive around the small village she's lived in all but twenty of her ninety-five years. "The Lovetts' house once," she'd say. "No more."

*   *   *

Another house: "Martin Mortimer's place. Three wives."

"What was he like?" I asked.

"Dreadful snob," she said.

Another house. "Handsome Don Ransom's house," she said.

"What did he look like?"

"A chipmunk."

You get old, you hoard your verbs.

*

Of course if you were born in 1896, your world has shed its skin five times or six, and you're the oldest person you've actually met. When was the last time you dreamed of anyone being alive?

*

Rebuilt. Retool. Remarry. Change your life. Do we index that last one under Life, you must change your, or under Change your life, you must? Why, whenever I hear that half-line of Rilke quoted, always solemnly, do I wonder how large a diaper I'll need?

*

Gossip: a way to afflict the sadness you fear on others. Or, even sadder than that, the happiness you fear.

*

One lure of gossip consists in how much work it takes, and how enjoyable that is, to change the known world to fit a theory about it. ("But if she's recently inherited money, and doesn't want us to know about it, that would explain. . . .") In that way, gossip resembles detective fiction, or most literary criticism.

*

Gossip: I know it's true; I heard it from you.

*

Art: You know it's true; you heard it from me.

*

He left a rose behind her head,
   A meat axe in her brain.
A note upon the bureau read:
   "I won't be back again."

                        —Raymond Chandler

*

More from Chandler:

1) If you don't leave, I'll find somebody who will.

2) I left her with her virtue intact, but it was quite a struggle. She almost won.

3) Goodnight, goodbye and I'd hate to be you.

Exit lines, ends of paragraphs, ends of chapters: Chandler was the imprisoned master of the last word.

*

Why do I read that stuff? The rusted slang, the clumsy expositions ("I turned west on Pico, but I couldn't shake a dozen unanswered questions that stayed on my tail"), the mushheart-toughguy imitations of Samuel Johnson (Hammett: "The gaudier the patter, the cheaper the hood"), the snakes-with-their-bad-tasting-tails-in-their-mouths plots, the slinky and untrustworthy heiresses played by Bette Noir, the stripes and shadows of black and white like plaster and lath. . . .

(Does Pico run west?)

Describing why I ought not to like it, I have perhaps made it sound more attractive than it is, like a smoker talking about not being able to quit.

*

A yellow dress, a crusted spoon, an un-
watered begonia? The clue's only one

scrap in the world's rich litter and since you
don't know what it is nor how to guess
you're driving west on Pico, low on gas
and snappy patter. Moral dusk again
for the romantic loner: good doesn't count
until there are others, and then it's impossible. . . .

*

GRACE UNDER PRESSURE

There's no other kind: pressure makes it
grace or else it's charm, as in "charm bracelet."

*

THE POET'S END

He paled, he wrote more poems, white heat,
etc. Then he grew worse.
The grand tour to the last resort
often leaves an exhaust of verse.

*

Death is the mother of beauty? No doubt. Also of blackmailers, deb-
utantes, baggers of groceries, corrupt cops, babies, funeral directors,
and all the shrinks who live in, or rent office space in, the building
on Central Park West that houses more shrinks than the entire state
of Montana. Death loves her children equally, all her pretty ones.

*

Hamlet, with Yorick's skull in hand: "Where be your gibes now? your
gambols? your songs? your flashes of merriment, that were wont to
set the table on a roar?"

Laughter is the father of beauty.

J. D. McClatchy

 *I have from time to time kept both a notebook and a jour-
nal. They are very different things, as different as a recipe and
the plat du jour. The one book I've scribbled in consistently,
though, is my commonplace book, a sort of ledger of envies and
delights. "By necessity, by proclivity,—and by delight, we all
quote," says Emerson. But there is more to it than that. The
sentences I hoard are—to be literally figurative about it—images.
And as G. K. Chesterton once wrote, "The original quality in
any man of imagination is imagery. It is a thing like the landscape of his dreams; the sort of world he would like to make or
in which he would wish to wander; the strange flora and fauna
of his own secret planet; the sort of thing he likes to think
about." The bowerbird in me is forever collecting colored threads
and mirror shards to make a sort of world. My secret planet is
populated by Diana Vreeland and Dwight Eisenhower and Al-
exander Pope and Sergei Rachmaninoff and John Cage and Jean
Henri Fabre and Dizzy Gillespie and Elizabeth Bowen and Ed-
gar Degas and hundreds of others: a sort of Mad Hatter's tea
party of brilliant conversationalists talking over and at odds with
one another. I don't use their remarks in my poems; I sometimes
quote from them in my prose. But for years now I've been collecting them. I collect them for their own sake. I collect to admire, not merely to appropriate. I collect phrases because of the
way, in each, something is put that is both precise and surprising.
Twice-distilled poems? No. But an abstract model for the poetic.*
 Perhaps one day I shall make a small book of them. Fifteen

years ago, I would have included aphorisms of my own. (Here's one that comes to hand: "Memory's like a cherished old neigh-borhood. After a time, the wrong sort of people move in.") Today, phrasemaking bores me. I had lists of words that intrigued me; catalogues of "other voices overheard" while poems by Crane or Stevens or Warren were read out to me after a dose of hashish; lists of ideas from Wilde or Proust or Valéry; bits clipped from newspapers are tipped in. Nowadays, the entries are less frequent, more bemused, less intimate. There's a recurring character, named X, to whom phrases happen. What follows are a few excerpts, more or less randomly chosen.

"Those who have free seats boo first."　　　—Chinese saying

*

Thoreau, in his Journals, on how hard it is to read a contemporary poet critically: "For, we are such a near and kind and knowing au-dience as he will never have again. We go within the fane of the temple, but posterity will have to stand without and consider the vast proportions and grandeur of the building."

*

An example of literalism. When Lord Cornbury opened the New York Assembly in 1702 in drag—in the style of Queen Anne, in fact—and was challenged, he is reported to have answered: "You are all very stupid people not to see the propriety of it all. In this place, and on this occasion, I represent a woman, and in all respects I ought to represent her as faithfully as I can."

*

—his squeeze-box
—but less of that anon

*

"For the last third of life there remains only work. It alone is always stimulating, rejuvenating, exciting and satisfying."

　　　　　　　　　　　　　　　　　　　—Käthe Kollwitz

*

"When the axe came into the forest, the trees said: the handle is one of us."
                                                                —Turkish saying

*

Apropos the work of older artists becoming more spare, it should be noted that this is not always obvious. *Parsifal* is the thinnest of RW's scores (in terms of printed bulk, that is).

*

—*frère-ennemi*
bel canto > *can belto*
Eadward Muybridge sequential photographs > *Egyptian two-dimensional figures*
—X's ideas seem to have been lifted from fortune cookies
—*limae labor* (Horace), "the work of the file"
—scrape X off my shoes
—*bougereauté*

*

"All literature is to me me."
                                                                —G. Stein

*

Van Eyk's motto: "As I can but not as I would."

*

"Il faut choisir: une chose ne peut pas être à la fois vraie et vraisemble."
                                                                —Braque

*

12.ii.87. On Joyce Carol Oates' office door, she's taped up a card on which she's typed out this remark by Robt. Louis Stevenson: "To be idle requires a strong sense of personal identity."

*

On the overemphasis of clarity in writing: A. J. Liebling said the only way to make clear pea soup is to leave out the peas.

*

"Cinema is simply pieces of film put together in a manner that creates ideas and emotions."
                                                                —Hitchcock

*

"Rome, Italy, is what happens when buildings last too long."

—Andy Warhol

*

Ravel, on his critics: "Does it not occur to these people that I may be artificial by nature?"

*

"Verse that is too easie is like the tale of a rosted horse."

—Gascoigne

*

On a postcard from the old, ailing Auden to a composer who'd asked him for a libretto: "Too sad to sing."

*

Hemingway said there are two ways to spend an evening. Get into your Buick, shut the windows and sit near the exhaust. Or go to a cocktail party.

*

Frost said he was "content with the old-fashion way to be new."

*

The story is told—I think of Brahms—that the master is made to listen to a new score by a young composer. As he did, he kept raising his hat. The young man asked him why. "I'm just saying hello to old friends," he replied.

*

Told that a certain poem resembled an older poem, Allen Tate replied, "It had damn well better."

*

Poussin, from a letter to a friend, 1642: "The beautiful girls you will have seen at Nîmes will not, I am certain, delight your spirits less than the sight of the beautiful columns of the Maison Carrée, since the latter are only ancient copies of the former."

*

Fernando Pessoa's heteronyms: Alvaro de Campos, Ricardo Reis, Alberto Caeiro

*

hanami—[the season of] cherry blossom viewing

*

Which mandarin has the longest fingernails?
—bread and circuses
—X's work is like a Grinling Gibbons carving
—mutton dressed as lamb

*

Coleridge described himself as a "library-cormorant"

*

Poe distinguishes between obscurity of expression and the expression of obscurity

*

Du Bellay: *"rien ne dure au monde que le tourment"*

*

Res tene, verba sequentur   —Cato the Elder

*

Virgil Thomson, watching a beautiful woman walk toward him down Fifth Avenue, turned to his companion and whispered: "It's at times like this I wish I were . . . a lesbian."

*

Philip Sidney wanted from poetry a "heart-ravishing knowledge"

*

Mallarmé said that the French word for "day" sounded like night, and vice versa.

*

"Who plans suicide sitting in the sun?"   —Elizabeth Smart

*

The Marquis de Sade is descended from the same family as Petrarch's Laura.

*

Paul noticed this bumper sticker on the LA Freeway yesterday: "The meek are contesting the will"

*

—sottocapi
—X is copperbottoming his career
—The Flat Earth Society

*

Dylan Thomas's blurb for Flann O'Brien's *At Swim-Two-Birds*: "This is just the book to give your sister if she's a loud, dirty, boozy girl."

*

On his passport, Stravinsky listed himself as "inventor of sounds."

*

Maria Tallchief, withdrawing from the New York City Ballet in 1965: "I don't mind being listed alphabetically, but I do mind being treated alphabetically."

*

"Outside of a dog, a book is man's best friend. Inside of a dog, it's too dark to read."   —Groucho Marx

*

Emerson referred to "the Poetry of the Portfolio—"the work of persons who wrote for the relief of their own minds, and without thought of publication."

*

Klimt said that to write anything, even a short note, made him "seasick."

*

Lao-tzu: "The Way that can be spoken of is not the True Way."

*

—X got up on his hind legs and . . .
—X is filling a much-needed gap
—backbencher; ward-heeler

—*un mutilé de guerre*
—frog-marched

*

optima dies prima fugit

*

Motionless, deep in his mind lies the past the poet's forgotten,
Till some small experience wake it to life and a poem's begotten,
Words its presumptive primordia, Feeling its field of induction,
Meaning its pattern of growth determined during construction.
                    —WHA, note in "New Year Letter"

*

"Some people think that luxury is the opposite of poverty. Not so.
It is the opposite of vulgarity."   —Coco Chanel

*

"Technique in art . . . has about the same value as technique in
lovemaking. That is to say, heartfelt ineptitude has its appeal and so
does heartless skill, but what you want is passionate virtuosity."
                    —John Barth

*

"Drawing is not form, it's the way you see form."   —Degas

*

"Exuberance is Beauty"   —Blake

*

To the wounds of his victims Torquemada applied thistle poultices.

*

Euclid defined a point as having position but no magnitude.

*

Roethke had submitted "The Lost Son" to *Horizon*. Sonia Brownell
(later Orwell) returned it with this remark: "It seemed to us that your
poetry was in a way very American in that it just lacked that inspiration, inevitability or quintessence of writing and feeling that distinguishes good poetry from verse."

*

"Poets are jails. Works are the convicts who escape."
—Cocteau, diary, 23.iii.53

*

11.xi.90. In line with Jane for a movie at MOMA. SM approaches, said he'd been at the NYU reading last week and been struck by my new Bishop poem. Did I remember the Cambridge reading of long ago? he asked. I did. Did I remember talking with Lowell about Bishop? I didn't—but he had been listening in. He overheard me asking Cal what might account for EB's popularity. "All the fags like her" was his answer.

*

Tom Paulin refers to an Irish word *thrawn* to mean a poetry or language where there's "something a bit difficult, a bit contorted," as in Donne or Hopkins or Browning (or Frost, he adds, and Hardy).

*

For the Greeks, memory was "the waker of longing."

*

Happiness is what I most know in life, but grief is what I best understand of it.

*

Harold Bloom: "My favorite prose sentence by Mr. Ezra Pound is in one of his published letters: 'All the Jew part of the Bible is black evil.' And they ask me to take that seriously as a Western mind."

*

"What constitutes adultery is not the hour which a woman gives her lover, but the night which she afterwards spends with her husband."
—George Sand

*

A British critic described Beverly Sills' voice, later in her career, as "part needle, part thread."

*

—rust-proof
—X has floured his sauce
—the talking classes
—fan de siècle
—a slash of gin

*

The Japanese ideogram for "noise" is the ideogram for "woman" repeated three times.

*

"*All* must have prizes," said the Dodo.

*

Schoenberg's transcription of "The Emperor Waltz" for clarinet, violin, cello and harmonium—an image for *translation* in general?

*

My old college teacher Elias Mengel once showed me his copy of Wallace Stevens' *Collected Poems*, which WS had inscribed: "Dear Elias: When I speak of the poem, or often when I speak of the poem, in this book, I mean not merely a literary form, but the brightest and most harmonious concept, or order, of life; and the references should be read with that in mind."

*

O. Wilde: "only mediocrities develop"

*

Robert Pinget, on his own writing: "You might call it a kind of automatic writing carried out in a state of total consciousness. . . . I am now convinced that in a work of art we do not try to conjure up beauty or truth. We only have recourse to them—as to a subterfuge—in order to be able to go on breathing."

*

"I have played with quite a few musicians who weren't so good. But as long as they could hold their instruments correct, and display their willingness to play as best they could, I would look over their shoulders and see Joe Oliver and several other great masters from my home town."
                                                                    —Louis Armstrong

*

Balanchine: "*Apollo* I look back on as a turning point of my life. In its discipline and restraint, in its sustained oneness of tone and feeling, the score was a revelation. It seemed to tell me that I could dare not to use everything, that I, too, could eliminate."

*

"The closer the look I take at a word, the greater the distance from which it looks back."   —Karl Kraus

*

Freud on the surrealists (from the journal of Princess Marie Bonaparte): "They send me all their productions. They think I approve what they write. But it isn't art."

*

The measure of a poem's "immortality" is the later life it has in other poems. Imitation, appropriation—dismemberment and regeneration —by new poets give the old poem its purchase on life.

*

Braque on Picasso: "He used to be a great artist, but now he's only a genius."

*

Andrew Lloyd Webber is reported to have once asked Alan Jay Lerner, "Why do people take an instant dislike to me?" Lerner replied: "It saves time."

*

Pope, on his *Brutus* (of which an outline and eight lines remain): "Though there is none of it writ as yet, what I look upon as more than half the work is already done, for 'tis all exactly planned."

*

"A book is never a masterpiece. It becomes one."
                                    —from the Goncourts' journal

*

—*pompier*
—Boot Hill
—majaism (Levine?)
—X's poems are *objets de vertu*
—X's grasp exceeds his reach
—wings-and-flats
—which is the quick brown fox and which the lazy dog?
—a musical term: the dragged glissando

*

Jean de Reszke's voice was described as having *"le charme dans la force."*

*

Age is a caricature of the self (or the self's body and features). To make someone look funny—or do I mean merely to make fun of someone?—make him look older.

*

About his wife Camille on her deathbed, Monet writes: "I found myself, without being able to help it, in a study of my beloved wife's face, systematically noting the colors."

*

Nietzsche held the "refinement of cruelty belongs to the springs of art."

*

Tu nihil in magno doctus reprehendis Homero?   —Horace

*

Nabokov, *Look at the Harlequins!*: "In those days I seemed to have had two muses: the essential, hysterical, genuine one, who tortured me with elusive snatches of imagery and wrung her hands over my inability to appropriate the magic and madness offered me; and her apprentice, her palette girl and stand-in, a little logician, who stuffed the torn gaps left by her mistress with explanatory or meter-mending fillers which became more and more numerous the further I moved away from the initial, evanescent, savage perfection."

Cynthia Macdonald

*N*otebooks are like attics, a place for treasures which some-times turn out to be junk, but take you anyway to another time and place. Ah, my Giants' bat signed by Mel Ott. Scott's Boys' Day carp kite which flew in our garden in Tokyo. Two minia-tures of my father as a child, one an inferior copy, one in which there is depth and sadness. A stiffly boned strapless dress, gray satin with a carnation-pink satin and sequined bodice in which I sang at the San Francisco Opera Auditions. A mahogany table with one leg missing. My mother's College Board results. Jen-nifer's second-grade painting from York House in Vancouver. And this—what is it?—white metal object with a sharply pointed turnscrew in the center of a hollow cylinder. A torture implement for dolls?

Or perhaps a notebook is a second brain, the mind's miscel-lany caught in ink before it is forgotten. Part commonplace book, part work notes, fragments, observations, and ideas for use in work already under way, or for possible work-to-be, some entries close to diary passages, but not much that is personal and inti-mate. A place in a book to note matters of possible interest. A place to put matters of note for a book. A book to write notes for a sonata.

Poem fragment—There are far too many of these, representing my fragmented life as writer, teacher, therapist, and person having a personal life. These lives fit together most of the time, one feeding the other, but in switching between them, too many poems get started and then abandoned. Some are failures, as are some completed poems, the ones where you think, after the first draft, this is terrific, experiencing sometimes a small frisson. Then the next day: disappointment. I copy many of what I consider the more promising incomplete poems into my notebook. This fragment had its genesis in the real story of a man who taught mime and killed his lover, then himself: The Ballad of Claude Caux: Mute Claude Caux, master of mime / who made us believe you could climb air, / mute Claude Caux, how did you go / about killing her? Prickly Claude Caux, fencing master / charming épées from the tip of your sword, / cutting the air into patches / to close wounds. Money talks, Claude Caux, and so / do you, mute only on stage. / Yet where did talk get you / when you found her out?

Then the question: is there enough life left in this, or other incomplete poems, to reconnect so that work goes on with the complex and mysterious interaction between poet and poem that there was at the beginning. Without this interaction, I cannot write.

*

I've begun thinking about "my" cantos—VII and VIII—for a new translation of Dante's *Inferno*. Dan Halpern has asked twenty poets to do one or two each. I begin by reading all the verse translations I can find. From horrible—Dorothy Sayers—to good—Mandelbaum, Musa. Should my translation lean toward a prose-based line which allows for more accuracy, or lines which are poetry and may, if I can get them right, come closer to the poetry of the original?

*

Thinking about my work as a therapist with people who have writing blocks, I realize all of them are prose writers. Isn't that strange? Perhaps not strange with the "I've-always-wanted-to-write-but-can't" patients. But what about those in the have-written-successfully-but-are-now-stuck category?

*

I've just returned from a reading Bob Hass and I gave in Berkeley. He read the virtually finished draft of his cantos. I haven't even begun! We talk about the "wrong" solution to the metrical problems of trying to match in English the Italian feminine word endings: use lots of articles, prepositions and conjunctions. But that yields "dead poetry," the opposite of Pound's ideogram. Or Dante's text.

*

I would like, in all my writing to spell rhyme, rime, even though the word comes from the Latin rhythmus so spelling it rhyme more accurately connects rhythm and rhyme. But in this day and age when both r & r are still, in spite of the New Formalists, primarily used in flexible or hidden ways, I think it's useful to distinguish more quickly between them and to remind ourselves that they are not Siamese twins. Besides I like the sense of white frost (rime) at the rim of the endeavor.

*

Immersed in Dante, but still struggling with formal decisions. Free verse? Too far from the original. Blank verse? Not quite; I want rime traces and the sense of the way rime links the stanzas— beads linked into a chain by rime. I decide to rime middle lines (abc,dbe,fgh,igk), a trace of linkage though not a true chain. To tie off this ghost chain I will end each canto with a complete terza rima stanza, preceded by the necessary first and third line rime in the penultimate stanza.

*

Virginia Woolf said of Max Beerbohm in an essay titled "The Intellectual Imagination": "But was not his passion for loading his lines, like the fingers of some South American beauty, with gem after gem, part of his boldness and brilliancy and strength?" The ridiculous music of Beerbohm's name—yields this quatrain: Mr. Beerbohm and Mr. Sasson / Played a duet upon the bassoon / Ump-pah-pah, ump—"how lovely they cried / And every one else is quite out of tune."

My poem "Victoria's Secret," begins with the lingrie catalogue and continues with Queen Victoria. I had a lot of difficulty achieving both sense and music in a stanza using Woolf's description of a lunch with Beerbohm where they talk about his story in which a very successful woman novelist writes a novel that a critic throws into flames in the fireplace. The book won't burn, no matter how much he prods it or pushes it further in. I wanted this material in the poem. I prodded and pushed. But it wanted to be a prose lump in the poem's throat. I hope that finally I got it right.

*

My Italian is that of an opera singer which I used to be. It is fairly useless for everyday tasks, for example renting a car, but it proves much more adequate for the Inferno. Accursed sinners, suffering, tears, blood, fear, betrayers, dismal foes . . . these are the stuff of opera. Anyone who has seen the wonderful documentary about mezzo-soprano Frederica von Stade and watched her enact the pre-scribed faces and motions for *orrible* and *terrible* will immediately understand the connection. I'm beginning to feel I'm inhabiting Dante's poem. But the choices to be made are, as my adult kids say, awesome: *orribile, terribile.*

Why are all prose translations of Dante so inaccurate? Surely the point of translating poetry into prose is that you can stick more closely to the original. Singleton, whose notes are essential for the non-Dante scholar, makes weird changes from the original in his prose translation.

*

Adrienne Rich in *What Is Found There: Notebooks on Poetry and Politics:* "*Misprision.* I first learned the word in a Shakespeare sonnet I memorized in school. An Elizabethan word, rarely used today. It means 'mistakenness,' 'to have taken something wrong'—misapprehension or 'misperception' we might say today." She goes on to relate *misprision* to events in the Soviet Union and the Gulf War, then applies the word to power, meaning, "To have taken something wrongly, to have mis-taken, to have ill-used what was taken, what ought not to have been taken, to misrepresent, misapply, divert to other means what ought to have its own rhythm and purpose. *Misprise:* to value wrongly. To value wrongly—the worst misconduct by a public official . . ." The word itself has intimations of "prison," "pry(pries)," and prize. All seem appropriate to what Adrienne says about the word.

*

Translation is compromise. Again and again. Perhaps warring factions—the Bosnians, the Serbs, the Croats; the Israelis and the Arabs, and so on, should be forced to translate each other's poetry. Perhaps

the Guelphs and Ghibelines, even though they spoke the same language, should have.

*

Richard Howard has just shown me his Dante translation; it is very
fine. He and Wilbur are the only two who have translation as a second
skin. How amazingly lucky I am to have had Richard in my life for
over twenty-five years. Summer, 1966. Bennington College. Richard
walking toward me down the path, he with Max, his English bulldog;
I with my children, Scott, age 7, Jennifer, age 10. The occasion, a
two-week summer course for alumnae and families. Having written
in almost total isolation for the previous six years, first in Vancouver,
BC, then in Tokyo, I was desperate to have exchanges about poetry.
When the man with the bulldog held out his hand and said, "Hello,
I'm Richard Howard," my life was changed. Yes, I know that sounds
melodramatic, but it was, as if I'd met Glinda the Good on the path.
He became my mentor. For a number of years I showed him almost
every poem of mine that I considered finished. And four years later,
as we were walking from his apartment to a restaurant to have lunch,
he said, "I'm going to be the editor of a new poetry series that George
Braziller is doing. Would you like to be the third in it?"

*

Bob Hass' essay "What Furies" in *Twentieth Century Pleasures*: "The
meditative poem can step a little to the side and let the world speak
through it, and the world has no need to cry 'Let be! Let be!' Because
it is. It has a mind of winter or, as the Zen teacher Robert Aiken has
said, a mind of white paper."

*

My cantos are finished. I'm working on the notes. Want to include a
quote from the Mandelstam essay in which he describes Dante's
process of creating terza rima, "the forming instinct." But it doesn't
relate specifically to VII and VIII. He says that to think about terza
rima "one has to imagine how it would be if bees had worked at the
creation of this thirteen-thousand faceted shape, bees endowed with
instinctive stereometric genius, who attracted still more and more
bees as they were needed. The work of those bees, who always keep
an eye on the whole, is not equal in degree of difficulty at the various
stages of the process. Their cooperation broadens and becomes more

complex as they proceed with the formation of the combs, by means of which space virtually arises out of itself."

*

Joy Harjo responding to a question about her family life, tribal life and life as a writer, in an interview with Marilyn Kallet: "Well they are not separate really. Though the way I've come to things is very different from say, Beth Cuthand, who is a Cree writer from Saskatchewan, or Leslie Silko from Laguna. There is a tendency in this country to find one writer and expect her to speak for everyone and expect her experience to be representative of all Native women and all Native people."

This is such an important statement for all "typed" writers. And we all are, even Wasps. Because, although any writer may be geographically, ethnically, religiously, even economically typed, one kind of typing is never mentioned: being typed by class. Many responses to poetry are class-driven. Especially responses to diction.

*

Favorite contemporary ecstatic poets: Amichai, Dubie, Hirsch, some of Neruda (especially the elemental odes), Allan Grossman, early Kinnell, perhaps Ted Hughes. I suddenly realize there are no women in the group. And I can't think of any contemporaries who belong there, certainly no Americans. I have to go back to Dickinson, who surely does. Many poets, again mostly male, reach for the ecstatic as a way to end their poems, but there is often a rote quality about these ecstasies, what I've termed "the all-purpose ending." I've given talks about that subject, but I should get the material into a finished essay.

*

On my shelves for over-size books, I find the large maroon and gold *Divine Comedy* that, at sixteen, was the first one I read: "A New Translation into English Blank Verse by Lawrence White, with illustrations by Gustave Dore." Four years ago at a storage warehouse in Massachusetts, going through the boxes of books I had saved several years earlier when closing my mother's house in Cambridge, I pulled out about twenty books from several hundred to take with me, expecting to ship the rest, along with furniture, in a few months. For various reasons, everything else still remains in storage. If I were a mystic, I'd say I took the White/Dore because I knew it would be needed.

I read the White version of "my" Cantos. It is excellent. Another excellent one is by Tom Phillips. Why are they virtually unknown? Who, what, decides what will become a part of the canon?

*

I've thought a lot about sestinas. I've read many (favorites: Ashbery, Justice, Auden, Bishop), taught them in forms classes (from which have come some excellent ones; a favorite: Leslie Adrienne Miller's "The Man in the Courtyard," the title poem in her book), but never written one I've considered successful enough even to finish it.

I collect end words for them in my notebook as Henry James collected place and proper names. I roll the words on my tongue, waiting for them to find the subject, the emotion which will make them cohere into the poem itself. They don't. Too forced, I decide (though I often play games out of which poems come). You must start with the subject matter and find the end words. But still I collect the end words.

Sestina Words: *die* (*death, and cast the*), *dye, lie, lye, lea, Lee* (my maiden name); *munificence, sense, cents*—possibly *magnificence, essence*, etc. How about *degree, filigree, agree, cordially*? How about *once, one, won,* (*won-ton soup at the Peking duck house/won-ton soup was so heavy this evening I can still feel it bumping against the Peking Duck House duck*)? How about *munificence/sense/cents/magnificence/essence*? *Miss, missed, mist, mistake* and all the other "*mis-*" words?

*

The 92nd Street Y Dante Reading. The company in which I find myself is grand and I am pleased to be of it. We read in the order of our cantos. Seamus Heaney goes first. His translation is very fine. The music of his voice, his accent make me think he could read Joyce Kilmer's "Trees" and make it sound like a good poem.

The order after Heaney: Strand, Halpern, Kinnell, me, Clampitt, Graham, Wright, Howard, Plumly, Williams, Pinsky, Mitchell, Forché, Wilbur, Merwin, Corn, Olds, Digges, Hass. What an amazing range of approaches to our task. Dante through the scrim of each poet's voice.

Those who read in the first half can sit in the audience for the second. Richard and I sit together. When Bob Hass reads the last lines about the ascent from Hell, I feel exultant and overwhelmed. Richard and I are holding hands. He squeezes mine and I see tears rolling down his face.

Rebecca Sinkler, *The New York Times Book Review*'s editor, described the reading in the *Review*: the genesis of the project in a Detroit restaurant, the making of a translation "for our time," which poet wore the best shoes, had the best hair, the best beard. But in the end she abandoned her rather chatty tone about the event as event, and had a reaction very similar to the one Richard and I had had: "Mr. Hass . . . paused . . . increasing the tension and drama in the last moments of the poem, then delivered the last lines of the last stanza: Dante and Virgil emerging from hell, glimpsing 'the night sky with the beautiful things it carries / And we came out and looked up at the stars.'

And we came out and looked up at a starless New York sky, we who had journeyed for four hours in the company of poets and the beautiful things they carry."

*

I've just found, in a box of unexamined memorabilia removed from storage, a spiral notebook of my mother's. It's shiny blue, about one and a half by three inches; I remember it was in the drawer of her bedside table. It seems to be a list of books she'd read though I recognize very few of the titles: *Descent into Hell, Mirror for Man, Sixteen Self Sketches, Spin your Web, Lady.* This last title is actually the way my father and his friend Humphry Bogart sometimes talked in the thirties and forties. I wonder where that kind of tough-guy speech came from? Not Dashiell Hammett or Raymond Chandler; they were contemporaries. Daddy wrote movies, mostly B-movies. Has anyone ever written poems in that dialect? Steven Dobyns comes to mind. No. Denis Johnson? No. I think I've read detective-story poems that caught it. Could it be used in any other way in a poem? A sestina?

I'm interested because, used with contemporary speech, it would provide a language collision, a language friction.

* * *

Back to my mother's little blue book. She read many mysteries; I guess that's what most of these are. I know she didn't read only mysteries; her bookshelves when we cleaned out the house attested to that fact, but there are over a hundred in this book. Then, suddenly on the top of a page: *Psychoanalytic Reader*, International Universities Press. The Press is a major publisher of psychoanalytic books. But I never heard her express any interest in that area. And she certainly didn't demonstrate much insight during her life. A mystery, and I can't ask her. One of the frustrations of the death of someone with whom you share a long, close history is what you can't tell them something no one else you know would be interested in . . . and what you can't ask them.

Whenever I see her handwriting, she is, for a moment, there with me.

*

From *Self and Others: Object Relations Theory in Practice* by N. Gregory Hamilton: "A 2-year old boy and his father walked back from the park one summer evening. They commented on their shadows stretched out before them on the sidewalk.

'That's my shadow,' the boy said, 'and that's my Daddy's shadow.'

'Yes,' his father answered, 'there they are.'

Shortly, he lifted his son to his shoulders. The boy laughed at the change in their shadows.

'What's that on top of my shadow?' his father demanded.

'That's me,' the boy said, giggling.

Over and over he said, 'That's me.' Previously, he had said it was his shadow. Now he said only, 'That's me.' His shadow had become a self-image.

'That's me' is what is meant by the self in object relations theory."

The shadow, which has merged the outlines of father and son, is now one. For the poem, and for life, it must be both one and two. And then there are the layers of what is under the shadow(s). The sidewalk, dirt, shale, etc. That is the poem, the only kind of poem that interests me. When the poem is just the merged shadow it may please on first reading. But I never want to return to it again and again.

Some fathers would have said, "What's that under my shadow?"

*

After the Dante "Y" reading, all the poets, plus many others from poetry and publishing, went to an Italian feast at the Dakota (the building John Lennon was living in when he was shot). Dan Halpern planned the menu. He is as inventive about food and wine as he is about editing and writing: he is a savorer.

The security about getting into the building was stringent, as we'd been warned it would be. On a par with getting into the White House for the party of a hundred poets given by the Carters (May Swenson almost was not admitted because she did not have a driver's license).

Once through the security you are on your own in this maze of buildings, with more mazes within each one. No elevator men or other attendants to help. I got lost three times.

When I left the party, the door, which led to the courtyard which led to the hall which led to the security desk and thence out, was locked. A sign said so and instructed: Take Elevator Down. I did and found myself in a capacious, brightly lit basement. Although its size and soaring ceiling made it the grandest NYC basement I'd ever been in, I couldn't see the way out of it. I looked for instructions. There were none. I went to every door and the four or five passages which led off the basement, but I didn't dare go down one for fear of not being able to return. There was a small room, more like a cage, in the center of the space which had a television set playing the David Letterman show with the sound turned to silence. The door to the cage/room was locked. Surely someone was about to return to watch the TV? I waited. No one came. I would have to go back to the apartment to get directions. The elevator had no handle on the out-side of the door thus no way in. Panic. One of the doors that I'd seen had looked different from the other, more like a front door. Yes, it had a doorbell! When I rang it a dog barked but no one appeared. There was a phone in the cage. I would try to break in. Couldn't. Rang the doorbell again. More dog barking. I'd left the place I was staying at 5:30 pm and it was now after midnight. I'd been in the basement forty minutes. Would I have to spend the night? Would I make my 8:35 morning flight? I was consigned to Hell, probably the one for gluttons. I didn't even have anything to read. Except cantos 7 and 8. More panic.

The elevator door opened. Three guests from the party. I yelled "Don't let it close," but before I'd gotten the words out it had. I outlined our situation. They could hardly believe it. But now there were four of us, reconnoitering was possible. Two left to try different passages. We rang the doorbell. The dog barked. We approached the cage. As the person with me began to see if she was a better lock picker than I, a voice said, "yes?" We turned to find the sleepy, disgruntled occupant of what were probably the super's quarters. Like the disagreeable boatman who ferried Dante and Virgil across the river to deeper Hell, he pointed the way. Across and up and out.

*

Idea for a poem, from a *New Yorker* clipping: "Mark Kindschi, a thirty-seven-year-old slack rope walker who has lived for the last three years on a tugboat moored in the Hudson, has decided to leave New York. This week, after more than a decade of street performing, he will be on his way, taking with him several large spools of five-sixteenths-inch steel cable, some rope, a dufflebag full of juggling clubs and drumstick-shaped torches, several iron braces, a three-hundred-pound forge (he is a self-taught blacksmith), a six-volume edition of the plays of George Bernard Shaw, and his fiancée, Mia, who is another slack-rope walker." What a great list. But, no. I don't think I can make a poem of it. These first two sentences are too good; what can I add? But I will keep the concept of slack-rope walking in my head and maybe it will be part of a metaphor. Remember, Cynthia, that almost all your poems abut these kinds of people—the tightrope walker, the plant which grew too tall, the fire-walker, the world's biggest man, Florence Nightingale—began with an image, a narrative intention, and a voice. The characters had to find a way to encompass these in order to continue. Invention was necessary in a way that fully-fleshed Mark Kindschi doesn't require.

To amplify the quick mention above of the way a poem gathers itself, I remember how that happened in "The Holy Man Walks Through Fire." I was driving to Sarah Lawrence from Westport, where I lived, and thinking unhappily about the war in Vietnam, about the way successive presidents had fucked up and how we couldn't now seem to extricate ourselves from the war.

The phrase "the point of no return" came to mind. And suddenly I saw a man walking through fire who discovered the pain of that and wanted to turn back, but was past the point of no return. Almost simultaneously his voice began talking: "They were looking (as they still looked at the flag and / Other residual emblems, feeling a crinkle / Of lost certainties) / For someone to show he knew what they needed / And I, who had three times tried / To kill myself but each time was saved by a quirk, / Decided I was being saved for something. . . ." What he was being saved for was to be the leader of the country. A failed leader. But I had no idea of what story the leader would tell, what shape his failure would take. Or that the last stanza, after he has walked through the fire, would begin: "I have limited / use of one / foot with which / I am writing . . ."

*

How many times I've failed at attempting to write about war, the homeless, etc. even though I care deeply about these topics. The more monumental the tragedy the harder it is to write about. Which Holocaust poems succeed? I used to think Louis Simpson's "The Bird"—which begins " 'Ich wünschi'ich wäre ein Vöglein,' / Sang Heinrich, 'I would fly / Across the sea . . .' so sadly / It made his mother cry"—was successful, and I still do, but now I find it uneven. Insofar as it works I think it does because it deals with the Hitler period through an individual, because it so thoroughly captures the sentimentality and horror of that period, and because the jingly form makes it sound almost like a children's story, i.e. the form clashes with the content, which, contrary to the cliché, can be very effective.

I had a student who visited one of the Concentration Camps—I think it was Dachau—and wrote about visiting it and thinking it looked like a summer camp. This choice struck me as brilliant. Unfortunately, her development as a poet was not up to her idea.

I, too, don't have the means, or haven't found them for those overwhelming subjects. The Vietnam war, which I worked to end, and went to jail to protest, yielded one effort which was barely possible.

Almost all my attempts, and those of others, suffer from what I used to call when I was teaching at Sarah Lawrence, "the-sitting-on-the-train-and-looking-into-the-windows-of-the-Harlem-tenements syndrome." A sort of Lady Bountiful stance.

One recent failure is called "The Overnighters." It begins with the speaker, lying on a couch, reading in the *The New York Times* about the children known as the overnighters. When I actually did read it, there were passages that broke my heart, as the article described how these children are sent to a different home each night: "They may, or may not get clean clothes or a bath," and "It is only after the lights are out that they cry." I thought I might, by acknowledging the speaker's privileged life and by using the quotes, make it work.

But, no. Many more attempts, each one revised many times.

Finally, I think I was successful because I was focussing on something completely different. I'd been puzzling over the question of a reality which always escapes being definitive. An image came to me: a very ill woman lying on a couch. I began with that, in a first section called "The Young Woman Who Lies in a Shoe." The first line is: "A woman of wool lies on a couch covered with pale shawls." That image becomes a narrative; the second section has another similar but conflicting narrative, and finally, in the third, I found my characters on the street. That poem, "The Woman on the Stone Couch Dreams and Wakes," was in *The Paris Review*. It's my best effort so far to deal with that kind of subject.

Only now, as I write, do I notice that the first line of "The Woman on the Stone Couch" ("A woman of wool lies on a couch covered with pale shawls") begins with almost the same words as the first line of "The Overnighters." "I lie on a couch in my friend's apartment./ The couch is taupe velvet with an airy, hand-woven Persian shawl/ draped over the back." Why this repetition of the setting? Don't know. Will mull. But as to differences that may make one poem fail and the other succeed, maybe the change from an "I" to a third person narrator is crucial.

*

I often copy a poem I particularly like, getting it into my fingers and thus, in a small way, into my body. Memorizing is the true way to get a poem into the body, but I'm poor at it. Wislawa Szymborska's untitled poem, translated from the Polish by Milosz, that begins, "I am too near to be dreamt of by him," is one I copied. It is an ecstatic poem by a woman. Does the search for ecstatic bliss, ecstatic release without accompanying pain dampen, even extinguish the ecstatic? How does the ecstatic differ from the sublime?

*

It is spring, and we are in Italy on our way from Perugia to Urbino. We detour slightly to go to the Fonte Avellana, a monastery in the Apennines which has been in continuous use since 979. Jennifer and Hillary will spend a couple of hours climbing while I read and enjoy the views. Then we'll go inside. Trees are flowering, a long bridge stretches over a ravine, the sky is brilliant. Once each hour for several hours a day visitors are allowed inside for fifteen minutes. A monk will lead us. I think of Browning's "Fra Lippo Lippi."

Inside it is intensely quiet in contrast to the noise made outside the several busloads of school children who are playing games waiting to have lunch in the snack bar. The scriptorium where the monks wrote and illuminated manuscripts still has its long table, but it's clear it's no longer used. The library is lined with books. Here Dante, exiled for so many years from Florence, wrote part of *Il Paradiso*. Yes, it would have had to be Paradise, not *The Inferno* that was worked on here. This place is suffused with the sublime. Or maybe I just want to believe that.

*

Gerry Stern in an issue of *Ploughshares* which he edited says of the ecstatic: " . . . it denotes a state of exultation in which one transcends oneself and, as well, a kind of dislocation. . . . I recall that the Buddhists thought of a state that is beyond ecstasy—it is called equanimity—and is characterized by knowledge and the bliss that goes with it. I love the idea of ecstasy transcended. Were it to take the form of writing, I'm afraid it would be realized in silence, by a blank page maybe." I think I don't love the idea of ecstasy transcended. It's too totally out of this world; the second shadow is not there.

*

I often include in a condolence letter Dickinson's "After great pain a formal feeling comes—" To me it so captures my response to death, and to other personal tragedies. Is it an ecstatic poem? I feel it is. Must the ecstatic always contain the Dionysian? Doesn't the end of the last line contain it: "This is the Hour of Lead— / Remembered if outlived. / As Freezing persons, recollect the Snow— / First— Chill—then Stupor—then the letting go—"

Heather McHugh

The notebok is a site of insecurable premises: it's where a writer can turn and return to the unprefixed. The notes entered in a writer's notebook—unlike these headnotes, and unlike critical footnotes—are no appendage; they depend from no foregone body of work. It is this unforegoneness that constitutes the sense of vividness in notebooks: the feel of an abruptly enterable, expandable presence. Speaking from neither head (the precursor) nor foot (the afterthinker), notebooks are constrained neither to oversee nor, necessarily, to understand: but they record, and that has heart at heart. By "heart" I mean the mortal, material, guarded innermostness of us, what works out of sight in seizures, outflows, surges, tentativenesses, spondees, and desponds.

There's a certain luxury in the physical relation a writer bears to her notebook. A notebook must be portable, must be filled by hand, at different times, in many leads and inks: to glance back over a notebook is to see colors and penchants, swellings and contractions, exfoliations of sketchwork and pastework, even ravages of ripwork and incision. One of my notebook pages was, with no mean trepidation, actually set on fire and then extinguished, a study in devastation; to another page was stapled a dollar bill, itself inscribed and perforated. Notebooks invite the writer to extra-semantic vagrancies; and in looking back over them, one has the sense that one is (itself, or oneself) not readily semanticizable: one is and has been many. And many are the selves one finds unlovable.

Chekhov's every note seems evocative of a whole (and skeptic) social narrative; descriptions of physical characters can't help

*sliding into revelations of moral character: "Her mouth was like
a slot: one longed to put a penny in it," for example. Or, "She
had too little skin to cover her face: in order to open her eyes
she had to shut her mouth, and vice versa." Keeping a notebook,
Chekhov kept company; he kept bad company well. The quirks
of the individual betray the streaks of the species.*

*A notebook is solitude's colloquy. The times I've kept a note-
book (a novel is released, but a notebook is kept!) were periods
when I was alone and uprooted, periods of relative homelessness.
Perhaps that accounts for the extravagant sense of intimacy that
attends, when I remember it, the thought of the notebook keeping itself: it was my retreat, it was where I felt most at home.
Entering its passages, keeping the time of day, and literally keeping it—dating it and deepening it—was most pleasurable for me
when I was stationed, far from home, in a public place: surrounded by strangers, free to be the unobserved observer. The
paradox is then most active: for a notebook isn't public writing.
Yet the circumstance of a milling public itself deepens a privacy,
extends an anonymity; one's privacy there is fiercer, more intent.*

*The engagement seems more than faintly touched with the
erotic; and it's full of fidelities, too. For me, a notebook was a
kind of husband: an occasion for loving and excerpting the world
at large (at large is where the human animal may not, until
death, forever roam).*

*The excerpts here are peculiar to the time surrounding and
following the death of a good friend in Florida. The poem that
follows the excerpt was one of a series in which I could not
transform, by any metaphorical mumbo jumbo, the atrocity of
his dying. I married a year or two after that death, and since that
time have never again kept a notebook.*

*To have a compatible and constant human intimate is, for a
time, to forget death; and to forget death is to forget one's first and
final premises. I shall have to come back to the notebook's domain, I imagine: that is, to the work of unforgetting. One tries to
get beyond the writing; one writes to get beyond the trying. Meanwhile, one can read the notebooks of others (like Kafka, Chekhov,
Beckett) for their seismographic status: their register of the de-
tailed and local grounds of the general human accidentality.*

1984

Idea: from the Greek: form, notion, class.

We've forgotten form's abstract. We tend to oppose it to content, which we suppose closer to idea, and in which "in" gets into the act. . . .

Form affirms, who said that? (Merrill?) Crystals are alive, radiation scares us partly because of half-life (the uncanny, says Freud, isn't the perfectly strange: it's the half-familiar). Science won't let us class things as inert anymore and hallelujah. If everything's alive we better broaden our respects. . . .

*

We think "class" the sign of a distinction: a high-mindedness at work. But it's also an exclusion, an ease: it's easier to think of fewer possibilities. But let me not too easily assume the truth is complicated, only, either; nature pulls back from the welter of minutiae and forms a spiral, too.

*

1985

January 21: There are so many ways to be unwise, not the least of which lies in being too smart, too quick off the block, too full of one's own to listen to anybody else's. The longer I live the less I like glib, can stand to be or hear it. . . .

*

March 16: Charleston, Illinois, 1:48 AM. Hearing of Mitchell Toney's nearing death.

And when he had opened the seventh seal, there was silence in heaven about the space of half an hour. . . .

And I heard a voice from heaven saying unto me, seal up those things which the seven thunders uttered, and write them not.

*

March 25:   Jacksonville, Florida

Illness is the night-side of life, a more onerous citizenship. Everyone who is born holds dual citizenship, in the kingdom of the well and in the kingdom of the sick. Although we all prefer to use only the good passport, sooner or later each of us is obliged, at least for a spell, to identify ourselves as citizens of that other place. . . .

—Susan Sontag

*

April 14:   We live in a forgetfulness, a distraction. All the little irritants, flat tires, hurt fingers, laundry, complaining co-workers, become (or pass) our lives *for us.* And on the dining room table in the house where Mitchell lay (or, less frequently, walked), dying, were spread the annual income tax papers of his parents. . . .

*

April 25:   Individually we die out and it's not the *moment* of dying that's intolerable, it's the *endlessness.* . . . No one with a mission or a big hope helps. What helps is humble: a gratuity, not a salary. On the bus, a woman smiles and asks am I all right; in the fast food place a man offers extra coffee; I mean happy is only lucky (I used to say I was lucky and mean for life! Characteristically lucky! But hap *is* chance). Happy is lucky like that, only for a relative second, before the second splits. . . .

*

May 18:   Air near Denver
To live with a more constant attention to the depths, not just the surfaces of experience. To work without loss of heart. The last words Mitchell said, according to Charles, as Charles was trying to feed him a spoonful of water and trembled while trying, were these: "Keep calm." In the long lovelessness, not to disdain the ordinary, ever. Not to get suckered back into shallow businesses . . . old fears and vanities seem petty . . . have I a greater capacity for courage now? greater motivation for it? This all sounds trite to me. It's for poems to save such ferocities of feeling from death by commonplace. It's for poetry to shake the saying. . . .

*

May 24:   All this homilizing and resolve of mine sicken me. Most of the time I just feel sore, I haul around the animal of my shot passions. It hurts to breathe. . . .

What women call a period is really a semi-colon, meaning more to come. . . . Blood out of men, all at once, might be a period.

*

May 14:   1st dream: letter from the dead: "No love, no words, no apples, no oranges. No pairs."

*

May 22:   2nd dream: Mitchell, sick, asks me to reach into the top shelf of a closet for gifts he wants to give people. Each gift has a name. I'm supposed to deliver them. When I've gotten the last one down I am disappointed to notice it isn't for me. Then I realize what my gift is: I'm the giver.

*

July 6:   (in the air, en route from Boston to North Carolina)
Life can be awful for children, I think—the containments must seem endless. As we get older, we contain *ourselves*, invoke ends to make unpleasant presents *pass*able. . . . This doesn't prepare us well for death, this comfort-by-living-in-the-future. In planes I think most often of death, and my dead friends—the perspective is so out-of-this-world. . . .

*

July 7:   My waking life is still a constant attempt at dialogue with Mitchell. I'd talk to mediums, scryers, crazies, priests, or mynah birds if they said they could talk with the dead. Every dark, every sky, every altitude is his dark, his sky, his altitude.

It's no consolation to be told he survives in our memories, or in his work. It's his experience I can't stop wondering about, mourning after; one feels so close to someone—how can they just GO OUT, as a fire goes out? Surely it's *my* incapacity that separates us. I can't believe life's complication could come to so obliterating a simplicity. We can't live in ourselves alone.

I share St. Augustine's regret at "selling the art of words" to pay off debts (he's speaking of teaching rhetoric, of course). . . . In two years I hope I'm done with universities. It is monastic life I half-crave, with its studies, solitudes, illuminated texts (and well-bred—never sour— grapes). . . .

I visited Mitchell's home town, Jacksonville. Rented a car and spent some time at the beach, a stretch of throbbing vacancy edged by foam, littered by the come-and-gone, and lettered by commercial bi-plane ("How about an ice-cold Busch?"). At dusk one particular mile of boardwalk was purpled and hearted, pumping music, cruised by families, lovers, jacks and jills, dancers, desirers—I was almost the only white one there. I liked that neighborhood of urgencies and tones. . . .

But the grave was a bald spot in the grass. Florida grass isn't much to write home about anyway; the grave is marked with no stone yet, and in dead sun. . . . I wish I could plant trees, roses, a whole fucking Eden where he is.

*

July 15:   Mitchell's mom and dad got up at 6 AM to see me off at the airport. His father's horoscope this morning read: "It may seem the events since early May were designed to test your spirit. Now it will become apparent you've been freed from a narrower way of life." The early morning in Florida is clear and warm and dewy, with a pink cast on water and leaves.

If anything could turn me into a Christian churchgoer it would be black gospel music. When that music comes on I can't stay still, my liveliness leaps, I actually feel great joy and great capacity for tears. Deeper, farther back than any other music in me goes that one: I came from it, I'm headed for it. . . .

*

July 27:   Home in Maine, I think of Mitchell and of death daily, half the time in wonder. There's a blessing (the French word blesser means to wound) in it but I miss the man; I miss men. But I love Eastport, my niche; it's my grounding and joy. And even that will be lost, huh, God, old buddy, old pal? The water's beautiful, also the islands, proportions, clouds (which are air-islands, matched to their partners in the Passamaquoddy Bay below), boats. I'm drinking bad Chablis on the Cannery Wharf, where the ferry (a funny tug-and-scow affair) comes and goes each hour. It's bright blue and white and breezy and the big gulls are healthy and clean. But every moment of every day I am sad for the dead.

In general, I crave to share my lucks and passions with someone, but want to let things take their course: half the forces I ever exerted (of personality, will, wish) finally seemed unwise. And now I may not flirt or wave at death, with any flag or flourish, red or white. A long unease and then a real disease, that's the prospectus. At the bottom of this cup is embossed "Sweetheart Plastics." "Red!," said Mitchell, "Where do you get your reputation? (You leap from lips to leaves in fall. Not until we leave do you stay. . . .) What do you mean in cemeteries where, plastic, you last?"

*

November 19:   Is happiness in life by chance *mal*adaptive? I wonder. Is death a moment or an enormity? (I can't prepare for it with my old addictive joy in futures. Or it that just what I'm doing? Constructing a plausible form of future to digest?) When I'm happy I look forward. I forget death. Is this then poor happiness or poor understanding of death? Or do we need both, the love and the relinquishment of futures, each in its time?

The main trouble in my life is this struggle with death. My almost constant attention to it—my reluctance to approve its purest democracy: utter arbitrariness in time. Since Mitchell died I can't rest without coming to some peace about this (i.e. I cannot rest). Perhaps rest will finally mean letting it go—I keep examining my own willingness to die (I need an electron microscope to see it).

The work of my life has been to live well (but what 'well' means has changed—not to distinguish myself anymore, now it must be to be *with* and *like* others, even—this change of emphasis is surely salutary). Last night reading something incidental I fell into such a weep-ing *it wept me*; I couldn't keep reading. I went to bed with no hope in my spirit, only a sense of the common horror, what we spend our lives ignoring but are headed for—our only outcome. . . .

I do think time is my big blindness—it's such an unacknowledged tyrant, its arbitrariness so man-made, its terms so universally assumed (I remember how I resisted learning to tell time as a child—it went against my grain, and took forever [!] to swallow)—once you enter that world, as though you'd entered the world of language, you leave all other worlds behind, you actually *contract* (engage *and* diminish) experience to match it.

So now may death free us to the unspeakable not only in its social/local/vernacular sense (as horror) but also to the unspeakability which, simply, preceded language—to the unspeakable which is too great to be shrunk into any one human language—(unspeakability that could yet become a tribute!). Unspeakable understanding is greatened understanding, not amputated, in an instant adding another dimension (not just the two- or three-D axes we imagine, but a depth freed of our characteristic biological speeds). Timelessness in that second we thought the last. . . .

*

Book title: *Done For* (generates nice readings but nasty reviews, too tempting for bilious critics).

*

Translation tip for Bulgarians visiting America: Whenever anyone on TV (except a whore or hotelier) says "Take care of them," he means "Kill them."

*

1988

March 15:   "Him you do not teach to fly, teach to fall faster."
                                                            —Nietzsche

*

August 8:   My lilac, lilies and potentilla are all spreading! Two years ago, they started as little snippets, rootlets, really, at my hand; but now their own nature takes over and they spread. . . . Last month I dreamt there was no self, except in the faint sense of a presiding uneasiness; otherwise all was otherwise; no selfwise existed. This effect was quite literal in the dream. Like a great deal of my dreaming since 1985, this was more of an illumination than a narrative. It was a sense, an experience, I never had awake.

Awake, nevertheless, I'm in a peaceful niche of life, here at home in Maine, with bright flags of kitchen towels on the line (my prayer flags) and the yardwork showing fruits (at last this year 4 small pears on one of the trees).

*

1989

October 29: Syracuse, NY
In my solitude again (these semesters away from home are getting harder) I'm grateful for Chekhov's journals and Kafka's diaries. They are oddly contrary to expectation: in the former, a swift and lacerating outline of character ("She had too little skin to cover her face: in order to open her eyes she had to close her mouth, and vice versa"); full of mortal over- and under-toning; while in the latter (Kafka) the most prominent feature (after the constant self-denigration and complaint) is the glimpses or snippets of people *seen*—utterly free from moral coloration—"young little girl, 18 years old; nose, shape of head, blonde, seen fleetingly in profile; came out of the church"; or "old father and his elderly daughter. He reasonable, slightly stooped, with a pointed beard, a little can held behind his back. She broadnosed, with a strong lower jaw, round distended face; turned clumsily on her broad hips." My gratitude to the former is for the quality of his judgment, and to the latter for the quality of his freedom from it (not at all what I'd expected from their respective fictions). Those glimpses of Kafka's, so spare and structural, like sketches for a painting, but always poised in three or four dimensions (of which time is more obsessive than the other three), particularly astonished me. Glimpses of strangers, saved as gestures, turns of head—people through a window or a door (Kafka's window or door!) A glimmer arises for me of that sense of "realization" I study and crave and so seldom can actually feel flame up in my life—the deepest understanding that ANOTHER PERSON LIVED, I mean so lived as I do, the feeling so deep it's free of tense—we fail *to believe*

in ("realize") those around us *in the present* as absolutely as we do anyone in history. So when I say these glimpses turn now and then to realization in me, the equivalent is out of time: "this person *is* alive" (not only "this person *was* alive"); and even "I *am* alive" (a sentence in which every word means the same thing). This last realization, the sudden shuddering understanding "I am alive" is so foregone we leave it till the last: it is achieved better the nearer we are to death. "I am alive" can most honestly be said when it's about to be untrue.

Yet the presence I am groping to characterize amounts to a *solidarity* with all other human experience, and not an *exile* from it. In my solitude I come closer to human being than I ever can in close-ups and absorptions—(am I excusing myself? comforts of abstraction? Never actually helping the sick child through the night. . . . Not that I don't have the instinct: I don't have the occasion).

But I must more precisely imagine what IS: the sick I *don't* see, they exist. And must need help. Do I not hear them? I hear clearly the call of the dying, but I haven't gone to their side. Instead I sit somewhere with manuscripts and drink coffee and consult with those paged sensibilities (read the dead). How much good could I do?, the shirker asks; every act excludes more than it includes (is this true? not if infinities are nested everywhere! What's *more*, then?—or as William Bronk puts it, "What would more *mean*?") And how could "good" have a "much" before it? The debate must keep arising in me out of a sense of wasted life: my sense of selfishness—powers bounded by material safekeepings. Shall I someday have the courage of my yearnings? to rid myself of job, pride, houses, decades of attachment? Decade, decadence. What's of moment? (Be born now, not *then*.)

WHAT HELL IS

Your father waits inside
his spacious kitchen;
his corpulence is
powerless.   Nobody seems
to know exactly

how your illness spreads; it came
from love, or some
such place.   Your father's bought,

with forty years of fast talk, door to door,
this fancy house you've come home now to die in.
Let me tell you what hell is, he turns to me:
I got this double fridge, all full of food,
and I can't let
my son go in.

*

Your parents' friends
stop visiting.   You are a damper on
their spirits.   Every day you feel

more cold (no human being here can bear
the thought—it's growing huge as you
grow thin). Ain't it a bitch, you joke, this

getting old?   I'm not sure I should laugh;
no human being helps, except,
suddenly, simply

Jesus.   Him
you hold.

*

We're not allowed to touch you
if you weep or bleed.
Applying salve to sores that cannot heal
your brother wears a rubber glove.
With equal meaning, cold or kiss
could kill you.   Now what do I mean
by love?

*

The man who used
to love his looks
is sunk in bone
and looking out.

Framed by immunities
of telephone and lamp
his mouth is shut,
his eyes are dark.

While we discuss despair
he *is* it, somewhere
in the house.   Increasingly
he's spoken of, not

with.   In kitchen
conferences, we come
to terms that we can
bear.   But where

is he?   In hell,
which is the living room.
In hell, which has
an easy chair.

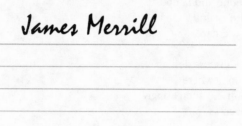

James Merrill

How did we live in the Golden Age? We kept notebooks, journals, commonplace books full of odds and ends—which of course got mislaid, sometimes lost forever. Not that the computer, when it came along, was infallible; my first, overprogrammed one broke down last year, was pronounced brain dead, and had to be, as they say, disposed of thoughtfully. Still, some such arrangement beats living, as I would otherwise do, in a welter of places and people, undated drafts, cryptic jottings. Keeping these between covers provides a faint illusion of tidiness, and the thought of so many opposing impulses sleeping peacefully face-to-face when the book is shut, remains oddly satisfying.

Postage / Gestapo
Proust / stupor
Neruda / unread
manatee / emanate
Nashville / ill-shaven

*

After the first few games of Patience, the new deck understood that its life in your hands would be one of dire omens and cheating.

*

Crowded lecture hall, one of his last appearances.

Member of audience: Mr Cage, do you and Merce Cunningham have a homosexual relationship?

Long pause. JC (amiably): Well . . . I cook and he eats.

*

DJ's aunt in South Dakota, 1930s. One day an itinerant worker knocks—she's alone in the house—to ask if she could give him a meal in return for a half day's work. She agrees, and off he goes to the field. By noon she has laid out a spread of leftovers which they both find wanting. The man nevertheless cleans his plate.

She: I hope that was all right?

He: Yes, Mam. Delicious—what there was of it. (This sounds wrong, so he keeps going.) And there was plenty, such as it was.

*

The various commentators on TV, lest their rating drop, vie with one another: how best to sensationalize today's disaster? Reported flatly, the disaster is already bad enough. Let's have these media people tested, like athletes, and expelled from the club if the rhetorical steroids in their urine rise above a certain level.

(Cf. photo of Saddam jovial beside grim 9 year old hostage. Headline: BRITISH BOY SUBJECTED TO REPEATED HAIR-TOUSLINGS.)

*

The bold diction of expiring sense.

*

Rossini's "Musique Anodyne"—multiple settings for solo voices of a single brief text (Metastasio). By turns tragic, romantic, mocking, these little songs suggest how many different tones can channel a given statement. As if what we have to say were negligible compared to the saying of it.

*

(Athens, 1985) Ruth Somebody at dinner: tall, blonde costume-jewelry Dolly Sister type. Sixty, looks 45. She waited till her children were grown, then came to Greece. Now ending her 2nd fairly disastrous love affair "with a man who had mistresses all over Europe," and has just one more session—this one in church, not the Greek priest's house—to complete her exorcism. Session One left the priest ill for days, and Ruth's toes scorched by the thwarted, exiting demon. The priest's sofa was scorched, too.

*

Always to have suffered fools gladly.

*

Italian activists insist that the Pope refer to his would-be assassin as "a human being." Poor simpletons—as if the human being weren't capable of anything.

*

"His subject is Man, his tragic fate and heroic defiance in the face of extinction"—Bruce Chatwin on Malraux. Why do I so loathe this kind of talk? I heard it first, I think, from Kimon and took it even then with distrust. Meanwhile it emerges ever more vividly that we ourselves have all along been contriving that tragic fate: extinction is nothing if not manmade.

*

As the ship pulls away, a panorama: the slopes of Piraeus mantled in sulphur yellow. It's the miasma everyone deplores in this country without public spirit. But through the smog burn grids of tiny redgold baguettes—far-off windows catching the sunset at our backs; while high above, pearly in dark-blue evening, a full moon has risen. To be remembered always.

*

What is my type? Crafty italics, tall thinking caps. . . .

*

Dream: I am carrying a half-mile-long cloth "kraken" in triumph through the streets. At every corner, a vendor of "Volcanic Ices." I have won!

*

Wings that bore me, bear me hence
Into that timeless zone
The written page, the perfect tense—
                              (on the plane)

*

Dinner with a shrink.

Q: What does dying mean to you?

A. Acceleration of the aging process.

*

Newly discovered poetic fragment by Stesichoros: the "proto-Oedipus." It antedates Sophocles, and by a somewhat cooler telling of the story (Oedipus lives on, blind but fed & cared for, while Jocasta just goes on reigning upstairs) shows the more famous poet as over-reliant upon the loud pedal. . . .

*

"Earthenware with lead glaze which has degraded to iridescence during burial." (Label in museum.)

*

The gods of rock and tree, their masses celebrated by Cézanne.

*

Alpine valleys, meadows around Barbizon—genre painters virtually Hindu in their worship of the cow.

*

Bruce M. mishears the topic of an Art History lecture at London Univ: Pierrot's Flagellation.

*

The hat motheaten, the bathtub of zinc,
The parrot-droppings on a speechless perch
Acrumble in green sunlight speck by speck
Wonder naively why Toulouse-Lautrec
Should not have left them rich. So paupers think
Of an old flame's estate left to the church.

*

After Dartmouth reading & question period, a student (blond, in tank top) comes up: Who *are* you? Are you American? What sort of English are you speaking?

*

X remained vernal throughout his long life—past sixty still enticing, graceful, fragrantly in bud. Old Mrs Y—older, that is, by only a few years than himself, but whom the generations had bent and gnarled into a leafless trunk—said it was a scandal. (Ending for novella ca. 1900.)

*

Postcard of Pompidou Center—all multicolored pipes and vents. PH: You should hear it when the Hunchback's at the console.

*

Watching the fire,
An ironwood log splits into blazing discs
on its bed of ashes—not discs, letters
They spell DRUMIAEL (a 99th rate devil)
Nearby a little incandescence crab, Kabuki-faced, pulses,
its claws open & shut, diamonded for the dance.
Signals of terrible complexity. Computer chips,
hot barnacles at the Red Sea's bottom—
Saurian roast
        Alligator luau!
              [psychedelic mushroom]

*

Hank: You're treating me like a servant!

Mrs Porter: You don't know how servants are treated. I'd never ask a servant where he went last night & what he did. That's no business of mine. I *can* ask my lover these questions. My lover may prefer not to answer them, but I'm within my rights—as I am when I draw my own conclusions from his silence.

*

Christmas 1984. Mary Lou [Aswell]'s obituary in the *Times.* No surprise—she'd been dimming rapidly—just pure grief. We were alike in our love of amusement. Like me, she aged without maturing. Or rather, could still, at the end, shed the . . . opacity, and simply sparkle. DMc had written how, bedridden, blind, but receiving the sunset's last communion through a prism on the sill, she threw her arms wide & exulted: "There it is—my *source!*"

[Added later.] Charlotte tells a not dissimilar story of the elderly Frenchman met at Notre Dame during the Fauré Requiem. Years ago, as a boy, he'd sung bits of it to his mother in a car driving South. She loved it so, he promised to sing it to her when she was dying. Fifty years pass. At her deathbed he begins to hum the melody. Slowly, from the old woman, a ravishing smile.

*

SCHUBERT BUTCHERS
WAGNER'S NEW RAGS
(anagrammatic headline in the Entertainment section of *Afterlife.*)

*

Dronning is the Danish word for <u>Queen</u>.
A walker near the Palace will have seen
Her driven past, in picture hat and poils,
Making that gesture only known to Royals,
A kind of . . . wave? "Young man,"—her smile is stunning—
"I'm much farther out than you think, and not waving but
                                                    dronning."

*

. . . but vive la difference! Your kissoff could be my jacuzzi.

*

The new pack of cards: slick, disco-slithery.

*

Alexandria. An exchange between old friends [ca. 1960].

Germaine: So-and-so called me 'Christine' when we met the other day. I was very annoyed.

* * *

Christian: I know. Somebody called me 'Germain' not long ago & I threw up.

*

Everyone is responsible for his face.
No one wears it undeservedly.
Will there be another war? Look at yourselves, Europeans, look
    at yourselves.
Nothing is peaceful in your faces.
All is struggle, desire, avidity.
Even peace you want violently.

—Henri Michaux in Asia, 1933

*

Dream: A music festival. I am seated halfway back in a crowded theater. Charlotte & her children are within sight. The lights dim. "The Magic Flute" begins in silence. Curtain rises on a gang of perhaps 25 ten-year-old boys racked like pool balls in a close triangle. Now they "break" and deploy rapidly through the audience, spraying at random a luminous paint onto people's faces. I am grateful to receive a cool quick-drying coat of it on mine. We are now the chosen ones—herded onto the stage (I touch Charlotte's bare shoulder and wave farewell) and into a mysterious world. My particular guardian here is a grown-up. It is clear that he and I are of different natures (different species?), yet a deep sympathy grows between us. Now we are crossing a long low wooden bridge. He falls into the shallow water & is instantly helpless, passively drowning. Since no one else will, I jump in after him & try to save him. He goes by limp in the jaws of a great fish. I manage to put a line into his hand, which hauls him back into the world. Now it is my turn to be lost underwater. A prismatic igloo of flesh-colored sand encloses me. I try to escape but every door is just one more reflection. House of mirrors. I hear my friend calling, feel him trying to reach me. I'm not afraid. I know he will.

[1974]

*

Awesome—Two Thumbs Up! (up what?)—wannabes—
Pustules of idiom we itch to squeeze.

What can the Muse do for the common weal?
Make an appointment for a facial peel.

*

[Istanbul] Evening after evening where we drink our wine we've noticed a . . . drunk? a lunatic? A rotund, scowling, twitching little person in his 30s—like the boy one teases at school, but tougher. Cigarette in his mouth, mirthless parodies of another customer's dance. Tonight, before our eyes, the riddle is solved. He approaches a table near ours, one of whose drinkers (tall, lean, sexy) presently stands, moves his chair across the way & sits down in it. Out come towel, soap, lather, a razor—our little madman is a barber! In between sweeps of the blade both he and his client light cigarettes, take swallows of raki, rise to do a few dance steps together. The razor harmlessly glittering in the dusk.

Susan Mitchell

*I keep many different notebooks, so many, it's possible I
have a notebook fetish. The notebook I take with me everywhere
is narrow ruled and 7³/₄ by 5: it fits easily into my pocketbook.
In this notebook, I jot down lines for poems, ideas for essays,
and thoughts that occur to me during the day. I have three other
notebooks identical to this one. Nuts & Bolts is a very technical
notebook where I write down my thoughts on craft and technique, along with lines from poems that I admire. In the notebook called Gradus Ad Parnassum, I set exercises for myself.
Then there is the Commonplace Book, in which I copy out passages from books that have particularly impressed me. Besides
these, I keep notebooks that accompany special projects—translations, a long poem, a heavily researched essay. The project
notebooks are leather bound, looseleaf, and measure 8¹/₂ by 11.
The excerpts that follow are largely from the 7³/₄ by 5 notebook
that is always with me. Most of the entries I have chosen are
from 1992, but after a while these run into dated entries which
record the beginnings of the poem "Music," included in this
anthology.*

1992

It would take tremendous energy to be the first person not to die,
the first person to live forever, simply because no one had ever done

this before. If no one thinks it is possible, then no one is going to try to figure out how to put eternity together like an airplane or a submarine or a rocket. Doing it the first time without a plan, without any manual of instructions would be the hardest, but after a while, it would get easier. Begin by imagining the impossible. A hummingbird trapped in a screened-in porch darts through the mesh. At the precise moment of passing through, it folds its wings, pulling them in tight against its body. It does this too quickly for anyone to notice. It is not possible to witness such events with the eye. But I remember a momentary break in the sound its wings had been beating. As if a song had passed through the eye of a needle. That break is a knot of silence no bigger than a drop of blood.

*

Last night around eleven, I went outside to have a look at the boats in the canal. Hearing something behind me, I swung around and took it by surprise, the glare of my flashlight in its face. Caught off guard, the darkness reared up like a horse. Within the circle the flashlight made, everything was ordinary. Beyond that circle, the darkness was chased further and further into itself. I had never seen darkness so clearly. It outlined the boats. It outlined the creaking of the ropes as the boats pulled against their moorings.

*

For my epitaph: "ready to be anything in the ecstasy of being ever."
—Sir Thomas Browne

*

"She said flawless so often, it sounded like worthless."

This line remembered from a dream in which I was looking through a book. The book consisted of drawings and maps, as well as writings. The maps resembled old-fashioned watches, the kind that men pull from their pockets on long gold chains. There were many intricate parts to the watches, or rather, to the maps. The maps journeyed in on themselves, delineating interiors not visible, but somehow present. The book impressed me, and I wished I had made it.

On waking, I thought: Well, I have made it since I dreamed it. But not really. It's the difference between the first mental draft of a poem and the written poem.

*

Originally, the word *site* suggests a place in which everything comes together, is concentrated. The site gathers unto itself, supremely and in the extreme. Its gathering power penetrates and pervades everything. The site, the gathering power, gathers in and preserves all it has gathered, not like an encapsulating shell but rather by penetrating with its light all it has gathered, and only thus releasing it into its own nature.

—Martin Heidegger

I know that the poems I am writing are going to make a book when I feel that they are all breaking off from the same site. The site is not any one of the poems taken by itself. And the site cannot become a poem. The book of poems is the site. Or it is a map that allows the reader to create the site in his or her imagination. For a long time, there was a poem I kept trying to write, but each time I tried, I ended up writing a different poem. At last I understood that the poem I could not write was the site. The site was nonverbal. When I imagined it intensely, I wrote poems that were broken off from it. I could point to images that made up that site, but it would be best not to point. Even gesture would begin to disturb a silence that needs to be preserved. I need to keep secrets from myself, perhaps? Or, I need the site to remain visual if it is going to have the power to generate language.

Whenever a book of poems is very powerful, it creates a site that other poets begin to draw on. Instead of working from their own sites, these other parasitic poets feed off this Ur-site. So a curious kind of theft takes place, the theft of a power source in the imagination.

*

Whenever I read Walter Benjamin's "A Berlin Chronicle," I experience the world of his childhood through my knowledge of what will happen to him later in life. I read his chronicle through those losses still in the future: what will happen to him as a Jew when Hitler comes into power. So I am always reading this essay differently from the way Benjamin intended. I read it through the tragedy of his suicide. Could I learn to read it in a more innocent way? Or will Benjamin's Berlin always be a ruin for me? But doesn't this also happen when I reread a novel or a poem and know how it ends? If the work ends tragically, then when I reread it, its end is always present for me in its beginning.

There is a kind of love that always contains loss—as premonition and as remembrance of the past.

*

Why is it that pain can wipe out all memory of pleasure while in pleasure there is often some intimation of loss, however vague? Is there pleasure that abolishes all memory of pain for extended periods, not just the few seconds of orgasm? For me, this would have to be sleep, a dreamless sleep, but with remembrance on waking that I had been drifting into deeper and deeper sleep, dropping from one level of sleep to the next like a boat going through locks in a canal. Maybe it's odd to think of sleep as pleasure, but on waking from deep sleep, I feel as if I were actually separating myself from something physical that I had been intertwined with, something luxurious and soft and intoxicating.

*

Understand: to stand under, so as to take what streams directly into the mouth, the water from a waterfall, the drip of icicles melting

> Über Berg und Tal
> Ist ein Wasserfall

*

a noise of birds
a roof of birds taking off like tar paper
the birds (starlings?)
                    the roofs across the plaza, the
palm trees are overflowing
many have only the air to inhabit

Construct a life to provide for the idleness of sustained effort

*

It surprises me that so many people think of transforming themselves only after they have had a traumatic experience. So and so has
left them so they feel pressured to change. But why can't self-
transformation be a response to one's work? The work needs me to

change, so I will. For the work to become better, I have to become other than what I am. In a way, writing is trauma—sustained, ongoing, chronic trauma. Can I feel more, can I laugh more, can I go deeper?—this is what my work demands day after day. If I can't change, then my work will grow bored with me.

*

It is possible to enlarge a photograph of the face until it appears to be a blossom and further, until the blossom has stairways and pulpits. Who could have guessed all our possibilities?

*

If music had its way with us, language would become a thing of the past.

*

Sometimes there is a clitoral intensity to seeing, as if an optometrist kept adding more and more lenses, turning them this way and that. *Is this better? Or is it better this way?* Sharper and sharper until it almost hurts. Those drops Milton has the angel put in Adam's eyes until Adam swoons from seeing.

*

That feeling I had for a long time after surgery, that the universe was empty, flat, that I was pressed up against a wall, the wall the end of the universe, the limit against which: bare, blank, cold—that feeling is finally gone. The universe is full again, exciting, achingly so. What seemed like a terrible revelation no longer has meaning. Is either view correct? Are both views correct? Neither? Niels Bohr says, "The opposite of a shallow truth is false. But the opposite of a deep truth is also true." And happiness is not thinking about any of this. Probably, it was pain that led to the invention of language. Pleasure is pure immersion.

*

When I am certain that I have nothing in common with a person, I tell myself that we both know what water tastes like, and neither of us can describe that taste.

*

It was late afternoon when we entered the church by the side door. We had stopped for tea first, and Odette had poured milk into my cup and then the steaming Lapsang Souchong, a smoked tea I have loved ever since. The tea room was very warm, and the babble of French around us made me drowsy. The French Odette spoke seemed heavily outlined because she spoke slowly for my benefit. Odette kept her hat on. The hat was a dark color indistinguishable from the color of her coat and her dress. ide, it was almost dusk, the streetlamps, the headlights of cars already on. We had come to the Isle Saint Louis because Odette had wanted me to seee a painting by George de la Tour that was in the Eglise Saint Louis, that splendid Baroque church Le Vau designed. Today when I wanted to verify the name of the painting, I could not find any mention of it in the five Paris guides I consulted. Perhaps the church sold it. I know, though, that it was there in 1963. When we entered the church, the lights were off. There was only a faint glow around the altar where candles were lit. Odette asked the priest if we could use one of the altar candles to illuminate the painting, and in response to something he mumbled, she dropped a coin in the box and dipped a candle in flame. When she held the candle up to the painting, light jumped out at us. The candle that George de la Tour had painted seemed to take fire from ours. I even thought I heard that flap of wind when flame catches and flares up. In the painting, a girl with bowed head sat before a candle. There must have been more, but that's all I remember of it now. That and the sound of one candle catching fire from the other. The painting made me forget momentarily Odette's philandering husband and something she always said when we passed his photo in her living room—*Mon Ange!* and then to me in English, *Never marry for love.*

Why did I suddenly think of this today? Why remember something I have not thought of in years? Now that I have remembered, I am obsessed with it, especially with that sound of the flame flaring up. There's a glaze over the memory, the kind of glaze that Van Eyck used. Even the obscure, smoky places in the memory, even what I don't see clearly is highly glazed and shines as if a candle were held to it. Even that sound, that flap of air, breath catching— shines.

*

Today in Liberties Bookstore I began to hear the tinkle of the little silver bell my aunt would ring when she wanted the next course brought to the dinner table. As I turned pages of books, the bell kept

ringing. When I got home, I napped for a while and dreamed that I
called my mother to ask her if she still had the bell. *Do you want to
hear it?* she said to me. When she rang the bell, it sounded more
tinkly than I remembered, but I think that was because my mother
let the bell dangle from her fingers. My aunt rang it with more
force—from her wrist and with a specific purpose in mind. The slight
difference in tone makes me think of something that Artur Schnabel
wrote in his edition of Beethoven's piano sonatas: "The key which
is touched by the third finger should produce a tone hovering between reality and imagination—but must be heard, none the less."

*

August 17, 1992

MEMORIZING THE SONATA OF KINGDOM COME

> Which is a sonata yet to be written and listening
> to the ———, I know the one most likely
> to compose this is not yet born

> I want to learn this by heart which will be
> like learning another heart

> This is the unbound sonata, not yet scrolled, the time
> not yet decided with imbecile signatures

> A bigness unending

> it had broken off from, and what it had
> broken from could still be felt

August 21, 1992

> How anemic the eye that looks outward
> immersed in blur and bludgeon. Give me visions
> that whir the optic nerve

December 25, 1992

> The bird cracking the same note, smashing
> it against rock,
> lashing at it, splitting

it down the center
where inside another note just like it,
the same DNA, the same three notes
streaming out of one
or a note like a fig
its many seeds
filling the ear
lodged in the ear
    buckshot

April 15, 1993

JOSEPH BEUYS AT MOMA

  . . .
s/c/ore   2/ implement—to score
               to keep score
               musical composition
  scorch
    arch
to score = to cut, incise, notch
            to get revenge

August 9, 1993

"MUSIC"

        The rose closes on it
        the rose closes its mouth
            on it
        so the thumb can
           almost taste itself
             tasted
singability
    dolphin clicks

the rib cage

February 25, 1994

and those things for which I haven't
  a name

exist like a hum, a field of
    cicadas
a crescendo
they are loud around me

*

Pulling oneself up by the roots of one's hair, by one's feathers—is
that what hope is?

March 26, 1994

What does it means to draw
to draw the voice out of
    the long solitude

The rib cage opening and closing
    on it, as if testing
the wings of something
just broken through its chrysalis
Or it's the sounds that do this, opening and closing
their leaves, their buds

It has the string on
    which to string
        itself along
on which to lose itself
        and find its way back

Steps—
        And it seems
light years waiting
for the intervals
to return a universe
in which the slow
scrawls, the measured
violets and blues of
dusk, autumnal underwater
in which a child bathes
from its window

*

As we take, in fact, a general view of the wonderful stream of consciousness, what strikes us first is this different pace of its parts. Like a bird's
life, it seems to be made of an alternation of flights and perchings.

—William James

[At this point, I switched from my notebook to my typewriter and
over the next couple of days wrote the rough draft of "Music."]

Music

1

    sucked into the nasal cavities.

    , which doesn't mean I am smelling this music
    like an iris haunting my head, taking
    over a room with one explosion after another.
    To live among flowers is bewildering
    after a while, and challenging.

    To keep opening. To have that as one's
    life work, all those crinkles
    of the rose, those petals, and how exciting
    for the thumb ever so gently to
    and then extract itself

    slowly, the rose smacking its lips, it
    can almost taste itself tasted,
    or is it the thumb?
    What the thumb has entered
    is time, is tomorrow and tomorrow, but not
    yet unfurled, the flags and umbrellas
    still wrapped tight, and that,

    I'm told, is how a theme came to Beethoven,
    not melody, but a single note
    he went at with his beak
    cracking it like a seed, then the two
    halves, then those halves, the music getting

smaller as it grew bigger, as
if to get the entire score he had

to hack back to core and from core extract
ore, and what I love
is the way it's possible to carry
all that in something as small as a nut,
and just thinking about this
I feel it enter me like buckshot, each note
a fig, the many seeds
lodged in my ear.

when I was nineteen, something happened, I

a froth where the music was starting
to leave itself for air
or darkness, as a violin's bow over the string,
glissando or with gasp and fret,

wax to make slippery, so as not to stick
as the hummingbird, obsessive,
sticks to the air

                    attacking,
the nest more scratch than notes.

Listening, I could hear how little
of my life I filled, the long shadows the possible
cast as it flew off like birds into
another language   by dropping

stones down a shaft, someone could hear
the distances, the music not yet
scrolled, the time not
decided with imbecile signatures.

;   or houses open
on one side to receive the ocean thundering
hundreds of feet below, to be lowered
into the dangers

I wanted to sleep close to that and hear it
mumbling, a girl with one long dark
strand of hair in her mouth,
so I couldn't understand what she was saying, all
her underwater reverberations
through the caves of the cavernous and obscure,

especially the disruptions, the long pauses
when nothing was said, only the
bulging of a wave starting to fill up

I could call it Sonata of the Future
that silence, and all the
pieces of broken churned up and polished

clouds are a part of it and passages
are, vast fields of air
for which the word <u>oscuro</u> is entry

as to a smoke-filled bar or a steamy
that's pitch and polluted
the dark murky, the turnpikes and malls of, say, New Jersey

2
Lately, I've been thinking about the problem
of what is singable. Is everything
singable? And what does it

mean to sing when the intervals are like arches
spanning a river and the river
is transported bodily, its bubbles
breaking, the glass from which
one drinks these waters
breaking?

universe in which the measured violets and blues

and all those things for which I haven't
a name existing like a hum
a field of crescendos

opening and closing
as if testing
wings of something just broken through
a chrysalis, the sound, that hum opening
and closing its leaves, its buds about

protracted, if necessary,

as if the diaphragm were a chrysalis

its buds all along the about to

3
What does it mean to draw? To draw
the voice out of the long, each column of air
ictus and glide   And if it has the string on which to
string itself along, on which to lose
and find itself back to

4
one has to be ready to record
what one doesn't understand and even what
one doesn't hear, like Webern

in his bagatelles, to include the silences, to start
with them because someone else
might hear the inaudible for him, below
the level of hearing, though
going on, a crackle or persistence, a gate

through or something metal knocking
against something metal
or plastic, noise
of birds, many   what he

broke it off from, a jaggedness
where he struck and kept striking, some of it

its stopping only another way of continuing

and if one langauge no longer, then rushing
at once to where another, like a spring
starting up   and will

feel their way along

a rope ladder, swaying above and slippery
and those places where the nails
hammered down have fallen out, the orange swirls
still visible in the waves below

or consumed as smell, the vapors, the fumes
rising up out of, to breath that
if there are no

steps for the voice to follow and one has to
swing out again and again
like a spider throwing its lassoes of spit

like a bird glancing the et cetera of light

Lisel Mueller

Unlike poets who use a notebook as fodder for their poetry, I think of mine as a corollary. Most of my notes are reflections on poetry and the writer's relationship to the world, as well as observations on language, especially American English usage. (My notebooks also contain extended quotations from other writers, but they are not included in these excerpts.) This is material that engages me deeply, and I trust that it serves my consciousness as a writer. If I were good at writing longer pieces, I could write essays on these subjects. As it is, I enjoy clarifying and defining them for myself in brief nuggets. It has been suggested that I am uncommonly fascinated with the implications of langauge because I switched languages at the age of fifteen. I wrote these notes for myself only; whether they are of value to anyone else, I can't say.

1991–1994

Marie Luise Kaschnitz wrote that it might be instructive for a poet to examine her work and make a list of words she has favored, as a way of finding out about her preoccupations. In her own case, she found to her surprise that her imagery is dense with chestnut and plane trees, but not conifers; that she favors clouds but not stars; that wind and water are ubiquitous, but snow almost absent; that certain flowers keep recurring; that birds always show up in migratory flocks.

Of course she soon gave up; the game became boring. I wonder what such a dictionary would tell us about ourselves, and whether it would lead us back to childhood.

*

The beginning of a poem by a child in a pediatric hospital, where long-term patients are encouraged to write:

> I was born between God
> and Jesus.
> My father was a heart,
> my mother was a bow and arrow.

*

Found poem:

> What place is there for the soul to go after death?
> In heaven there's no more room between the stars.
> Who builds the houses of the angels?

(Translated excerpts from a German review of *Heaven: A History* by Colleen McDonnell and Bernhard Lang.)

In "Lucifer in Starlight" George Meredith calls the stars "the brain of Heaven."

*

In response to criticism that his fiction was negative and pessimistic, Max Frisch replied that it was much more negative not to suffer by not presenting negative things, because if you suffer it means you want something else, something more, out of life. Praising things as they are is just giving in.

Speaking of painters who understand tragedy, Michael Brenson of *The New York Times* said something similar. He said that if they did not understand tragedy they would not understand hope.

*

A friend tells me that lately he finds it hard to write poetry. In order to write poetry he has to love the world, he says, and the world has become so unlovable.

Yes, the world has become extraordinarily violent, corrupt, cruel and shallow. When societies divide into people who despair and people who couldn't care less, and the power in the hands of the last group keeps growing—in the United States as well—anger is easier to come by than love. How to do it, how to turn anger against brutality and injustice into great poetry; how to burn like Blake, like Yeats in "The Second Coming"? How to deal with the suffering of others in a genre that has traditionally been a projection of the self? And how can we be presumptuous enough to identify ourselves with victims of horrors we are sheltered from?

*

Who am I to speak for the homeless,
I have a house to live in;
who am I to speak for beaten women,
I am not one of them

What right have I to raise my voice
like an angel proclaiming the gospel;
who am I to palm off my poems
as loaves and fishes

What right have I to say *my life*
as if it were singular,
as if it could be distinguished
from the life cycle of my species

How can I praise the light
as if I had no need for darkness;
how can I speak of darkness
and keep still about what is done there

What good is my safehouse of words
to the millions of people dying
on the rootless roads of our century;
who am I to speak for them

What can I say about courage
when my back has not been to the wall;

how can I speak in the name
of anyone but myself

when I know that is not enough

*

Still, love *is* the impulse from which poetry springs. Even dark poems. Especially dark poems. To know the worst and write in spite of that, that must be love. To celebrate what's on the other side of the darkness. Truly great poetry has always sprung from love-in-spite-of, like love for a deeply flawed person.

And if it's true, as Williams wrote, that people die from the lack of what is found in poems, then poetry must not be trivial, peripheral, ivory-towerish, as it is often accused of being; then we have a responsibility to speak to and for others. Certainly that means acknowledging suffering. But it also means to heal, to bring delight and hope. It implies consolation. How to console without being false, shallow or sentimental: I find that the hardest challenge.

*

Yehudi Amichai demands that every poem should be the last poem, written as if it contained the last thing the poet would ever say, shaped to contain a condensation of all the messages of his or her life. It should be a virtual will.

*

Note on language: Our everyday speech is so suffused with metaphor that we can hardly say three consecutive sentences without using it, never mind the fact that it is overwhelmingly "dead" metaphor, i.e., no longer felt as such. Not by a native speaker anyway. But for a foreigner, even though he has absorbed dictionary and grammar book English, it can be a hurdle. I am imagining a conversation between two businessmen, one American and one a foreigner. At one point in the conversation the American leans back and says, "The ball is in your court." The other man looks bewildered. "It's your turn," the American explains. The foreigner turns around. "No, I mean it's up to you." Up? Why up? He casts his eyes toward the ceiling. The American tries once more. "It means it's your move. Like in chess."

Ah. His visitor's eyes light up. He knows chess. He understands. But what about the ball?

*

"It speaks to me," we say about something that touches us in a special way. Language, communication; Martin Buber's I-Thou relationship operating even when one of the two is a speechless object.

*

H. writes to me about the sad state of her 93-year-old bedridden mother, a stroke victim. "There's only one thing to wish for, but of course one must not say it," she writes. As if words were still magic, and—though she wants to spare her mother further meaningless life—she does not dare be the agent of her death.

*

When I give a reading I sometimes read "Late Hours," a poem from my recent book, which refers in part to my husband and me reading Chekhov's short stories together, and whose last lines are

> What luxury, to be so happy
> that we can grieve
> over imaginary lives.

I like to read the poem because I feel these lines so strongly, am so aware of the (undeserved) luxury of happiness. I've never had a direct response to them from a listener and don't know how audiences feel about them. But recently I've had a response from a reviewer living in Tel Aviv.

She quoted the lines and added her comment: "A luxury poets cannot afford!" So I am directed back toward the real sorrows of the real world.

*

Note on language: I wonder how much the meaning of a word influences our attitude toward the object it denotes. Since German was my first language, I grew up with the name "Flügel" for grand piano, so that instrument is for me a dark, shiny wing, not necessarily grand, but capable of soaring, bearing music upward and outward, releasing it to air and freedom. And even now I can't think of the mullein as an unglamorous, oversized weed, since in my childhood language this proudly erect plant is called "Königskerze," a king's candle, and I grew up with a notion of its dignity. I've learned to my satisfaction that there are more respectful common names for it in English too, such as Jacob's staff and Aaron's rod.

*

Nostalgia doesn't do any good, but old people have always indulged in it. What is new is that even the young are nostalgic these days. People under 30 write novels and poetry collections and memoirs about their childhoods. Never have we been so aware of the fleeting moment. Writers take notes, artists sketch, videotapes roll, each recording the blip of the present, more of a blip all the time.

*

"Poetry is in love with the instant and seeks to relive it in the poem, thus separating it from sequential time and turning it into a fixed present."
—Octavio Paz

A poem is to keep a now for then.
—Felix Pollak

*

Outside the house language keeps changing. Now that it's August cicadas decide it is their time; they fill our ears all night. The birds are no longer raucous; mostly they twitter like old ladies, though the catbird continues its impeccable imitation and the crows are irrepressible. The bullfrogs in the little lakes next door are gone; we miss their cow-like moos. The bees hum discreetly, and the flies, newborns this month, are beginning their black buzzing. The trees are a long way from rattling yet; still heavy with summer they offer us the language of silence.

"When you've got a stoned baboon, all bets are off." Sounds like one of those incomprehensible aphorisms, like, "If you've got an elephant by the tail, you'd better let him go," or the question about the sound of one hand clapping. Something funny to say at a party. But in the story in which the sentence occurs, "Way Down Deep in the Jungle" by Thom Jones, it makes perfect sense. It has to do with doctors attached to an African mission and features a baboon that enjoys whiskey and pot. *Context is all.*

*

Amazing, what a country's language reveals about its culture. Amazing, and in the case of American English, alarming. American English is riddled with idioms of violence. We make a killing on the stock market, and go to a party dressed to kill. We are gunning for someone, as we may be outgunned. We shoot a picture, write a shooting script. "Shoot!" the well-bred lady exclaims, since she wouldn't be caught dead using a four-letter word. The top gun of the corporation may or may not be a straight shooter, but he definitely calls the shots. We suspect criminal conduct but can't prove it, since there's no smoking gun. Economists speak of a trigger mechanism. I hear a baseball announcer wishing out loud that one team would beat the other's brains out, hardly appropriate for the mild sport. Our two-fisted, double-barreled, take-no-prisoners frontier past is stuck in the language we use so casually.

*

Note on language: **Zoo.** 1. A park or institution in which living animals are kept and usually exhibited to the public. Also called *zoological garden.* 2. *Slang.* A place or situation marked by confusion and disorder: The bus station was a *zoo* on Friday. (*American Heritage Dictionary*)

In February 1993 the authorities decided that all four New York borough zoos would be renamed Wildlife Conservation Parks. They were bothered by the pejorative flavor of the word *zoo.* An interesting case of the secondary meaning of a word usurping its primary meaning.

*

Two possible autobiographical notes:
1. I am not yet the author
   of my life. I am still
   its unenlightened protagonist.
   This is not the epilogue;
   this is still the thick-and-thin
   of the plot, unraveling.

2. All of the gaudy clothes have been burned.
   Now I can go as I am,
   nearly naked.

*

The pronoun "we," in the large sense of the human race or a community, a shared culture, is hard to find in poetry these days. When
"we" is used, it usually means a personal plural, such as the speaker
and his/her lover. This is the age of the first-person singular. A poetry
of persuasion is not in favor; neither is the social and cultural stock-
taking that Auden, for example, was engaged in. Younger poets seem
to stay inside the boundaries of the self, and I don't mean the traditional lyrical self. Keats could assume that the song of the nightingale, a bird fraught with magical significance for all of his readers,
would evoke a responsive cry of the heart in them. Whitman's "Song
of Myself" was about everyone. But the new "I" is the "I" of a
splintered age, a community of one. It's neither inclusive nor invi-
tational and does not cloak itself in dramatic or mythic disguise. It is
naked and insistent on the authenticity of its specific, even exclusive,
autobiography. Ideally, the distinction between speaker and poet, per-
sona and person, is eliminated, though of course that is never entirely
possible.

Surprisingly, it is precisely those poets who show their most private,
least replicable selves who have the largest readership. And I don't
think that prurient interest has much to do with it. It's as though all
the injured selves out there in the audience have been waiting for a
powerful speaker to give language to their own pain. The poet's circumstances may differ somewhat, but the feelings generated are the
same. We are one species after all. And so, ironically, the most self-
centered poets turn out to be the most universal.

*

Imagine you were the last person on earth to speak your language
and you knew it. The horror of that. Ishi, the Yalu Indian, is the most
famous example, and he at least could pass on some language to his
anthropologist friends. I read about a woman who did not have even
this opportunity.

If I had been the lone survivor
of my Tasmanian tribe,
the only person in the world
to speak my language
(as she was);

if I had known and believed that
(for who can believe
in an exhaustible language),
and if I had been shipped
to London, to be exhibited
in a cage (as she was)
to entertain the curious
who go to museums and zoos,

and if among all those people
staring and pointing and laughing
and making their meaningless sounds
there had been one thoughtful face,
a woman's say, sympathetic,

who might have instinctively understood
the one word I could not let die,
the indispensable word
I must pass through the bars
of mutual incomprehension,

what word would it have been?

*

In one of Grace Paley's stories, the narrator, a writer, says she has
always despised the narrative that starts with "There was a woman
. . ." and then is followed by a plot, drawing a line between two
points. She despises it because it takes all hope away and she believes
that even an invented character deserves the open destiny of life.

*

Evidence in defense of surrealism: I don't remember the dream I had
last night, except that at the end a telephone kept ringing and ringing. No one answered it; I don't know why not. You don't question
what happens in a dream. You accept everything. But then I woke
up and realized that the telephone I had heard was the gentle, rhyth-

mic snoring of the sleeper beside me. In fact, the telephone sound had been a kind of rasp rather than a bell-like tone.

*

Note on language: First it was *capitalism,* but after a time that must have sounded too crude, so for many years it became *free enterprise.* In the 80s it shifted to *free markets,* and after the fall of communism in Europe, it turned into the *market economy.* Where do we go from here?

*

Around eight o'clock one summer morning I saw a low branch reaching out of the dark wall of buckthorn bushes, reaching into sunlight like a hand. One hand, extending from its dark body, splendid in its isolate illumination. A few minutes later it was in shadow, as if it had withdrawn, retreated into the indistinct tapestry of leaves and branches from which it had come. Of course I knew that it was the sun, not the branch, that moved, but reason does not destroy the image: that great hand dipping into the sunlight as if of its own volition, as if it had a need for warmth and beauty.

When I tried to make a poem from what I had seen, I failed utterly. The perception was what people call "poetic" because of its very wordlessness. I couldn't translate it into language without having it veer off into the silly or the portentous. Maybe it's that very struggle of translating the wordless into language that keeps poets going. In love with language as we are, don't poets always work against its resistance; isn't the struggle toward the poem always to lose as little as possible in translation, to make the language so transparent that it disappears and reveals the experience itself? Not that we can ever fully succeed. "Dance the orange," Rilke commanded, dance being probably the most direct, least mediated, way of transmitting perception and feeling. I envy painters, but perhaps they feel that paint and canvas get in the way as much as I feel language does.

> O, to speak raspberry canes,
> whisper berries into your ear,
> the red ones that dropped on the moss.

> —Günter Eich

Mary Oliver

For at least thirty years, and at almost all times, I have carried a notebook with me, in my back pocket. It has always been the same kind of notebook—small, three inches by five inches, and hand-sewn. By no means do I write poems in these notebooks. And yet over the years the notebooks have been laced with phrases that eventually appear in poems. So, they are the pages upon which I begin. Also I record various facts which are permanently or temporarily important to me—when I first see certain birds in the spring, addresses, quotes from books I'm reading, things people say, shopping lists, recipes, thoughts.

Some of the phrases and ideas written down in the notebooks never make the leap into finished prose or poems. They do not elaborate themselves in my unconscious thoughts, apparently, nor does my conscious mind pluck at them. This does not necessarily mean that they are of a casual or fleeting order of things; it could be that they are seeds broadcast on a chilly day—their time has not yet come. Often I find the same idea will emerge through several phrases before it gets worked on.

I don't use the pages front to back, but randomly, in a disorderly way. I write wherever I happen to open the notebook. I don't know why this is. When the notebook is fairly full, I start another. In the spring and fall notebooks especially, there are pages where the writing is blurred and hard to read. Spring and fall are the rainy seasons, and almost all of the entries are made somewhere out of doors.

What I write down is extremely exact in terms of phrasing and *of cadence. In an old notebook I can find, "look the trees / are turning / their own bodies / into pillars of light." In a more recent notebook, "the refined anguish of language / passed over him." Sometimes what is written down is not generally understandable at all, but is a kind of private shorthand. The entry "6/8/92 woof!" records for me that on this day, and with this very doggy sound, I first came upon coyotes in the Provincelands. Both the shorthand and the written phrase are intended to return me to the moment and place of the entry. I mean this very exactly. The words do not take me to the reason I made the entry, but back to the felt experience, whatever it was. This is important. I can, then, think forward again to the idea—that is, the significance of the event—rather than back upon it. It is the instant I try to catch in the notebooks, not the comment, not the thought. And, of course, this is so often what I am aiming to do in the finished poems themselves.*

Who would tell the mockingbird his song is frivolous, since it lacks words?

*

Do you think the wren ever dreams of a better house?

*

Though you have not seen them, there are swans, even now
tapping from the egg and emerging
into the sunlight.
They know who they are.

*

When will you have a little pity for
every soft thing
that walks through the world,
yourself included?

*

When the main characters of one's life die, is there any replacement?
Or, is there anything *but* replacement?

*

I hope I don't live to be a hundred
in the arms of my family.

*

When you first saw her—beauty, the dream—the human vortex of
your life—or him—did you stop, and stand in the crisp air, breathing
like a tree? Did you change your life?

*

The small deadly voice
of vanity.

*

It's better for the heart to break
than not to break.

*

Elly Ameling during a masterclass at Tanglewood, talking to a young
singer "No! No! No! Make it like peaches in your mouth!"

*

All my life, and it has not come to any more than this: beauty and
terror.

*

Something totally unexpected,
like a barking cat.

*

Sharpsburg: "One well-read member of the 9th New York wrote long
afterward: The mental strain was so great that I saw at that moment
the singular effect mentioned, I think, in the life of Goethe on a
similar occasion—the whole landscape for an instant turned slightly
red."

—B. Catton, *Mr. Lincoln's Army*

*

The sword, after all, is not built just to glitter like a ribbon in the
air.

*

But I want to say something more uncomfortable even than that.

*

"And then, who knows? Perhaps we will be taken in hand by certain memories, as if by angels."

—M. Yourcenar

*

Molasses, an orange, fennel seed, anise seed, rye flour, two cakes of yeast.

*

Culture: power, money and security (therefore).
Art: hope, vision, the soul's need to speak.

*

All culture developed as some wild, raw creature strived to live better and longer.

*

Dreams don't have time/space constriction. Of course, in a way Adam naming the things of this world was narrowing his horizons.

Perhaps dreaming is meditating, before language existed. Animals certainly dream.

*

Language, the tool of consciousness.

*

The line is the device upon which the poem spins itself into being. Verse, versus, vers, turn the plough, turn the line. It is impossible to measure the frustration I feel when, after making careful decisions about where the lines should turn, an editor snaps off the long limbs to fit some magazine's column-girth or print-line. Most especially in those instances when it seems so inexplicable—when the criminal act is accomplished not by an editor but by a poet/editor. To make a fuss to a friend is so painful. But I will fuss and fuss, and keep the little leaping goat in his wide pasture.

*

Who are you? they called out, at the edge of the village. I am one of
you, the poet called back.
Though he was dressed like the wind, though he looked like a
waterfall.

*

F. has been to visit us, and now he is gone. The power of last resort,
is the power to disrupt.

*

M. arranging the curtains in the next room. "Hello there, darling
moon," I hear her say.

*

If you kill for knowledge, what is the name of what you have lost?

*

The danger of people becoming infatuated with knowledge. Thoreau
gassing the moth to get a perfect specimen. Audubon pushing the
needle into the bittern's heart.

*

I took the fox bones back into the dunes and buried them. I don't
want to hold on to such things anymore. I mean, I'm certainly full
of admiration, and curiosity. But I think something else—a reverence
that disavows keeping things—must come to us all, sooner or later.
Like a gift, an understanding, a more happy excitement than possession. Or, of a sudden—too late!—like a stone between the
eyes.

*

Everybody has to have their little tooth of power. Everybody wants
to be able to bite.

*

About poems that don't work—who wants to see a bird almost
fly?

*

With what sugar in your voice would you persuade
the beach plum
to hurry?

*

After a cruel childhood, one must reinvent oneself. Then reimagine
the world.

*

van Gogh—he considered everything, and still went crazy with rapture.

*

A snapping turtle was floating today on Little Sister Pond.
Goldeneyes still on Great Pond.

*

Laughing gulls fly by the house laughing.
Maybe a hundred pilot whales off the point.

*

All July and into August, Luke and I see foxes. An adult fox with a
young pup. The adult serious and nervous and quick. The young one
trailing behind, not serious. It reached up, swatted the pine boughs
with a black paw before it vanished under the trees.

*

To Unity College, in Maine, and back. We stayed in Waterville, saw
two bald eagles flying over open rivers, though there was still much
ice, and snow. A good trip, friendly people, an interested audience.
Luke and Bear were quiet throughout, except that Bear threw up on
me just as we arrived in the parking lot. I hope he learns to ride
better than that.

*

Hundreds of gannets feeding just offshore, plunging, tufts of water
rising with a white up-kick. Scary birds, long wings, very white,
fearful-looking beaks. We opened the car windows and there was no
sound but the sound of their wings rustling. They fed at three or
four places, then were gone much farther out. We were at the right
place at the right time.

*

"I am doing pretty well, gathering energy, working . . . and every now and then *timor mortis* descends over me like midnight."

—Letter from D.H.

*

Just at the lacy edge of the sea, a dolphin's skull. Recent, but perfectly clean. And entirely beautiful. I held it in my hands, I was so excited I was breathless. What will I do?

*

Three deer near the path to Oak Head—of course now they always make me think of Luke. Happiness by association.

*

Who knows, maybe the root is the flower
of that other life.

*

Money, in our culture, is equal to power. And money, finally, means very little because power, in the end, means nothing.

*

Lee, as he was dying, called out, "Strike the tent!" Stonewall Jackson said at the end, softly as I imagine it, "Let us cross over the river and rest under the shade of the trees."

*

Today I am altogether without ambition. Where did I get such wisdom?

*

You there, like a red fist under my ribs—
be reasonable.

*

little myrtle warblers
kissing the air

*

Let's not pretend we know how the mule feels.

*

Hearing a crow, the first one in a long time. I listened to it, deeply and with pleasure. And I thought: what if I were dead, lying there dead, and *I heard that!*

*

Which would you rather be, intellectually deft, or spiritually graceful?

*

The sugar of vanity, the honey of truth.

*

When I was young, I was attracted to sorrow. It seemed interesting. It seemed an energy that would take me somewhere. Now I am older, if not old, and I hate sorrow. I see that it has no energy of its own, but uses mine, furtively. I see that it is leaden, without breath, and repetitious, and unsolvable.

And now I see that I am sorrowful about only a few things, but over and over.

*

Fairy tales—the great difference is between doing something, and doing nothing. Always, in such tales, the hero or heroine does *something*.

*

The new baby is all awash with glory.
She has a cry that says *I'm here! I'm here!*

*

Give me that dark moment I will carry it everywhere
like a mouthful of rain.

*

There is a place
in the woods
where my swift
and stout-hearted dog
turns and wants to climb
into my arms.

*

Don't engage in too much fancy footwork before you strike a blow.

*

So much of what Woolf wrote she wrote not because she was a woman, but because she was Woolf.

*

I would like to do whatever it is that presses the essence from the hour.

*

A fact: one picks it up and reads it, and puts it down, and there is an end to it. But an idea! That one may pick up, and reflect upon, and oppose, and expand, and so pass a delightful afternoon altogether.

*

From my way of thinking, Thoreau frequently seems an overly social person.

*

The cry of the killdeer / like a tiny sickle.

*

The translation of experience into contemplation, and the placement of this contemplation within the formality of a certain kind of language, with no intent to make contact—be it across whatever thin or wild a thread—with the spiritual condition of the reader, is not poetry. Archibald MacLeish: Here is the writer, and over there— there is "the mystery of the universe." The poem exists—indeed, gets itself written, in the relation *between* the man and the world. The three ingredients of poetry: the mystery of the universe, spiritual curiosity, the energy of language.

And what is the universe, as far as we are concerned? Leo Frobenius: "It was first the animal world, in its various species, that impressed mankind as a mystery, and that, in its character of admired immediate neighbor, evoked the impulse to imitative identification. Next, it was the vegetable world and the miracle of the fruitful earth, wherein death is changed into life. And finally the focus of attention lifted to the mathematics of the heavens."

*   *   *

Art cannot separate from these first examples which willed it into existence. Say such forces belong now only to dream or nightmare or to Jung's (our) collective unconscious—or to the ecologically sensitive—I say it's entirely more primal than that. Poetry was born in the relationship between men of earth and the earth itself. Without perceptual experience of life on this earth, how could the following lines be meaningful?

It is the east, and Juliet is the sun.   Or

And what rough beast, its hour come round at last,
Slouches toward Bethlehem to be born?

I think as an ecologist. But I feel as a member of a great family—one that includes the elephant and the wheat stalk as well as the school teacher and the industrialist. This is not a mental condition, but a spiritual condition. Poetry is a product of our history, and our history is inseparable from the natural world. Now, of course, in the hives and dungeons of the cities, poetry cannot console, it carries no weight, for the pact between the natural world and the individual has been broken. There is no more working for harvest—only hunting, for profit. Lives are no longer exercises in pleasure and valor, but only the means to the amassment of worldly goods. If poetry is ever to become meaningful to such persons, *they* must take the first step—away from their materially bound and self-interested lives, toward the trees, and the waterfall. It is not poetry's fault that it has so small an audience, so little effect upon the frightened, money-loving world. Poetry, after all, is not a miracle. It is an effort to formalize (ritualize) individual moments and the transcending effects of these moments into a music that all can use. It is the song of our species.

*

Hasn't the end of the world been coming absolutely forever?

*

It takes about
seventy hours to drag
a poem into
the light.

*

delerious with certainty

*

It's almost 6 am. The mockingbird is still singing. I'm on my way to the ocean, with the sun, just rising, on my left shoulder, and the moon, like a circle of pale snow, lingering on my right.

TOAD

I was walking by. He was sitting there.

It was full morning, so the heat was heavy on his sand-colored head and his webbed feet. I squatted beside him, at the edge of the path. He didn't move.

I began to talk. I talked about summer, and about time. The pleasures of eating, the terrors of the night. About this cup we call a life. About happiness. And how good it feels, the heat of the sun between the shoulder blades.

He looked neither up nor down, which didn't necessarily mean he was either afraid or asleep. I felt his energy, stored under his tongue perhaps, and behind his bulging eyes.

I talked about how the world seems to me, five feet tall, the blue sky all around my head. I said, I wondered how it seemed to him, down there, intimate with the dust.

He might have been Buddha—did not move, blink, or frown, not a tear fell from those gold-rimmed eyes as the refined anguish of language passed over him.

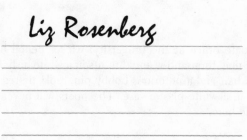

Liz Rosenberg

I have been keeping journals since I was ten or eleven years old, so this form of writing is deeply ingrained. For these excerpts I drew both from my "writing journal"—a small and lightweight book I carry wherever I go—and from special "Eli journals" I have been keeping since shortly before the birth of our son. (He's now six.) "The Poem of My Heart" came directly out of an Eli journal; it was, in fact, the last "entry" in that particular book: a larger book than the writing journals, roughly the size of an average hardcover library book, with a light plaid cloth cover. Most of my poems begin in journal form, sometimes in very rough form, sometimes nearly finished. "The Poem of My Heart" I thought very rough when I jotted it down in the journal, but as it turned out—though I revised it fifty or sixty times—the finished version was very close to the original notes. This is often true, I've found, of the poems that cut closest to the bone.

1986

I've been thinking about my own generation, what we were as teenagers: a watchful decade; aloof, observant, suspicious, self-absorbed, compassionate, uncertain, hopeful and cynical by turns. Our great weapon was humor, as against the largely humorless 60s, the ambitious 80s. We saw the flower children fail, and empathized with our parents—we waited to see what would happen. Mostly we're still waiting.

*

The graduate office at the university: wicker pencil holder in the shape of a dog, thousand-year-old mints in a white dish. Women with short dark hair and a notorious bobby pin, a plastic red rose or pink carnation in a white plastic vase. The poets will never be welcome or at home here.

*

Stories or poems—Van Gogh's brother, Freud's attachment to & defense of then recanting of cocaine, the story of Mrs. Washington Roebling who lost son & husband to the building of the Brooklyn Bridge & then finished it herself.

*

The student poets came creeping into the auditorium, all of them wearing black clothes—most of them in long black coats. And a shadow fell over the audience.

*

Fiction requires a certain accumulation or weight to work. First paragraph is proposition for the story and last seals it off.

*

Emily Dickinson *cuts into* her poems with a welder's arc. If there's a daintiness in that, think of the strength and agility required!

*

How shall we let the dead bury the dead? When we all know it's the dead who bury the living!

*

Of John [Gardner]—I am thinking of Dave Smith's charge against him that he had no sense of humor—and of the outlandish, clownish dances he used to perform with just his feet—lying on his back in the living room listening to music. It was elegant and comic to see those clodhopper boots move like whole dancers—it was Chaplinesque. But everything he did was art.

*

1987

Last Sat. took a pregnancy test and to my amazement—delight, awe, a touch of horror—found it positive. Occasional drowsiness, like a fit of vapors. Feel too as if I am racing against time on my own work—as if I were in low-lying land and could feel the fog rolling in.

*

A hero is one who in the face of danger pushes the highest elements in himself to the maximum limit. Isabel Archer—bravery and commitment to truth, confronting Madame Merle. Shackleton's bravery, endurance and stewardship in Antarctica. Always in heroism there is the presence of actual physical danger or of failure.

*

Crazy Eddie on TV, making faces at the camera, his face all bloated and distorted saying, "Crazy Eddie's prices are INSANE" & his eyes are little & cunning & greedy & so shameless you realize he really *is* insane.

*

Van Gogh's painting of the asylum—he gets the medicine-y colors & feeling of desolate space—in the arches. If you have vision, everything else takes care of itself. With art one is always thinking, what a simple, what a wonderful solution! As in Van Gogh's rain—blue lines.

*

This is the way I am, my husband opposite. We see an old couple doddering down the street, he says, how nice, look how long they've been together while I say in the same breath, Look how old they are. Soon they'll die and have to lie apart.

*

Cormorant on a lake stump. A most flexible and ever-moving neck, velvet black back & large spread wings with gray tatters like the old coat of an elegant aging gentleman. He points with his neck—I suppose constantly searching for food. Japanese grace and absurd balance. It seems his wings would ache from holding them outstretched like that. The way some people do.

*

Most important, Eli [son] is here, sleeping peacefully in the plastic hospital bassinet to my left, the image of perfection, hands folded toward his mouth. A baby is like a poem—self-absorbed and containing in himself the universal breath, and needing constant tiny cares & adjustments.

*

At a poetry reading. First night out alone without Eli or David— dreamy and gone, as if on drugs. Looking around at this carpeted university room, full of students in blue jeans, so much alike, so bedimmed of their animal joy. I remembered the Sufi expression, A pregnant woman is always right and thought: A new mother never lies. So I see this place clear, for once. God help us! We're writing in a dead language. And I can't stand to think that Eli will ever learn to be muffled, polite like this. We write a poetry of the cultured— we should be writing out in the street, down into the earth.

*

I see my reflection like a passing cloud speeding over the faces of students eating their lunch. The boy with missing hand. A man with bloody eyebrow brilliant red. The multiforms of humanity, the grown-up babies walking past me.

*

Two men in restaurant talking about wine—a valiant wine, bold, courageous yes but unpretentious, vital, straight-forward, virile. The men are crazy, of course.

*

Last lines of poems—complete yet kinetic.

*

I wish that everyone would look at me with eyes like the eyes my newborn son has in his head.

*

Is post-modernism an extension—another phase of modernism—or a break with it? Most literary periods defined by wars. Consider the kinds of wars and you'll see the differences in the literature.

*

It's never too late to rise up & be a flame. It's not too late as long as you're breathing, as long as your eyes are jerking back and forth the lovely way they do, reading. It's never too late to stop wasting your life.

*

I believe most poets are in search of beauty and mystery—& nowhere have I seen those two principles evidenced so perfectly as in Eli when he sleeps. To write a poem with great breath (like Whitman) is one accomplishment—but to write one with a baby's breath is yet another.

This is my love affair with Being.

*

1988

Eli eight months old today—sitting upright for the first time as we stroll, a fine spring day, cool and sunny and green.

*

The hours I wanted to escape from teaching, or took my break in a dark empty classroom—the fumblings, the wise thing almost said when headache or phone call intervened. The dying woman who interrupted my class with her pale face—not till after the funeral did I understand her urgency to thrust at me a few last poems. *I Dreamt I Dwelt in Marble Halls*—which is a song about death.

*

Feeling really dismal—out of proportion gloom. Iron-cold weather, both of our cars dead at once. The day shot—about to go get Eli from sitter. "How small is that with which we struggle; how great that which struggles with us." Rilke.

*

1989

In Wilson Hospital Intensive Care Unit, Eli asleep in the stainless steel crib attached to tubes, resting more comfortably tonight. Gurgle & hiss of the tubes a white noise. Watching the red numbers of his pulse monitor, the green waves of his heartbeat like a man running or Hebrew letters forming right to left. I am thinking about Eli—and myself—and how though I think of myself as a good mother I am impatient—covetous of my own time and work. What am I doing that's so important or wonderful? When I have all this time to sit here, I sit and stare at him or at his monitors.

*

Funny how you learn to live with hospital sounds—soft ringing and bleeps and hissing—and to live by shifts, waiting for the nice nurse to come on, dreading the shift of the cranky ones like the reign of a bad king. You learn to live in eight-hour clumps—all three of them. About half the people in medicine shouldn't be here—doctors and nurses who are harried, brittle, bitter, sharp-tongued, lazy, indifferent, clumsy, resentful—and the other half are geniuses. We have had more good than bad. But you occasionally see the nurses who just want to sit in the nurse's station and eat or talk on the phone, or flirt with the young male doctors in an almost-motherly way, putting their arms around them and laughing a lot. Nurses who say everything in a loud piercing voice as though illness were distance and you had to raise your voice to shout over it.

*

The peaceful, even sound of Eli's breathing fills the car. This is my work time, while he naps, but I know if I bring him upstairs he'll wake up and probably not get back to sleep again.

*

I write for insomniacs, grievers, depressives, lonely-hearts, hopefuls and children. I wouldn't say that I write in order to comfort or distract them, exactly—but to give a voice to what is already in them that needs a voice.

Also I write in order to make God repent of His sins.

*

I turn away from some acquaintance, laughing inanely, only to hear my two-year-old echo my nervous chuckle, his arm lifted like mine in some half-assed gesture of farewell, his shoulders hunched like a whining beggar. Better to bite the woman on the shoulder or wrap my arms around her legs and wail, or toss a ball at her head and run, or say to her "Move!" or "Don't go!" or "Go!" but never to make a liar of this vibrant creature tripping at my heels picking up scraps of every lunacy I drop behind.

*

In the midst of this nothing then, something—like the light rising off the day, a green mist. To fear the earth is not to stop loving it. Darkness, if not nowhere then everywhere—no one else on earth is so extreme except for man, so extremely anxious to get off it, to get on with it, to name everything with a word and so tame it with his ferocity.

*

The truth is maybe somewhere in between, in glimmering.

*

This is someone's real name: True Willing Laughing Life Bucky Boomerang Manifest Destiny.

*

1990

How do you expect me to work like this? You clumsy oaf of a god— how could anyone have thought you were a woman? You don't give a damn about children, injustice, the world—it's all a green ghost to you.

You wait to be served, hold out your empty plate, your pipe, your boots on the back of my neck bowed over a book. Are you listening to me, damn it?

I'm talking to myself again.

*

The endurance of vision—the significance of details—the importance of good directions.

*

Sometimes the day opens out like an alley of green lights up ahead.

*

1991

Three is the age of independence for Eli. He can walk, run, climb, slide alone and this allows him to enter his own world. What's gruelling, early on, is when one must follow along behind end-lessly, watching out, rescuing and worrying—constantly centered on the child's world which is to an adult often boring or silly—a good thing in small doses, but not a constant diet, not to entirely usurp the privacy of one's own adult world—thoughts and ideas, ob-servations, feelings or sensations. This I consider a fundamental hu-man right. Even ritualized religion, in its rituals, allows for private prayer.

*

Blink and it's 11:30 at night—always. No matter how early you start the evening. Have been thinking—any time a parent makes a child cry in an emotional situation, that's probably the parent's mistake. But the strength and stamina and patience to find another way, that's the hard part. It helps if you close your eyes and just listen to the child's voice. The wild faces and gestures are dis-tracting. I sometimes think the voice is the most honest organ of the body. If there is any way to see a child more clearly, it's to *hear* him.

*

Have instituted a month-long plan to buy nothing that isn't vital (food, medicine) or maintenance (batteries, etc.) Also to stop all sell-ing of self—writing for money, submitting work. Just to see what could happen if I remove myself from all that—to see what's left. Not to buy or order or covet or browse. Tremendously hard work—laying waste our powers becomes a habit of thinking and doing.

*

Sitting in rectangle of white sun, in quiet house, very happy. The ballpoint pen makes a star of light against the shadow of my hand moving across the page below. Happy for once to *be*.

*

For me, motherhood is all wild swings up & down—exhilaration, then crushing boredom, adoration or fury, delight then frustration— sometimes both at once. To be a mother seems to require subsuming one's self—and that is what's so hard, especially in art.

My friend Sheila said, When I do have 5 minutes alone to myself I don't know what to do anymore, how to think like an adult. My mind's a blank.

I remember that feeling so well—having nearly escaped it I feel I've escaped a jail. "I would give up the inconsequentialities for my children—my money, my life—but I would not give up my self." Edna Pontellier—*The Awakening.*

Recall Betsy Aswad's good advice—get an hour alone, no matter what you have to do to get it.

The problem being that an hour is not enough. Not for art. Maybe not even to regain one's right mind.

*

Realized tonight—I no longer expect that anything I do will turn out a success. Whatever one does. It vanishes, like throwing a stone into a deep well. Or a scrap of paper. You don't even see it or hear it sink but you know it's sunk. And then your life fills up with stuff to disguise the emptiness. Is there poetry in silence?

*

One can rush through a whole day—month after month—without one single moment of quiet thought or reflection. So it goes with me. Fear & anger are the enemies of art.

But I also thought today, if one could just write without them, anything would be possible.

THE POEM OF MY HEART

> But an old man
> Can know
> A kind of gratefulness
> Toward time that kills him,
> Everything he loved was made of it.
>   —Galway Kinnell, "Spindrift"

The milk-spray glitters on our newborn's cheek.
A power surge plunges us into darkness for half a mili-second
and then I hoist him by his footed suit and lower him like
         a boom into his crib.
In the dim, Christmasy nursery light,
the San Gabriel azaleas are opening their rose-pink petals
         as slowly as the mouths of women
about to say something wonderful.

Snow glitters on the new year in a wave tossed over from
         the old.
Time almost palpable, time twittering through the air
or gliding down a pole into a crowd of tens of
         thousands
cheering—incredibly, cheering on—the passage of their
         lives;
blowing horns and wearing paper-cone hats, like children
at that ecstatic instant when the cake is served,
before it is eaten.

Tonight we strolled him to a high-school parking lot
where we spend all our New Year's Eves—
as last year this night, a multiplying cell he rode
inside of me, learning the loop-the-loops of locomotion,
the way I walked and rocked him all that spring,
walked miles, as if by constant motion I could slowly
pull him forward with me out into the world—
till he's learned to distrust stillness,
and as soon as we'd reached the parking lot,
and sat, he woke and cried
and we stood up and walked him home again.

Welcome to the new year! you to whom everything is new.
The first flakes of a snowstorm stung like sea-foam in
        our faces,
turning the sky murky the way it does
that instant before it dissolves
into the floating world on which we stepped, duck-footed
carting our bundle of laundry-looking
        bunting
up and down streets where teenage boys
stepped out from New Year's parties to their cars
taking long steps, like timber wolves, and looked
at us, and in those always-surprisingly gentle voices
wished us a happy new year.

I was ten years old on New Year's Eve when my death
        terrors first struck—
all those people in Times Square celebrating
were going to die,
even the great Lombardo, and his band;
but worst of all myself and everyone I loved—
hypo of terror like a salty wafer on my tongue,
brushing the back of my head with fire—
But what is the use of hating time
when everything we've ever loved is made of it?

I've always thought that we could live forever,
coming to terms with the tyrants who live in us.
I've hoped that love would have the final word
and slowly, by accumulation, perhaps it will,
at first by a simple majority,
since anything learned by one is soon accessible to all,
and everything imaginable is real.

I'm not so sure about me
but you, little bear, must go on forever . . .
beautiful swimmer who sky-dived into time—
with your sweet-smelling skull as fragile as a china cup,
your sleeping hands curled toward your heart,
and the blue vein at your temple mapping a new country.
With your butterfly dreams of milk and motion,
your nose pressed in the flannel for the smell of the earth,

your scruffy cradle-cap and feather hair blown in the wind
     of our breath,
with your neck that flops your heavy head from side to side
thirty or forty times before you settle into sleep.
Beauty and mystery her snoring softly at my side.

The year's first dawn floated from black
to peacock blue stained-glass of sky
through which I saw our neighbor's roof, freighted with snow,
and then day broke—gray-gold and violetpink
—and Eli woke crying from his hunger for the world.

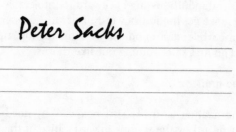

Peter Sacks

A *foyer. The place for introductions—some otherwise impossible. And for such contradictions as between prospect and refuge: as prospect, a would-be open channel or lightning rod through which current may be drawn; as refuge, neither water- nor fireproof, but a first enclosure within which something may be begun, sustained, temporarily buried. A widened margin, at times a threshold, at times the only path, the only ground. Also at times a vehicle (solitude-machine, or sidecar for the otherwise unmanifest companion/stranger), equipped both with accelerator and brake.*

In punctuation, a colon.

In politics—of the self, the word—a colony?

A shadow-cabinet?

For quotation, "I am come into deep waters, where the floods overflow me"; or self-quotation, "I have found my own true illness, exile tremens: though a snowfall wads the glass, recurring fevers burn back to the fires of my own country. . . ."

As fragment of a never defined wholeness, the illusion of unstoppability.

A running epitaph.

1991

Cape Town, May 12: The fire mantling behind closed eyes. And then the fire itself. Always that margin and excess, upleaping, chewing

245

at the wood, whatever's cut and dried burned back to the glowing scroll, the dead mouth hissing backward to intolerable pain: speaking out of where we go, the journey out of nature? deeper in? and of the catching up? while all around—above this tearing, ripping—images of peace. The first stars coming out like thorns.

What is the fire?

Bees in the heather, and the surf below. Why not be drugged and carried downward by the sounds toward a hive of their own making? Yesterday, after seeing [my father] in the hospital, I drove out to the beach and swam out past the waves to deeper quieter waters where the ocean swung and held me. To the body's pain and question, give only the body's wordless answer lulled and carried in the melting light.

Not that such an "answer" calms the question or the need:

—new growths in the spinal cord so that he's paralyzed from the waist down, spontaneous fractures in the back and shoulder; and everywhere the skin so thin it breaks like tissue, unable to hold him up for washing without breaking the skin, worrying we'll break more bones . . .

perhaps it simply makes a shore-like point of meeting—wash and friction—where our pain and ignorance and *lack of faith* meet something equally pressing, huge, but indifferent and absorptive, not differentiated and piercing. Wide instead of narrow, narrow, narrow. Doesn't *anguish* at its origin mean narrow, straits?

*

May 13:   Asked him what he'd read in the paper: "violence, violence, slaughter, burning . . . *terrible* bloody business," rolling his rrs—this morning's pre-dawn raid in Swanieville, the hostel "dwellers" rampage through the shantytown, 27 dead, the photo of a corpse left in the street, a charred arm stiffly raised, the left arm, charred club of the hand. . . . For what? rivalry for an approaching power, the who gets what? or sheer ecstatic rage, ecstatic grief—a bleeding woman screaming out her grief and terror by her husband's corpse: Mrs. Elsie Mvokwe, blood trickling from beneath her *doek*, would not go to the hospital until the corpse had been removed—if no sudden mutuality then a harder butchering, more killed in this violence than in opposition to the government, easier to risk and squander life in this rampaging fury (even if manipulated by "third force") than in deliberate resistance/revolution; sheer rage vengeful and exultant (or just grimly satisfied to settle accounts or to provoke another matching rage and grief)—killing those who share a misery that's now become intolerable, a furious attempted speeding up of change, the self-annihilation from despair—from deprivation, crowding, living in a world of trash, to war against these consequences not the cause?

and looked up *anguish*, kin to anger, hence to grief, and ancient words for strangle. The "answer" gives us breath so pain and doubt have something still to choke. So the torturer: Sigaret? And the walls take in the smoke.

altar, sacrifice: smoke ascending mediates between the realms, they said, earth and heaven, man and god. I say between the pained and the indifferent. Before his time, Cain's knowledge, reaching for the stone. Why is the first murder in scripture tied to a rejected sacrifice?? What if both had been accepted, or both rejected? Why should the differentiation—great enough to provoke a brother-murder—be via sacrifice? Why is it Cain's descendants who invent the instruments of music? How to know what Cain knows and be *kind*—not murderous, exclusive, moving always in a rage, the forms of anguish? Abel knows what Cain knows.

For the poet now, i.e. since the death of sacrifice, is form itself the figure and the work of anguish? Such that even free verse or the varying opennesses are ways of breathing whose apparent freedom and release exist only as functions of the stranglehold? the smoke, the screen, the blind, and then the fire.

I used to think the lyric was a way of altering the breath so that we could be alive and dead at the same time, the time of poetry—breathing and posthumous, body and acknowledged spirit; that poetic form might be death's homeopathic cure and exorcism of the death instinct. Something more uncanny than memorial. Why even think about it now he's in such pain?

Because I want to think about sacrifice, the way an earlier generation wanted to think about God after the supposition of His death. About sacrifice because I know two kinds of certainty without knowing how to connect them: of anguish—his dying, the country's trouble, the natural world's; and of joy, whose stubborn wildest inner-outer reach is one of blessed reverence, touched by something that is at once greater than the self and that feels at moments benign, recoverable in still greater fullness, a (religious?) joy—whence immortality, political hope (to change the human heart), our chance of rescuing the earth. The two can't be convincingly connected just by an aesthetic strategy or form, unless these mark some prior hinging function such as sacrifice? And held by the community as effective. Not scapegoating, not private magic.

From this comes my present difficulty with writing at all, especially writing for others *of my own time*. [What if the old sense of fame (an audience in posterity) (or for me altered, posthumous breath) were merely the side-effect of an unbearable, in many ways disabling, and self-isolating rage and grief *and* joy, as these issue through a medium that is itself inhuman?]

And so this increase of notebook work (and decrease of all other writing), which is somehow *not* yet in that state of tension/issuance, but which exists partly in the hope of opening the door to poetry, of accelerating towards it. Not yet, because lacking the *hinge* that lets the door swing between anguish and curative joy. If the hinge were once a kind of sacrificial procedure, and if my sense of lyric and of any poetics can't free itself from that origin, then part of my work now to continue writing will be to find-form-invent-undergo a credible experience of sacrifice that is as true to pain as it is to joy, while capable of transformatively linking the former to the last. For me now suffering has lost its meaning, while my joy is of a weird, unhinged nature, one which has no grip on pain, and which defines itself by utter distance from whatever circumstances give me time, space, inner life, to feel something beyond circumstance; and one whose far out solitude feels too selfish even in its apparent shedding of the self. Unless by such (*such* is the give-away, metaphor—the symbolic transfer broken down: the poet may now have to act, as well, beyond poetry to satisfy this part of the call and free the other, though where's the line?) unless by such an act of surrender (as poet's to poem, force, will, call-past-self), be it via pain *or* joy, the knife will strip you of whatever seems to keep you from still greater life, and thence: a dying person feels past agony and death the quantum in us that can't die, feels recognized as such; those with the power to oppress share from a recognition of what we all share, radical and sentient as breath; we take the weight of our greed off the planet, source.

I can't write without worrying about this—to do so would risk impoverishing my notion of what poetry does: though again, when the stuff comes, the rest of this gets sidelined though it's no doubt *pressing on the line*, pressing from a region that's then almost unconscious, since conscious and unconscious will have nearly traded places. I can't write poems out of worry, though I can worry *between* poems as now. Worry. The word's odd enough (why now?) to look up; it too goes back to *strangle*! So perhaps that was all or half-wrong up there about anguish and the forms of poetry etc. When truly writing, no matter what the grief or anger, I'm writing also (maybe *only*) out of joy? no poem without the hinge, tho' it's there on its own terms. So why theorize about the act of writing as if I were buying the poem rather than being given it?!

Dante re joy, the form of surrender-sacrifice that is joy itself. How else start *Paradiso* with Marsyas as figure of received inspiration! Flayed by Apollo. And later, in the sphere of Venus, *per letiziar lassu folgor s'acquista / si come riso qui*, by joy up there brightness is won, just as by a smile on earth; but down below the shade darkens externally as the mind saddens. And *Non pero qui si pente, ma si ride—* i.e. not repent but smile. All as if joy might be a form of return, of reascent. Not penitence but joy. Dante's graduated ascent, every step or flight upward brought about by part of his belief; and the entire *Paradiso* constantly about the smile.

And now recall Dad saying to me (strange how he went back to Afrikaans, as if more intimately rooted there) "*Moenie so lyk nie. Jy moet glimlag.*" Don't look like that (here he mocked my frown). You must smile.

And then *his* smile.

[*folgor*, a flashing flame, as lightning out of thundercloud]

His room open to the garden, lawn, oaks, flowers, sweeping breeze. Just now sleeping: downturned mouth opening to a dark inverted horseshoe, hands crossed over the swollen belly, covering the plastic bell-switch; voices from the corridor—Xhosa flowing over English words wheelchair, bunny blanket, trolly, we're just going to do her dressing; and Afrikaans natuurlik, nou-nou, vreeslik—tinkle of a tea-spoon in a glass, his light snore draining, draining; a train accelerating out of Kenilworth. Not he, *You*, father, it's only you this moment, how existence all of it heaps over you, a concentration of intensity but without meaning.

In the breeze a dead moth, upturned, rocked on the linoleum. I'm wondering how to draw the line: will your dying and your death now be associated with *everything?* Should there be borders? Death's full tide over the shore, the current rocking, turning to the spiral of what sinks. They called the hoist above you a monkeychain—a short trapeze hung from its hook. Watch fastened like a gold crab on your wrist.

leafage of the creeping rose, the stems tied spiralling around veranda columns, new growth leaning outward, leaf-veins branching. And a blown leaf hops across the lawn, leafage of the creeping rose, pressed on me, for the having, like a reassurance though I can't say why— new life aging in *one* season, shadows drifting on the brick.

where do my impulses begin? out of the remembered land? leafage, creeping rose. What says breathe deeper, or bring me to the image of long oarstrokes and the water moving backward in wide reaches —leaf and leafshadow now stripped of you or me or any of us, riding mingled with the wake?

beauty in the natural world, the breath I breathe—love for this life despite the knowledge now never more pressing of the body's self-betrayal; of being part of this, composed of it, dying back into it, soil of the rock, and of the mountains all around these seas, the lives brief as the flare and sinking of a struck match, white-caps on the sea, knowing here within these words some trace of salt, of mineral, tide-line, and avowal, you now riding this—and we who follow soon, waves further out but travelling after, unrepeatable but following the same fate, the part that gathers carries what it can—our calling is our unique way of breaking

oil of autumn, hooded wisdom of the flesh
oil of the lamp, unhooded wisdom of the flesh

and then that single stirring under me and through me of the *single* wave that is *all* waves, the one wave flowing outward through all time:

atom, gene-light, quantum, what spins lifted in the rhythm under us, our words, *your* momentary constellation still entirely here—smile, eyes, the hand that still takes mine or rather holds itself straight out unclosing for a moment in my own—an odd suspended phrase— until it clasps; and voice—your face unfolding, gathering, this and no other, against the breaking line.

*

Langebaan, May 14: sun down over Skaapeneiland (sp?), arched af- terglow as from a large fire on the far side of the island, seagulls moiling mid-lagoon, choristers released, released—that odd insistence not just of what they are but an appeal, dissonant as from within a margin, open, sheer, between the world and themselves; from the ebb-line, silhouetted, the fret-water now black on silver, a single fish- erman in orange waterproof rows out, leans back into the offing.

twilight turns the water to a granular screen the color of lit pewter: two boats remaining, and a buoy, the low island across the water to the west—each silhouetted with a presence so intense they seem to have been thrust up through the fabric of mere visibility, as from another world. Two wooden dories at anchor, swinging slightly but in place against the moving water, ride the motion as eternity rides time or time eternity, death life . . . mother's words to him "think of the happy times we've had"—he waist-deep in slow dying—our *mak- ing* what to say, all amateurs in grief . . . pushing through the fabric, sounds too, birdcalls entering the silence, through the sound of lap- ping water, as from the other side of silence or of audibility, the door of our comings and goings through this world

the sacred ibises fly home, they ride a swell of air up, up, then coast down in a long slide to their island roosts . . .

a calm hand levelling the spirit; or beckoning it out of the level?

earlier I breathed in time with the sigh and lapse of the lagoon, almost *hearing* the daylight recede, relapse.

a gull walks to the water, walking on until its weight is taken from it
... Rilke's swan ... others riding further out, one perched on a buoy

the near boat darkening still further,
hooded indigo lurks there, the memory of blue now
smouldering from its hull, oozing out like smoke; the water
so bright by contrast in the later twilight, more
luminous than daylight could have been, gulls carried
outward by the ebbing tide, their cries hitting the same
note so repeatedly the sound's unstoppable until the
repetitions slow to a last creak, sticking fast in silence.

Stars out, first dust of the Milky Way, Scorpio, Southern Cross, Or-
ion's slow spreadeagled fall into the west.

—That smouldering, as of Lethe or some counter-lethe, hooded or
unhooded essence, I now nervous that I'll always be in debt or
leagued with its weird blue, not knowing whether I'm consoled or
troubled by it, everywhere, the smoky/oiled color of whatever flares
and abides within the shadow or excessive brightness of a life, sloe,
plum, livid foison, pouring from the hull, gentian fuming; its slide
and swirling prior, subsequent, following from under ... marbling,
as fire burning behind alabaster, mantling, so Anchises' shade; pitch-
blende; *the glowing violet*

and of *things*, the actual wooden hull, its number visible by day,
SBH97BN, the orange inner rim and thwarts, the rope that disappears under the water

and of words, images, these too rise *from under*; can they be saved, can
we unmoor them still charged by the long waveline ... as chosen words
do carry the pressure (passion) and shaped residue of breath and thought
... to charge such creatures with the force of their emergence, our out-
casting and the casting of all things, all names, all emanations

—[now in this space, the unseen LEOPARD of the Cedarberg's enlarged and roaming, smoke-like, maculate, half-hidden fur of flame
and shade, the leopard of both worlds]—

As a living body casts a shadow, so this body-soul casts its odd lit
issue past iself toward an unknown end (or origin of its own pulse

breath source) (outer wall of time, expansion, *accelerating* outward to catch up with the enlarging shell or unshelled wave—*not circumscribed but circumscribing*). the haunting inner shadow-life, languid, ruinous but promising within itself another kind of light, reserve, reserved, expressed, held only as *held outwards* and issuing, *hope* . . .

actinia; actinic; *actinism*—the property of radiant energy esp. in the visible and ultraviolet spectral regions by which chemical changes are produced:

lyric, sea-anemone, ghost-offering of life, of *this is how we live*. dark-lustered mineral, of twilight, of the doubled star of consolation. And if my hinge, like Yeats's truth, can't be known only embodied, then think again of passion and the Passion—Christ, Dionysus, Marsyas, Orpheus, metaphor and pharmakon, the singing head and ferry. ARDOR in *Paradiso* XIV, radiant energy in the spectral regions by which chemical changes are produced.

Dionysus and St. J the Baptist both with *leopard* skin, the flesh of resurrection, lyric pelt, the garment of both worlds. What is the force that lets me see this now?

*

May 15: when others' words, however loved, will do no good. Though still the heart flows outward, now the anguish of the frightened voice must find its clarity past fear, unmuffled, memorable, with its hard edge of calling *not* from or out into the distance but near, near—I need the thread wound tightly around *my* finger, and unwound, the white grooves in the flesh return to an intenser red. What is the true *direction* of my words beyond foreshortened movements on the page, this furrowing tug and push off from the margin. . . .

knowing that soon the thread, wound or unwound, will make no difference to your finger, or after my own death to mine; your warped rheumatic index finger against which you tied so many suture knots. . . .

a floating cormorant dips down into its underwater dive, the rail splashing a small broken crown of light into the air

so little I can make of this, my finger pressing on the words, *mortal, mortal, mortal, burning, loved.*

*

Massachusetts, July 10–11:   Realizing as I copy out the pages from
May, and dwell on them, something in them ferrying me, transport-
ing, translating—actinium—transforming violet—realizing part of
what was and is going on: the pressure now of what has happened
between—my flying back from S. Africa to L.A. in early June, then
back again for the funeral, the funeral, his face in the coffin—all as
the very self's moulded and remoulded in ways not even evident in
whatever I wrote down between mid-May and now—the pressure of
his actual death, of his changed presence—so that now there's further meaning in the earlier pages, (that *further* may be a kind of
smouldering itself?) Through language to rework the self.

How afterwards it rained into the grave, and I lay sleepless in a small
room, under a rain-beaten skylight, under the same rain—until my
body also started falling inwards through itself into the earth.

In those pages, hesitant stitching, the loose working of threads without yet seeing the whole. Just as in absence of the grand schema we
can do some near piecework that may have within it, *without our
knowing*, required threads of a design. The poet's task now, despite
doubt, ruined schema eg. re sacrifice, vision, transcendent order, is
to surrender to the surviving impulse regardless of lack; and to do so
not in the merely ironic postmod playful manner that risks too little:
submit, the surrender is required precisely *because* of our not knowing
(even when they knew it, still it called for surrender):—in fact this
may link to lyric knowledge or *poetic* knowledge, which is not initially
only cognitive, is more a way of embodying or investing via ardor,
investing but also stripping, something re (un)clothing and revealing,
something re the medium, and rhythm. And to trust you're finding
or being found by truths—as pre-philosophical identification wasn't
cognition though Plato tried to take its ecstasy and ritual up into the
light of reason . . . the earlier wondering re sacrifice has some kind
of response here, with other responses pressing up from further
movement re joy

I'm also now pressed by slow rereading of *Paradiso*, throughout re
smile, joy, and esp XIV sequence from love to its bright garment for
the spirit, to ardor, to vision, to grace (the unearned light that lets us
see the highest good), and back to love, all in relation to the later

resurrection of the body. All this joined with my growing confidence re that glowing emergent flame which first burned as sheer uninterpreted image in mid-May, and with the tracked leopard, the half-imaginary actinic violet at Langebaan etc.; and the *smiles* throughout *Paradiso* joined now with Dad's smile and his saying *smile*—all the way back to his imagined spirit two years ago at Galisteo urging me to be more joyful, especially in what's near at hand. And how all this merging and emerging within love and ardor as the mantling flame within all incarnation.

that such ardor is itself a kind of answer, hinge, it's with the travelling single wave, it's sufficient, and within the embodied world—where now I'm sensing it more fully moving via Cedarberg and Langebaan and via words from—of those places to here at Merry Farm, the field uncut and golden, coreopsis, cosmos, the surviving olive, and the oaks. Having taken him into me in this and *as* this—greater ancient mind—joy/emergence/seeing the lasting and accompanying light. Has his suffering with such selfless grace, such strong retention-and-yet-giving of his spirit, forced us to recognize more fully the spirit in the flesh—a kind of passion. And how our last conversation was of love, the hardness of such love.

Wishing I could say this to him now that I'm seeing ahead as by acceleration toward a more accomplished joy—knowing there's still sorrow between—a *circum-scribing* joy.

sweetness in the field, under the oaks, breeze and birdcalls rising on an unseen wave, and thread by thread the wide net of the heart is set to lift and hold the light, and then the light's the net; and then there is no net, only the pouring light

that earlier image (from last year) of his presence in the backlit face of the breaking waves, connected then to that first blessing after the wave breast and heave shoulder—*The Lord lift up his countenance upon thee, and give thee peace.* Here, in the world.

in the working with these notes, a kind of *preliminary* crushing, offering, burning and distilling out of them/myself—so that forward via hope to catch up with *Par* XIV which is also (by what providence?) the canto of accepted sacrifice: *e non er'anco del mio petto esausto / l'ardor del sacrificio, ch'io conobbi / esso litare stato accetto e fausto—*

and not yet from my breast was drawn out *the ardor of the sacrifice* before I knew the prayer had been accepted and with favour.

Sacrifice not of the other, but of the self. An offering *to* the other.

Now, trying to find Yeats re the rose brings her thorn, the Absolute walks behind (?)—not finding the quote in my notebooks, reaching for *The Poems*, and the book opens first to where I'd years ago underlined Y's commentary re funeral poem for Parnell: "I ask if the fall of a star may not upon occasion, symbolize an accepted sacrifice."

the first stars coming out like thorns, our love within a larger will, his face, the unearned light, a mound of underglints, halo and threshing floor, the field loosely crowned.

*

July 12:   And now the harder work

GRIEVING

Silent, I went out under the stars,
my own life surging until time itself
lay buried in immeasurable drifts of light.

No world more real than this, for I was everywhere.
And still the words emerging,
This is death, I am not dying: where else can I be?

Laurie Sheck

When I was in my mid-twenties, I was lucky to be given the notebooks of Simone Weil by someone who knew I was interested in her work. They were a revelation to me, and I have kept them by my side ever since. In two volumes, one witnesses her work out the thoughts that inform her finest and most moving essays, struggle with contradictions, pay homage to the things that have moved her: poems, philosophic writings, folktales, etc. Right now I open randomly to a page and find these words: "Since affliction causes everything to be called in question. . . ." Throughout these volumes are references to everything from the insidious and corrosive presence the identity card the workers at the Renault auto factory (where she briefly worked) were required to carry, to the Iliad (on which she wrote her famous essay), to the Bhagavad-Gita, George Herbert's poem "Love," mathematical theorums, fragments from Sappho, as well as her own stunning inquiries into the nature of affliction, of goodness and evil, of friendship, beauty, justice, and faith. It is partly the unpolished quality of the notebooks I find so beautiful. One finds in them the record of a struggle, full of rough edges.

It seemed to me from the time I came to her notebooks that, in trying to write poetry, I would need a place to keep not just the record of my own gropings but a collage of the things written by others, thought by others, painted by others, that moved me. That the notebook would become, as it evolved, my teacher and companion. Often when I choose a quote from a writer to put in the notebook I don't see at first (nor do I want to see) just *how it relates to the others. But over time various preoccupations announce themselves, make themselves manifest, so that the notebook becomes a repository and touchstone for the self that is both writer and reader. It is one of the many places one goes to learn things, to feel one's way along in the dark.*

1990–1991

Television sets, movie screens, scripts, news anchors, theme music, commercials, terms like "soundbite" and "spin-doctor" interest me more and more these days. In these images and ideas I see a way of focusing and exploring the world of my new poems, a world which mirrors what I have been experiencing in psychoanalysis: the disparity between the "official" story and the hidden one, the true one.

"What is hidden is more real than what is manifested"—Simone Weil

In a poem, it is not enough to tell the hidden story. The question is also how to look at the subterfuge, the cover, how power functions to block out what it can't absorb, what would undermine it.

*

Our eyes get used to things, our ears get used to things. I was reading today about DW Griffith's early use of close-ups. Instead of showing a whole person, he would zero in on a face. We are so used to that now, we don't even think about it. But when audiences first saw it, they panicked. It looked to them like pieces of hacked up people up there on the screen, horrible, fragmented, grotesque. To examine what it is we have gotten used to, and how it has affected us, changed us. The annihilation of slow time (MTV, Sesame Street, etc) for example, what has it cost us? How has it shaped us?

*

Henry James on skyscrapers: "monuments to the temporary": how does it affect us to live in such a world? World of weekly installments, of the "new and improved," of "updates," of the latest "in" disease.

*

The poet unmasks the language of power. The language of power is the language of the lie.

*

Cocteau's limping angels. Beauty limps, he says.

How to place that wounded beauty against the backdrop of what seems so monolithic, so cold and unhurt, so horribly beyond feeling?—James's skyscrapers, the airbrushed faces in advertisements, etc. Not to isolate each from the other but to look at the interaction.

How often I think of Simone Weil. When she was 18 months old her mother tried to wean her from her bottle. The child would not eat any solid food though. The mother insisted, the child grew more and more frail. The mother consulted doctor after doctor. Finally one doctor said, "Madame, if you insist upon feeding your daughter this way she will die." The soul's refusal; its mysterious insistence on a kind of purity, its own integrity. So the child was fed thickened liquid through a bottle, and lived.

Weil knew how easy it is to take away someone's dignity, to crush them. Not hard. Easy. It is frightening how easy it is.

*

And if Bartleby had lived? But how could he possibly have lived? And of course the story had to take place on Wall Street, enemy of the isolate mysterious hurt soul.

*

Poetry that takes the vulnerable self, its softness and confusion, its groping, and places it up against the sheen and hardness of skyscrapers, slogans, etc. That juxtaposition. And says: now what do we have here? What comes of all this? What specific types of degradation does the soul suffer in such a context?

"The vulnerability of the precious things in life is beautiful, because vulnerability is a sign of existence."   —Weil

"Purity is not invulnerable to pain, but eminently vulnerable to it . . . eminently vulnerable in the sense that every attack on the part

of evil makes it suffer, that all evil which touches it passes into it as
suffering."
                                                                    —Weil

*

The light of the world we live in: neon, frenzied, traffic lights, mar-
quee lights, ambulance light, high crime lights, television screens,
their flickering, and strobe lights, headlights. This quickness.

*

Ingeborg Bachmann: "I crawled from a womb of machines." Yes. To
examine that. And how our machines have changed and are changing, growing more hushed and swifter all the time: xerox machines,
fax machines, electronic surveillance devices. How this quietness ties
into the language of power, of lies.

*

If everything is to be "used," as in an extreme market economy, what
place is there for beauty, for the untouched, and if there is no place, or
only a marginal place, what specific types of degradation are suffered because of it? What does it mean to have a "self" in such a world?

*

Gregor Samsa the salesman. He was USEFUL to his family; he supported them. He was obedient. He carried his salesman's sample case
from town to town doing the bidding of others, bringing home the necessary money. His was a degraded soul. And it was that degraded soul
that finally showed itself when he woke up one morning in the shape of
a giant bug. His soul showed itself in the way that those who are not per-
mitted genuine spoken expression come to show themselves—through
the language of the body, just as the abused child who survives by consciously forgetting the abuse articulates the "forgotten" experience
through bodily suffering. And of course language is dangerous, the truth
is dangerous. Bodily suffering (like Gregor's transformation) the LAN-
GUAGE of bodily suffering, of psychosomatic illness, is easily misunderstood, and therefore safer. Embodied in Gregor was the longing to be
understood and the fear of being understood. The longing to make the
hidden manifest, and the fear of it as well. At the core of many poems is
the equivalent of Gregor Samsa—his damaged, rotting shell, the odd insect voice he does and does not recognize as his own. The self at once
shown and encoded. The music and silence of that damage, and the purity that stubbornly survives that damage, as Gregor did not.

*

Purity is the opposite of manipulation.

*

The color of Cassandra's scream.

*

Cassandra was most pure when she spoke not to manipulate, but when, at Agamemnon's palace, she knew she was beyond influencing anyone at all. I think she spoke then to experience her own purity before she died, to pay homage to her purity in that way; to the purity in herself and in others.

*

Simone Weil: "The troublesome horse pulls toward beauty (of whatever kind it may be) in order to feed himself pleasurably thereon. He has got to be hurt until he reaches the point where he fears the beautiful instead of desiring it. At the end of this training, his energy, which was pulling toward the beautiful, now offers a resistance; but at this moment the winged principle is in the process of growth and the very itch produced by the growing wings carries one on toward the beautiful. The resistance to be overcome in order to be carried toward the beautiful is perhaps a test of authenticity."

*

If one had no belief in human goodness, in tenderness, or any hope for it, could one feel terror?

*

If I am watching the 11 o'clock news and there is a person on the screen suffering, mutilated, grieving, whatever, and that person doesn't feel real to me, or only real in the most cursory and fleeting of ways, aren't I participating in the violation and degradation of that person? Poetry is subversive in that it stands in opposition to vicarious, distanced watching, to spectatorship and morbid curiosity.

*

Pound: "Where the dead walked / and the living were made of cardboard."

*

If I were to really look into the children's eyes, the sufferers' eyes
(How Soft this Prison is), If I were to feel them (Pain Has an Element
of Blank), If I were moved by them to take some action (our stapled
feet). . . . I was an anchorman (it was a dream, I was asleep); I looked
into the teleprompter. I spoke. My voice was steady. I straightened
my tie. I cracked a joke after we broke for a commercial. The commercial showed Timex watches doubling as beachchairs. The survey
said viewers found it amusing. Then the signal came on, and my face
came back to fill the screen.

*

The language of television and its implications: Brought to you by
(implied presence of money, corporations); Stay tuned to this same
station (competition); We'll be right back (time, quickness, speed,
each moment something to be filled); News that you can use (utility,
immediate applicability as opposed to genuine knowledge).

*

Arno Karlen on Cocteau: "poetry is a force rather than a form."

*

"Lad of Athens. Faithful be
To Thyself,
and Mystery—
All the rest is Perjury—"

—Emily Dickinson

*

1992–1993

Gray images on black and white TV screens, as if from the underworld. The TV screen as underworld. As Persephone's grove.

*

The figure of Persephone: the aspect of the psyche that descends
into the unconscious (the underworld), in order to retrieve its authenticity, to come to terms with its deepest drives and conflicts.

In a sense the figure of Hades can be seen as an aspect of Persephone as well—the part of her that facilitates her descent.

*

The underworld as a place of seeing, but the seeing is turned inward. And yet through this inner seeing, the outer world, and a sense of what transcends the merely personal, can come vividly to life, as in Rothko's paintings. Just as I have always loved how Jeffers could have Orestes say, in his extremity, to Electra, "What fills men's mouths is nothing; and your threat is nothing; I have fallen in love outward."

*

The underworld, for Persephone, is the place AWAY from the mother, the place the mother cannot touch. Knowledge and feeling is achieved in this space. But the danger is getting lost and trapped in that space, which also has about it a kind of sterility (the sterile willows of Persephone's grove) because it is by its very nature held rigidly apart from the sunlit world. This is why Persephone must come back for a part of each year to the surface of the earth—to feel the tension between the world outside her body and the world within. To feel the gap and connection between inner and outer. To not forget the world. Hermeticism that forgets the world becomes sterile, emptied of its texture, its tension. Persephone's story is a story of tension—between withdrawal and connection, hiddenness and appearance, the sterile and the fertile.

*

Maybe the world is most real to Persephone when she is apart from it?

*

Why do I never picture her with Hades? I can't really FEEL her unless I picture her down there in her separateness, in the haunted space which is the landscape of her own remembered and repressed memories, of all that is ghostly and fiercely present at once.

*

Persephone on earth barely interests me. And when I read in the Homeric Hymns of Demeter's search for her I secretly hope Demeter won't be able to find her. I want to hear Persephone's voice as the voice of the one apart. Persephone's voice is the voice of the unconscious; Demeter's of the conscious. Nor does Demeter's grief particularly move me, nor the idea that Persephone and Demeter are, in fact, two parts of the same female figure—mother and daughter, conscious and unconscious. It makes perfect sense, but it doesn't move me. What moves and interests me is the unconscious self torn from the conscious part, not integrated into it. (This split is partly where psychosomatic symptoms come from.)

*

Looking at the catalogue from Susan Rothenberg's 1987 show at the Sperone Westwater gallery. Since going to that show, I look at the catalogue several times a year. I feel like I'm trying to figure something out when I look at her paintings. I guess I'm thinking of the fragmented self, of Persephone, of the shadow gardens, of the city as specter of itself, as if it were alive and posthumous, both at once.

I look at her figures that seem to come apart and blend into each other in a whirl of space; or, in stillness, to be severely divided, severed, as in "Half and Half" in which a dark torso and head are placed, upright, to the right and in front of the detached legs and feet. As if wholeness were an anachronism. The features of the face are barely discernable, and something rectangular, with steps, is behind it. There is a severity to this. The feet are facing TOWARD the torso, as if they mean to be rejoined with it, are concentrating on it, as if they could think and desire. But they can't be rejoined. It's a done deal. There's no putting the figure back together. Yet, eerily, it doesn't seem dead at all, this two-part figure. This is how it must live: severed, detached.

*

Ann Lauterbach: "poetry is the aversion to the assertion of power. Poetry is that which resists dominance." Precisely.

*

D. W. Winnicott in "Playing and Reality" quotes another analyst, Fred Plaut: "The capacity to form images and use these constructively by recombination into new patterns is—unlike dreams or fantasies—dependent on the individual's ability to trust."

Winnicott: "The potential space between baby and mother, between child and family, between individual and society or the world, depends upon experience which leads to trust. It can be looked upon as sacred to the individual in that it is here that the individual experiences creative living. By contrast, exploitation of this area leads to a pathological condition in which the individual is cluttered up with persecutory elements of which he has no means of ridding himself."

*

In my poems, my Persephone figure is, on the one hand, trying to find in the underworld that potential space between self and other, self and world, and senses it as sacred. On the other hand, she is also all cluttered up, and is trying, in that space that is the underworld, to sort through the images that assault her. Her separate space is a mixture of the sacred and the assaultive, sensory deprivation and overstimulation.

*

Emily Dickinson in her room. Her white dress. Her desk.

*

I am interested in how this figure of the unconscious (Persephone) can be interwoven with contemporary imagery. What is the mirror of the broken and annihilated self we look into in this our world? From her separate space in the underworld of THIS world, what would she think and feel and, in her mind's eye, see? What images would assault her? And what, too, would be of comfort? Beneath the assaultive and the brokenness is a yearning for wholeness and a skepticism of it, and a yearning for the sacred space Winnicott speaks of.

*

Henry James: "One story is good only till another is told, and skyscrapers are the last word of economic ingenuity only till another word be written. This shall be possibly a word of still uglier meaning, but the vocabulary of thrift at any price shows boundless resources, and the consciousness of that truth, the consciousness of the finite, the menaced, the essential invented state, twinkles ever, to my perception, in the thousand glassy eyes of these giants of the mere market."

*

Roberto Calasso on Persephone in the Underworld: "The invisible would now reassert its rights over the body of the visible more strictly than before; their dealing with each other, long diluted and mingled together in life on earth, would find a new center of gravity."

Calasso, again: "When Persephone took her place on Hades' throne and her scented face peeped out from behind the spiky beard of her partner, when Persephone bit into the pomegranate that grew in the shadow gardens, death underwent a transformation every bit as radical as that which life had undergone when it had been deprived of the girl. The two kingdoms were thrown off balance, each opening up to the other. Hades imposed an absence on earth, imposed a situation where every presence was now enveloped in a far greater cloak of absence. Persephone imposed blood on the dead: not, as in the past, the dark blood of sacrifice, not the blood the dead used to drink so thirstily, but the invisible blood that went on pulsing in her white arms, the blood of someone who is still entirely alive, even in the palace of death."

Persephone as the eye, the "I."

Calasso: "Kore doesn't just mean 'girl,' but 'pupil,' too. And the pupil as Socrates says to Alcibiades, 'is the finest part of the eye,' not just because it is the 'part which sees' but because it is the place where another person looking will find 'the image of himself looking.'"

*

Mark Rothko on his murals: "They are not pictures." "I have made a place."

It is something I aspire to in my poems—to make a place—a landscape of psychological and spiritual texture. Not a narrative, but a place made of words.

Rothko's sense of the solitary as almost sacred, "when a crowd of people looks at a painting, I think of blasphemy."

"To be rooted is perhaps the most important and least recognized need of the human soul."—Simone Weil. Rothko, feeling deeply

lonely and exiled, sought, I would think, to find that rootedness in
his paintings—that place of belonging rooted in genuine feeling. As
if feeling could BE a place. And at the same time, in painting works
that evoke such a great sense of distance and transcendence, what
he evokes in me as a viewer, is an enormous sense of longing for
what lies at once within us and beyond us, so present and illusive at
once.

*

Rilke's letters on Cézanne:

"Surely all art is the result of one's having been in danger, of having
gone through an experience all the way to the end, to where no one
can go any further."

"One lives so badly, because one always comes into the present unfinished, unable, distracted."

" . . . for a long time nothing, and then suddenly one has the right
eyes. . . ."

THE BOOK OF PERSEPHONE

This darkness. And what rises up out of this darkness.

I open the book of lost entries—
how fraudulence moves like a wind through the world,
how there's no page that is not shredded,
and there is nothing pure but a forgotten thing.

I remember nothing. I remember the stars and moon,
the entries I burned and didn't burn, the entries
like crumbled terraces of stars.
Each page of gutted houses, curtains of violence and sighs.
A child's cry pressed in a pillow. The crossed-out words
that haunted the white page, and the syntax clamping down
too hard, like a locked box.
The water murmuring *was was was.*

I remember nothing. It is winter. There is a forest of bare trees,
a town consisting of forged documents

through which a child must walk.
There is a city of cries, the child's sealed mouth, its tired legs.
Out of the dark more dark, razored or soft.

It is winter. The withered gardens whisper their dry stalks.
The child kneels at a locked box. There are walls
that shudder like flea-bitten cloth, there are walls disappearing,
and above them the leaden movie-glow of dusk,
then the hours of larceny, of theft.

I remember nothing. I remember the scattered pages,
the mechanisms of sums, the cities accomplished
and spoiled, crumbling and re-made.
The candor of ruin and the gates. In daylight the businesses
go on, the bright calculations, the frantic advertisements
that masquerade as calm. So little evidence is left
of what has vanished. As if when the swan lifts off the liquid stare
it is the wind of our words it leaves behind.

I remember nothing. I remember soft faces streaked with fear,
the red and gold disclosures stuttering briefly
before they finally closed. And then a darkness falling
downward, all strobe-lit and reeling, then this flat darkness

like the pressure of a hand.

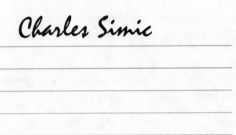

Charles Simic

I keep two kinds of notebooks. I use one kind to note down words, phrases, images and begin and abandon poems. The second kind of notebook is the place where I'll comment on something I've read, copy down favorite passages, and even jot down an idea once in a while. I must emphasize the almost total lack of order in the way my entries are made. "What a mess!" a friend once exclaimed on opening one of my notebooks. Very true. I regarded their lack of neatness as part of their attraction for me. Turning the pages, squinting to read my scribble, I find many things I completely forgot about that suddenly seem worth thinking about further.

Here is a sampling.

1987–1993

The ideal place to teach creative writing is a used books store, says my friend Vava Hristić.

*

I'm writing for a school of philosophers who will feast, who will be remembered for asking for a third and fourth helping of the same dish while discussing metaphysics. Philosophers who seek those moments in which the senses, the mind and the emotions are experienced together.

*

My hunch that language is inadequate when speaking about experience is really a religious idea, what they call negative theology.

*

The ambition of much of today's literary theory seems to be to find ways to read literature without imagination.

*

What all reformers and builders of utopias share is the fear of the comic. They are right. Laughter undermines discipline and leads to anarchy. Humor is anti-utopian. There was more truth in jokes Soviets told than in all the books written on USSR.

*

My old poems on Geometry (The Point, Triangle, Euclid Avenue, The Ballad of the Wheel) are my attempt to read between Euclid's lines.

*

New York City is much too complex a place for just one god and one devil.

*

The most original achievement of American literature is the absence of official literary language.

*

Where time and eternity intersect my consciousness is the traffic cop holding up a STOP sign.

*

Ethics of reading. Does the critic have any moral responsibility toward the author's intentions? Of course not, say all the hip critics. What about the translator? Isn't the critic, too, a translator? Would we accept a translation of Dante's *Divine Comedy* which would disregard the poet's intentions?

*

Gombrowicz, too, used to wonder, how is it that good students understand novels and poems, while literary critics mostly talk nonsense.

*

The ambition of literary realism is to plagiarize God's creation.

*

Seeing is determined not by the eye but by the clarity of my consciousness. Most of the time the eyes see nothing.

*

In their effort to divorce language from experience, deconstructionist critics remind me of middle-class parents who do not allow their children to play in the street.

*

Lately in the United States we have been caught between critics who do not believe in literature and writers who believe only in naive realism. Imagination continues to be what everybody pretends does not exist.

*

Many of our critics read literature like totalitarian cops on the lookout for subversive material, for instance, the poet's claim that there is a world outside language.

*

Poetry tries to bridge the abyss lying between the name and the thing. That language is a problem is no news to poets.

*

Poets worth reading usually believe things the age they live in no longer does. Poets are always anachronistic, obsolete, unfashionable, and permanently contemporary.

*

Can a timeless moment of consciousness be ever adequately conveyed in a medium that depends on time, i.e., language? This is the mystic's and the lyric poet's problem.

*

A good-tasting homemade stew of angel and beast.

*

One point of agreement between Eastern and Western philosophy: men live like fools.

*

Wisdom as measure, as a sense of proportion, as middle ground. If it's defined that way, one sees why there are only a few examples of wisdom in the entire history of the world.

*

If Derrida is right, all that the poets have ever done is whistle in the dark.

*

Like many others, I grew up in an age which preached liberty and built slave camps. Consequently, reformers of all varieties terrify me. I only need to be told that I'm being served a new, improved, low-fat baked ham, and I gag.

*

It's the desire for irreverence as much as anything else that brought me first to poetry. The need to make fun of authority, break taboos, celebrate the body and its functions, claim that one has seen angels in the same breath as one says that there is no god. Just thinking about the possibility of saying shit to everything made me roll on the floor with happiness.

*

Here's Octavio Paz at his best: "The poem will continue to be one of the few resources by which man can go beyond himself to find out what he is profoundly and originally."

*

The sense of myself existing comes first. Then come images and then language.

*

Being is not an idea in philosophy but a wordless experience we have from time to time.

*

Suppose you don't believe either in Hobbes's notion that man is evil and society is good or Rousseau's that man is good and society evil. Suppose you believe in the hopeless and messy mixture of everything.

*

I know a fellow who reads modern poetry only in the john.

*

Here's a quick recipe on how to make a modern poem out of an old one. Just take out the beginning and the end; the invocation to the Muses and the nicely wrapped up final message.

*

I still think Camus was right. Heroic lucidity in the face of the absurd is about all we really have.

*

Fourier, who planned a model of perfect human society, was known never to laugh. There you have it! Collective happiness under the steely gaze of a murderer.

*

A true confession: I believe in a soluble fish.

*

A school where the best students are always kicked out, there you have the history of the academy's relationship to contemporary art and literature. (I think Valéry said something like that.)

*

The prose poem is the result of two contradictory impulses, prose and poetry, and therefore cannot exist, but it does; This is the sole instance we have of sqaring the circle.

*

First you simplify whatever is complex, you reduce reality to a single concept and then you start a church of some kind. What surprises me endlessly is how every new absolutism, every one-sided worldview is instantly attractive to so many seemingly intelligent people.

*

My soul is constituted of thousands of images I cannot erase. Everything I remember vividly from a fly on the wall in Belgrade to some street in San Francisco early one morning. I'm a grainy old, often silent, often flickering film.

*

Only poetry can measure the distance between ourselves and the Other.

*

Form in a poem is like the order of performing acts in a circus.

*

One writes because one has been touched by the yearning for and the despair of ever touching the Other.

*

We call "street wise" someone who knows to look, listen, and interpret the teeming life around him. To walk down a busy city block is a critical act. Literature, aesthetics, and psychology all come into play.

*

Nationalists and religious fundamentalists all hate the modern city because of its variety and spontaneity. Stupidity and ill-will easily rule in a small community, but in a city one has many ways of eluding its grasp.

*

Hopscotch. Pierre leapt from Stalin to Mao to Pol Pot to Saddam. I hope, after the experience of this century, that no one in the future will still believe the myth of the critical independence of the intellectuals.

*

The lyric poem is often a scandalous assertion that the private is public, that the local is universal, that the ephemeral is eternal. And it happens! The poets turn out to be right. This is what the philosophers cannot forgive the poets.

*

How many literary theorists and teachers of literature truly understand that poems are not written merely for the sake of oneself, or for the sake of some idea, or for the sake of the reader, but out of deep reverence for the long and noble art of poetry.

*

We speak of rhyme as a memory aid, but not of striking images and unusual similitudes that have a way of making themselves impossible to forget.

*

I love Mina Loy's: "No man whose sex life was satisfactory ever became a moral censor."

*

Since democracy does not believe in the exclusive possession of truth by one party, it is incompatible with nationalism and religion, I tell my Yugoslav friends.

*

My aspiration is to create a kind of non-genre made up of fiction, autobiography, the essay, poetry, and, of course, the joke!

*

A theory of the universe: The whole is mute; the part screams with pain or guffaws.

*

I would like to write a book that would be a meditation on all kinds of windows. Store windows, monastic windows, windows struck by sunlight on a street of dark windows, windows in which clouds are reflected, imaginary windows, hotel windows, prisons . . . windows one peeks out of or peeks in. Windows that have the quality of religious art, etc.

*

Rushdie's case proves that literature is the dangerous activity, and not literary criticism and its currently fashionable notion that literature is merely propaganda of the ruling ideology.

*

Here's the totalitarian theory of literature from Plato to the Inquisition to Stalin and all their followers:

1. Separation of content and form, ideas from experience. Literature is primarily its content.
2. The content needs to be unmasked, revealed for what it truly is. The cop slapping the young poet and demanding to know who ordered him to write like that is the secret ideal.
3. Literature is clever propaganda for a particular cause.
4. Literature on its own terms is socially dangerous. Pure art is a blasphemy against authority.
5. The poet and the writer are never to be trusted. Trust the critic and the censor for their constant vigilance.

*

What is the difference between a reader and a critic? The reader identifies with the work of literature, the critic keeps a distance in order to see the shape it makes. The reader is after pleasure, the critic want to understand how it works. The erotic and the hermeneutic are often at odds and yet they should be companions.

*

A New Hampshire high school student reading an ancient Chinese poem and being moved—A theory of literature that cannot account for that commonplace miracle is worthless.

*

Another large group of cultural illiterates we are stuck with: college professors who do not read contemporary literature or know modern art, modern music, theater, cinema, jazz, etc.

*

Eternity is the insomnia of time. Did somebody say that, or is it my idea?

*

If poems were the expression of one's ethnicity, they would remain local, but they are written by individuals in all cultures, which makes them universal.

*

Both imagination and the experience of consciousness affirm that each is all and all is each. Metaphors, seeing resemblance everywhere, is internationalist in spirit. If I were a nationalist, I'd prohibit the use of metaphor.

*

For Emily Dickinson every philosophical idea was a potential lover. Metaphysics is the realm of eternal seduction of the spirit by ideas.

*

The individual is the measurer, the world is what is measured, and the language of poetry is the measure. There! Now you can hang me by my tongue!

*

How do we know the Other? By being madly in love with it.

*

Comes a time when the living moment expands. The instant becomes roomy. It opens up. Suddenly everything inside and outside of ourselves is utterly different. I know what I am, and I know what I am not. It's just me and It.

*

Is the clarity of consciousness the negation of imagination? One can imagine plenty in a state of semi-consciousness.

*

The highest levels of consciousness are wordless and its lowest gabby.

*

The tribe always wants you to write about "great and noble subjects."

*

When I was little, bad boys in my neighborhood advised me to grab my balls every time I saw a priest. It's the first lesson in the arts I was given.

*

Seeing the familiar with new eyes, that quintessential idea of modern art and literature, the exile and the immigrant experience daily.

*

Here's Konstantin Nojka's observation with which I agree completely: "Thought precedes the word—as in the example of a little kid who calls a strange man 'dad.' The adults correct him and say it's not daddy, but what the kid means is that he's like dad—has the same height, glasses, etc."

*

The academics always believe that they have read more than the poets, but this has rarely been my experience. Poets of my generation and the preceding generation are by far better read than their academic contemporaries, with exceptions, of course, on both sides.

*

Christ, like Sappho, challenges the tribe. Their message is, you have no tribal obligations, only the love for the Father in the first case and the love of your own solitude in the second case.

*

Consciousness: this dying match that sees and knows the name of what it throws its brief light upon.

*

Imagination equals Eros. I want to experience what it's like to be inside someone else in the moment when that someone is being touched by me.

*

I'm in the business of translating what cannot be translated: being and its silence.

*

Ars Poetica: trying to make your jailers laugh.

*

Two young birch trees wrestling in the wind. The crow in the snow refereeing.

*

Here where they make piggy banks with the face of Jesus.

*

Strafford, New Hampshire, Orpheus assuaging the fierceness of wild beasts with his new kazoo.

*

The day I went to make funeral arrangements for my father-in-law, I caught a glimpse of the mortician's wife nursing the mortician's new daughter. Her breasts were swollen huge with milk.

*

A sequel to Dante's *Divine Comedy*. The modern hero retraces his steps from heaven to hell.

*

I have a House of Horrors the size of my head, or the size of the known universe. It doesn't matter which.

Like everybody else, I'm sticking everything on a remote possibility that one of many lies will come true. I say to myself in moments of tenderness, perhaps you're more of a philosopher than you know.

As for the ALWAYS OPEN, always brightly lit House of Horrors, it's just a windowless room empty except for some trash on the floor.

*

The Gestapo and K.G.B. were also convinced that the personal is political. Virtue by decree was their other belief.

*

The closeness of two people listening together to music they both love. There's no more perfect union. I remember a summer evening, a good bottle of white wine and Helen and I listening to Prez play "Blue Lester." We were so attentive, as only those who have heard a piece a hundred times can be, so this time it seemed the piece lasted forever.

*

The lost thread of a dream. What a pretty phrase!

*

She's a passionate believer in multiculturalism, but she objects to all that fatty ethnic food. Especially sausages! No good for you.

*

Cioran is right when he says that "we are all religious spirits without a religion."

*

Eurocentricism is the dumbest idea ever proposed by academics. The notion that all European history—all its philosophy, literature, art, cuisine, martyrdom, oppression—is the expression of a single ideology belongs in *The National Enquirer* on the same page with "I was Bigfoot's Loveslave."

*

Even as I concentrate all my attention on the fly on the table, I glance fleetingly at myself.

*

America is the only country in the world where a rich woman with servants can speak of being a woman oppressed and not be laughed at.

*

What the lyric poets want is to convert their fragment of time into eternity. It's like going to the bank and expecting to get a million dollars for your nickel.

*

I agree with Isaiah Berlin when he says in an interview: "I do not find all-embracing systems congenial." I have a horror of minds who see all events as instances of universal rules and principles. I believe in the deep-set messiness of everything. I associate tidiness with dictatorship.

*

How to kill the innate poetry of children—the secret agenda of a conference on primary school education. I met teachers who fear poetry the way vampires fear the cross.

*

For a man like Teller, science meant new and much improved ways of killing people, and he was enthusiastically received in high places.

*

It is in the works of art and literature that one has the richest experience of the Other. When the experience is truly powerful, we can be anybody, a nineteenth-century Russian prince, a fifteenth-century Italian harlot.

*

Most of our political writers on the left and right are interchangeable. That's why it was child's play for so many liberals to become neo-conservatives. What serenity the day one realizes that!

*

Here's one firm law of history: truth is known at precisely that point in time when nobody gives a shit.

*

A poem is an invitation to a voyage. As in life, we travel to see fresh sights.

*

To be an exception to the rule is my sole ambition.

*

Twenty years ago the poem for me was still mostly an inspired and unpremeditated utterance. My friend Vasko Popa, on the other hand, was all calculation. A poem was an act of supreme critical intelligence for him. He had already thought out everything he was going to write for the rest of his life. Once, late at night, after much wine, he described to me in detail his future poems. He wasn't putting me on.

In later years I'd see these poems come into print one by one, and they were just as he described them that night.

*

Popa's metaphysics was Symbolist, and yet, it's not so much that he used symbols in his poetry, and he did. What he really wanted to understand is the secret of how symbols are made. Poetry is sacred action, it's been said. Popa's poems demonstrate how the laws of the imagination work.

*

"The salad bird" writes Lucian, "is an enormous bird covered all over with salad greens instead of feathers; its wings look exactly like lettuce leaves." For Popa, language was not an abstract system but a living idiom, an idiom already full of poetic invention. In that respect, his imagination and his poetry are wholly determined by the language in which he wrote. In his poems the reader enters inside Serbian language and meets the gods and demons hiding there.

*

Little said, much meant, is what poetry is all about. An idiom is the lair of the tribal beast. It carries its familiar smell. We are here in the realm of the submerged and elusive meanings that do not correspond to any actual word on the page. Lyricism, in its truest sense, is the awe before the untranslatable. Like childhood, it is a language that cannot be replaced by any other language. A great lyric poem must approach untranslatability.

*

Translation is an actor's medium. If I cannot make myself believe that I'm writing the poem I'm translating, no degree of aesthetic admiration for the work can help me.

*

The philosophical clear-sightedness of a man who is taking a long siesta on a day when many important matters should be attended to. As somebody said, cats know laziness is divine.

*

Blues musicians do not doubt that music touches the soul.

＊

My poem "Midpoint" is a reduction, the cutting down to a kind of algebraic equation of a ten-page poem on cities where I lived. The paring down occurred when I realized that all my future cities were the ghost images of a city where I was born. In my imagination I'm always at midpoint.

＊

To be bilingual is to realize that the name and the thing are not bound intrinsically. It is possible to find oneself in a dark hole between languages. I experience this now when I speak Serbian, which I no longer speak fluently. I go expecting to find a word, knowing that there was a word there once, and find instead a hole and a silence.

＊

I grew up among some very witty people, I now realize. They knew how to tell stories and how to laugh, and that has made all the difference.

＊

The restaurant is Greek. The waiter's name is Socrates, so Plato must be in the kitchen, and Aristotle is the fellow studying a racing form at the cash register.

Today's special, grilled calamari with fresh parsley, garlic, and olive oil.

＊

When I started writing poetry, in 1955, all the girls I wanted to show my poems to were American. I was stuck. It was never possible for me to write in my native language.

＊

I prefer Aristophanes to Sophocles, Rabelais to Dante. There's as much truth in laughter as there is in tragedy, a view not shared by many people. They still think of comedy as nose-thumbing at serious things in life.

＊

My second-grade teacher in Belgrade told me more than forty-five years ago that I was a "champion liar." I still remember being mortally offended and kind of flattered.

*

Only through poetry can human solitude be heard in the history of humanity. In that respect, all the poets who ever wrote are contemporaries.

*

A scene from the fifties French movies that I still love:

A fly gets shut in a room with three armed thugs and a woman gagged and bound who watches them with eyes popping.

In front of each man on the table there is a sugar cube and a pile of large bills. No one stirs. A naked bulb hangs from the ceiling by a long wire so they can see the fly count its legs. It counts them on the table, tantalizingly close to a sugar cube, and then it counts them at the end of someone's nose.

I have no idea if this is the way it really was in the movie. I've worked on the scene over the years, making little adjustments in it as one does with a poem.

*

My life is at the mercy of my poetry.

*

I thought "nosology" had to do with noses. Something like a science of noses. Many noses coming to be examined. The perfect nose in a lobby of a grand hotel lighting a gold-tipped cigarette behind a potted palm. The pretty nosologist examining my nose and almost touching it with her own.

Nosology, unfortunately, has nothing to do with noses.

*

O beau pays! The monkey at the typewriter.

*

In a neighborhood frequented by muggers and rapists after dark, I bring my soapbox and shout: "Everything I have ever said has been completely misunderstood!"

William Stafford

My father wrote before light each day, lifting a sheet of white paper out of a slender box and starting to jot down daily things—a dream, a scrap of conversation from the day before, a phrase from recent reading that had snagged his attention. On the last day of his life, he started his blank sheet with a question from an insurance agent on the telephone the day before: "Are you Mr. William Stafford . . . ?" As with all his daily writings, that fragment was both ordinary and profound: What if you had one last chance to answer that question? What would you say from so common a beginning? "Well, it was yesterday, / and that's when sunlight began to follow my hand. . . ." And so he ventured every day, his notebook a loose-leaf box of vacant space. Like a spider, he spun out his thread from the plain, sticky substance of the language rooted deep in the interior life, yet plain as day.

—Kim R. Stafford

1991

January 4: What moves me, what looms in my life, may not be what works in managing the material and political parts. So I learn not to depend on the innermost elements of my being, but to subordinate feelings and preferences. My success depends partly on my repression—

Even in politics, where I learn to calculate even as others do. As a result none of us clearly stands for what our most significant feelings would prefer. And the calculus results in conduct that may belie our purest feelings.

*

January 26: I must explore the revision that happens before you write anything down.

*

March 30: When you write you invite a reader to look in through a window on everything—and to feel, taste, hear, smell, *participate with* what is there. You can explain, but mostly you point out, part by part, and the sweep of the whole.

*

February 4: On the plane yesterday an insight about writing: you catch at the edge of a feeling or idea or glimpse or sound—and you don't let go. You merge along with it, almost as if your hands play over it, pushing, extending, turning it over, encouraging it. And all this activity awakes other feelings, ideas, glimpses, sounds. Things get exciting; you let yourself be persuaded that a unity is possible.

*

February 10: If you get important enough you even speak in italics. Others have to take a longer time to teach you anything, for they must contend first with your assumption that you don't need to learn.

*

October 5 (1990): It is usual in a speech to prepare the ground, to spread out assumptions, needed context, understandings needed for a foundation of whatever is put forward. Much of this the audience may already assume, base their lives on, and understand. That redundant part of a speech irks me, and some speeches never get beyond being a reminder. A poem may skip that, silently assume it, and abruptly make use of it, twist it, subvert it, *use* it.

A poem knows where you already are, and it nails you there.

*

January 7:   If legends, myths, and stories embody even the subconscious currents of people's wants and needs, then maybe gossip in a bar carries that kind of cargo.

Sharp Ears—Now what people say clings like rain to what the words mean. A remark won't fade but grows vivid as it curves to follow a speaker and plaster itself forever on the back. I'm afraid to listen: too much of the saved-up, too much of the concentrated story, spills out of the bottle and spreads out instantly all over earth and sky.

A tremor, they say, remains, a lasting heartbeat far down inside every atom. It can't forget what happened; it carries creation's pang forever, hidden but tremendously there. And that immanence lingers in all things, ready to tremble its helpless dance again in the presence of atoms like mine.

*

January 22:   In daily life, in living, I try to be in control. I act brave. I don't shiver. I level off extremes of excitement or apathy. But in reading or attending a theater or listening to music, or entering conversations that interest me, I lean into whatever is happening. I shiver when the wind blows, hoot the villain, cower at danger, embrace what is offered. The relief of participation changes my life.

*

January 11:   Art is a touch-and-go affair. Some things, when you learn how, you're not doing them anymore. For they are a gift; you can't demand them. You have no right, just the privilege, and it may be taken away or awarded all over again.

Kierkegaard tells how a head of lettuce, to have that succulent heart, requires time, leisure. He compares this to the meditation time, the dwelling in the inner life, that real human living requires.

*

January 20:   A thought came. I did not want to write the sadness of it. Hello, Today. Let's walk awhile together. Tell me your intentions. That way, we can help each other, and maybe forget tomorrow. You be today, I'll be tomorrow.

*

February 26:   On a recent trip to the East Coast I found that poets' revising goes so far as to have *others* monitor the needed changes. In effect, a committee is writing those poems. Being critics together, the writers manage to create texts that receive favorable reviews. Strange.

*

February 17:   Always do your writing in the wilderness—I was thinking that sentence when I woke up yesterday.

At first the pen doesn't know where to go. It has been away for a while and is now a little aimless. Besides, one of the world wars has begun somewhere off there beyond the horizon, making any random journey seem frivolous or even an act of treason—("What were you doing, Daddy, in that evident or more hidden war that is always going on whether you know it or not?")

So the pen, taking account of all that but unable still to do much about it, listens carefully to its own whispering and tries whatever direction the next word wants to go, meanwhile keeping in mind that sooner or later it will be necessary to spell out a meaning for all apparent meandering. (If you ever touch that real lost way you never even want to find your main path again; that's what bothers those who intend to guide you.) (What they're afraid of is, a new star shows up and all the old patterns turn into delusion and chaos.)

No wonder the pen tries to escape its past by pretending to have a future. There might be a way to escape, somewhere in the middle of things, if that awful responsibility of beginning and ending didn't haunt all who have to travel to live.

*

April 21:   About physics, apparently most of us (and maybe all of us?) can't encompass the scale and proportions involved in the realms of the very small and the very large. The realizations needed are *inconceivable.*

And maybe in the arts, too, a sense of the differences wrought by adjustments in sound, color, meaning . . . —this sense is unevenly distributed among people. Non-artists maybe just don't know how significant little changes are.

*

April 15: For a superior person, it is a little harder to believe in democracy. And if you are powerful, like an editor or something, and are selecting for a magazine or for publication you are liable to think of what you reject as inferior, whereas it may just be *other.*

*

If you think of the right questions, the answers are always being given.

If you are alert enough, every remark has a long vista.

The labyrinth you can't get out of is the one you create as you climb.

A gun can choose. A bullet has no choice.

It wasn't a place—time is where I came from.

*

February 3: For a long time they thought maybe there was a soul, that maybe lives had reasons, were sent from somewhere and found their way through the world and on with new duties and rewards and companions.

Maybe, in the evening when light changes and a day floods away into the horizon, that old thought comes again, settling quietly in the minds of survivors who lift their eyes from the ground and search earnestly through light, through shadow. Any friends or family who were taken away would survive somewhere in a better realm, restored, cherished, because life is precious and our joys and sorrows must have meaning.

So all your life you wonder. Sometimes a glimmering almost arrives. Your soul stirs in a gust that has come from nowhere and carries itself away, a promise of more, of revelation and rest.

THE TROUBLE WITH READING

When goats like a book, the whole book is gone,
and the meaning has to go find an author again.
But when we read, it's just print—deciphering,
like frost on a window: we learn the meaning
but lose what the frost is, and all that world
pressed so desperately behind.

So some time let's discover how the ink
feels, to be clutching all that eternity onto
page after page. But maybe it is better not
to know; ignorance, that wide country,
rewards you just to accept it. You plunge;
it holds you. And you become a rich darkness.

Rosanna Warren

A "poet's" notebook? Hardly. Rather, a compost heap. It's difficult to pitchfork individual hunks of material out of it, because they're all in the process of settling in together and undergoing a chemical/physical change that sometimes results in poems. Some of the hunks are study notes, the habits of an earnest schoolchild preserved in adulthood, crucial to my life but of no interest to outsiders. Others are gobs of family life, diary entries not to be shown to family members, let alone to outsiders. I don't keep a notebook as material for poems, but in order to live my life: without the remove provided by those blessed, narrowly ruled pages in their chaste binding, the onslaught of daily events and stray thoughts and unassimilated reading is unbearable. Once they have begun to find their way into words, however crude, the mind can find a purchase and trace patterns that gather shape involuntarily. There's a long way from the surprises in a notebook to the shaping power of a poem, but thinking about the notebook brought a modest perception about my poems: that they too emerge involuntarily, despite the conscious labors to bring them to completion; and that they emerge from the laboring mess of life itself, its unimaginable melding of disparate elements and the mind's effort to move among them.

1990

August: Vermont. From his study: A single dry beech leaf hangs from a branch of balsam by a spider web strand. I saw the same leaf last August, is it possible it has survived a winter of blizzards when a man has died?

Pond water glints through pine boughs. The mind of the forest: years and years of layered decaying leaves.

You brought me a small gray stone. I showed you an empty palm. To write the icon, slide cloudlight over the surface of the pond. It will adhere. We will read it together, years from now.

*

Tightening noose of a November afternoon. Sex on my fingers, honey from Mt. Hymettos on our thighs. I love this hour of erasure, this season stripping down in chill rain and gray. The trees are divested, the suburban
lawns are numb, the twigs
and vestiges are cast down,
And whatever small knowledge remains
Is to be cherished in the spine, the wrist pulse, the primitive *mons* which guards its secret against and into the circling down of night, the wheeze and shush of distant, hurrying tires.

*

from Marcel Schwob, *Le Livre de Monelle* (1895):
"Don't wait for death: she is with you. Be her companion and hold her close: she resembles you.

Die your own death; don't envy the deaths of ages past. . . ."

"Burn the dead carefully, and scatter their ashes to the four winds of heaven. . . ."

"Bequeath yourself nothing, neither pleasure nor sorrow."

"And she said, from afar: Forget me and I will be returned to you."

*

Dragging my innocence over the surface of the earth like a chain.

*

My spine a braid of pain.

*

Buber: "All real living is meeting."

*

Chiara, aged four, on Pierre from her day care: "Is he French, or a human being?"

To me, the other day, objecting to my reading aloud: "I *hate* it when you rhyme! Your mouth goes all wibble wobble and you look like a cow."

Later: "Drawing-writing is stronger than word-writing."

*

The father, in whom disease is chewing at lungs, brain, liver, and lymph glands, arrives to collect his young daughter from an afternoon of play at our house. He is thin, he wears a baseball cap and sunglasses. "How are you?" he asks cheerfully. "Fine, thanks," I reply, and in order not to ask him how he is, declare, with obtuse heartiness, "They played well this afternoon, they had a wonderful time." "Good, good," he says. His daughter, who does not know what is in store for them, gallops up: "Daddy!" He leans to embrace her, her arm is soft around his neck, her light hair falls over his shoulder.

*

Biography: a low mimetic mode. Precisely. By any means. So let it lead me. "We are saved by what we cannot imagine." (Ashbery) (Are we saved?) Give me your hand.

*

1992

June 27. Matthew 3:10. "And now also the axe is laid unto the root of the trees: therefore every tree which bringeth not forth good fruit is hewn down, and cast into the fire."

3:12. "[Jesus] whose fan is in his hand, and he will thoroughly purge his floor, and gather his wheat unto the garner; but he will burn up the chaff with unquenchable fire."

VIOLENCE (Transformations require destruction: like that Tibetan deity in the Museum of Fine Arts trampling on a necklace of skulls in his marriage with Wisdom. He has the slavering, fanged mouth of a monstrous bull as he leans over her, waving his forty-odd arms; she, in his lap, twists upward, her legs twining around his waist, melon breasts pressed to his chest. The museum label helpfully notes that the figures are "anatomically correct" and that they can be separated and fitted back together in their copulation. A crowd of schoolchildren tromps by the statue; two ten-year-olds linger to peer at it while their myopic and harassed teacher tries to shoo them into a farther room. "What's the bull doing to that lady?" asks one girl. "That's Asia," says the teacher, with a vague wave of the hand. "Come on." "Look," says the other girl, "that bull is *eating* that lady.")

*

July 2. Ezra 6–10. Sad, terrible and glorious rhythm. Return to Jerusalem. Ezra discovering the intermarriage of the Jews 9:3— "And when I heard this thing, I rent my garment and my mantle, and plucked off the hair of my head and of my beard and sat down *astonied.*"

Matthew 5:17. "Think not that I am come to destroy the law, or the prophets: I am not come to destroy, but to fulfil." And the impossible command, "Love your enemies." (5:44)

*

July 6. Esther 1–3. A fairy tale: powerful stupid king; cast-off queen; beautiful virgin; persecution. . . . Also, archetypal anti-Semitism: Mordecai the Jew in the king's gate is proud, does not bow down to the favorite, Haman. Therefore: genocide. "The posts went out, being hastened by the king's commandment [of slaughter], and the decree as given in Shushan the palace. And the king and Haman sat down to drink; but the city of Shushan was perplexed." (3:15.) Horrifying banal detail.

*

July 15. Job 14. The chapter of mortality: "Man that is born of a woman is of few days, and full of trouble. 2. He cometh forth like a flower, and is cut down; he fleeth also as a shadow, and continueth not." (I Peter 1:24. "All flesh is as grass." Isaiah 40:6. "The voice said, Cry. And he said, What shall I cry? All flesh is grass, and all the goodliness thereof is as the flower of the field: 40:7. The grass withereth, the flower fadeth: because the spirit of the Lord bloweth upon it: surely the people is grass.")

*

from *Zen Mind, Beginner's Mind*, Shunru Suzuki, p. 106, "Dogenzenji became interested in Buddhism as a boy as he watched the smoke from an incense stick by his dead mother. . . ."

*

July 21.   *Yale Review*, vol 80, #3. Richard Poirier on William James. Literature as "performing presence," enactment (but no #!**!! social normality rubbish as in Austin!). James: "Each word appears less as a solution than as a program for more work." (p. 77) James' attention to neglected transitives rather than nominatives. From James' *The Stream of Thought*: "All *dumb* or anonymous psychic states have, owing to this error [substantives taken as concepts], been coolly suppressed; or, if recognized at all, have been named after the substantive perception they led to, as thoughts 'about' this object or 'about' that, the stolid word 'about' engulfing all their delicate idiosyncrasies in its monotonous sound. . . ."

*

July 28.   End of Job. 41:18 "By his *neesings* a light doth shine, and his eyes are like the eyelids of the morning." (Great word.)

19. "Out of his mouth go burning lamps, and sparks of fire leap out.

20. Out of his nostrils goeth smoke, as out of a seething pot or caldron."

*

July 30.   Tillich, *Dynamic of Faith*, p. 100, "There is no faith without separation." (Max Jacob's love poems.)

*

August 4.   Proverbs. Themes keep recycling: punish children, fear the Lord, be thrifty and provident, care for the poor: combination of peasant wisdom and grim faith in righteousness rewarded. Concern with language: strictures against false witness. 15:4— "A wholesome tongue is a tree of life: but perverseness therein is a breach in the spirit." Women get it hard, especially in advice to wayward sons: 23:27—"For a whore is a deep ditch; and a strange woman is a narrow pit." (Ecclesiastes 7:26. "And I find more bitter than death the woman, whose heart is snares and nets, and her hands as bands. . . .")

*

August 12. Proverbs rises to crescendo. 30:15 " . . . There are three things that are never satisfied, yea, four things say not, it is enough:

30:16. The grave; and the barren womb; the earth that is not filled with water; and the fire that saith not, it is enough. . . .
30:18. There be three things which are too wonderful for me, yea, four which I know not:
30:19. The way of an eagle in the air; the way of a serpent upon a rock; the way of a ship in the midst of the sea; and the way of a man with a maid." (Practical advice gives way to poetry, to awe.)

*

October 15. John Butler Yeats' letters to Willy. August 6, 1906: "Poetry is written not by Intellect but by the clairvoyant faculty."

April 6, 1913: "Personality is born out of pain. It is the fire shut up in the flint." (p. 161)

*

Nov. 16. Return from D.C., conference on American Poetry at Library of Congress. Predominant thesis, that American poetry is a poetry of solitude, the new self in a new land. But my notion was different: and here I realized I'd hit on my own bent, tragic Virgilian eclogue as opposed to the intoxicant of "pure" lyric (Mallarmé, "Rien, cette écume, vierge vers"—Nothing, this foam, virgin verse). That in the U.S. we cannot be exempt from the blood guilt of our destiny, from Cortez to Puritans to Civil War to L.A. 1992. That ours is a *contaminated* lyric, no virgin, and that that is its force. The "self," yes, but the self in relation to God, to nature, to history. Good old WCW had it right in 1925 in *In the American Grain*: we must record these initiatory sacrifices. Remus cries out from the bloody ground (he is the great, lost figure in *The Aeneid*). The real eclogue is not safe from Caesar's soldiers: "*Tityre, tu patulae recubans sub tegmine fagi . . .*" (The first Eclogue: You, Tityrus, lying under the cover of a spreading beech . . .). And what is the Hebrew Bible but one ghastly long account of the fall of language into time? A thoroughly bloodied word, that covenant, with a berserk parent insisting on complete obedience, and the children forever lusting after the groves. The terrible repetitiousness of history, sacred history. A recurring dream.

*

Dec 7. Isaiah 29:4. "And thou shalt be brought down, and shalt speak out of the ground, and thy speech shall be low out of the dust, and thy voice shall be, as of one that hath a familiar spirit, out of the ground, and thy speech shall whisper out of the dust." This describes true poetry. Language suffering the condition of its utterance. Like Pier delle Vigna in Dante, "*si della scheggia rotta usciva insieme / parole e sangue, che io lasciai la cima / cadere, e stetti come l'uom che teme*" (So from the broken twig spewed out words and blood, so that I let the branch fall, and stood like a man in fear). All spitting and hissing, primal language of pain, original language. Language is a physical medium, needs blood or dust to come true. Poetry must whisper or gurgle.

*

From Hofmannsthal, *The Book of Friends*:
"We are so eager to possess and are made so happy by any sign of fidelity that we can feel something like pleasure even in a regularly recurring fever."

"Reality is the *fable convenue* of the Philistines."

"Singing is near miraculous because it is the mastering of what is otherwise a pure instrument of egotism: the human voice."

"What is culture? To know what concerns one, and to know what it concerns one to know."

*

1993

January 15.   Basho 1644–1694. The most "famous" Japanese haiku:

The old pond:
A frog jumps in—
The sound of water

(more literally—"water of sound"). Robert Aitken (*A Zen Wave*):
" 'Samadhi' means 'absorption,' but fundamentally it is unity with
the entire universe. When you devote yourself to what you are doing,
moment by moment—to your koan when on your cushion in zazen,
to your work, study, conversation, or whatever in daily life—that is
samadhi."

*

Snow today. Nino and I ran down Robinwood Avenue, almost silent
over the white, in the white: it was a soft feathering snow, light as
breath. The woods drew us in, we passed under a curtain of snow-
embroidered boughs and were in the "other" world: Silence, white,
no human forms, the path beckoned us on. Nino running—a black
arrow, nose slicing the wind, head low, tail ruddering straight behind,
plumes in the air. His small legs flew fore and aft. He's eleven years
old and sick with a tumor, but running in the snow, he's immortal.

*

Jan. 18.   Basho.

In plum-flower scent
Pop! the sun appears—
The mountain path.

Aitken: "In the *eihei koruku*, Dogen Kigen asks, "Without bitterest
cold that penetrates to the very bone, how can plum blossoms send
forth their fragrance all over the universe?' " p. 31

Kobayashi Issa (1763–1827). When his little daughter died:

While the dewdrop world
Is the dewdrop world,
Yet—yet—

Aitken: "We come and go, being seen off and seeing off. 'Yet—yet' is also the point. . . . Please stop at that point. Enter that point. Someone asked me how long it would take to attain *kensho*, realization experience. I answered, 'No time at all.' "

*

Feb. 9. Basho:

> Let my name
> Be traveler;
> First rains.

*

(At the Zen temple in Cambridge, an angry cold young man resident there, filled with pride of self-mastery. The Holocaust was a "cosmic readjustment of karma." Now there is someone with a petrified heart. What hell did he crawl out of?)

*

Feb 17. From Missal: "Memento, homo, quia pulvis es, et in pulverem reverteris" (Remember, man, that you are dust, and to dust you must return). All this turning / returning / con-version—Jonah, prodigal son, Hebrews.

*

June 3. From *The Crown of Thorns*, Austin Farrar, lent by A. G. For Easter: "We do not come to God for a little help, a little support to our own good intentions. We come to him for resurrection."

Easter III: "Unless we agonise at some time over the birth of faith, faith is not ours, it is not a personal possession, it is not the child of our own soul . . ." (p. 31).

*

August 26. Jeremiah 25:11. "And this whole land shall be a desolation and an astonishment . . ." 25:15. "For thus saith the Lord God of Israel unto me; Take the wine cup of this fury at my hand, and cause all the nations, to whom I send thee, to drink it. 25:16. And they shall drink, and be moved, and be mad, because of the sword that I will send among them. . . . [Bosnia, Somalia]. 25:33. And the slain of the Lord shall be at that day from one end of the earth even unto the other end of the earth; they shall not be lamented, neither gathered nor buried; they shall be dung upon the ground. . . ."

This desolation is MAN-MADE. God has no need to wreak vengeance: we author our own destructions.

*

Nov 27. In the detox clinic to visit X. More destructions. Thanksgiving. Glimpsed other inmates: anorexic, tall young woman—narrow foxy face; heavily made-up eyes; wore skintight leggings, highheeled sandals, bodysuit. She looked like a ruined Barbie Doll. Husband (?) and brother (?)—dumpy, helpless-looking young men—brought in two-year-old boy, who ran to her. "Sweetie! Did you miss me?"

In the waiting room near me, a middle-aged man with a bleary, bruised look sits with his visitor. Both men heavy. The inmate says he feels lousy, his mind's a "sieve," he can't hear what anyone's saying to him, his stomach's upset. "At least you're sober," says his friend. "You gotta give yourself that. One day atta time." "Yeah, one day atta time," replies the inmate gloomily. "What kinda life is that? No drinking, no smoking, no gambling, no going out with the guys —WHAT KINDA LIFE? WHAT'S TO LIVE FOR? It all seems so . . . mundane." "No one ever promised you a rose garden," says the friend, "That's life. Gotta accept it." "Yeah, no roses, sure ain't no bedda roses." Pause. Then the inmate: "What's worst is, now I'm sober, *I don't know what's going to happen.* When I'm drunk, I always know what's going to happen. But sober, I don't know."

*

1994

Feb 18. V's death. He was ninety-six, still composing.

My last conversation with him, three weeks ago: he asked whether I believed in the after-life. "I don't know," I replied. "Do you?" He said he was skeptical, but still waiting to see: "I won't say no, I won't say yes, I'll see . . ." He added, "But I think God is an oversimplification."

*

March 7. Home with rain patter, high snow banks melt into gurgle, wash into storm drains; mist hovers over all, a palpable cloud.

* * *

Numbers 25:1. "And Israel abode in Shittim, and the people began to commit whoredom with the daughters of Moab. 25:2. And they called the people unto the sacrifices unto their gods: and the people did eat, and bowed down to their gods."

Ends with Phinehas pursuing man of Israel and Midianitish woman into tent, "and thrust both of them through, the men of Israel and the woman through her belly. So the plague was stayed from the children of Israel."

Violence. This raging exclusive god. The need to slay all other possibilities. Psychically, depicts a mind in defensive spasm, almost a sexual spasm, "the woman through her belly."

*

March 9. Glaucoma. glaukommatos: gray-eyed. Glaukos, gleaming, silvery, bluish-green, gray. A poem of anguish: her arm, a twig wrapped in cloth.

Afternoon falls out of itself. Hypnotic snow. The arbor vitae hunches in the cold, clumps over. Rhododendron leaves curl inward, like cigars.

*

May 25. B.U. Student Union. Upstairs, those mortuary photographs of the Metcalfe teaching award winners: most of them look miserable in the camera's eye. Trapped souls: in the bulb's glare, the skin is caught in mortal fatigue, hairdos are helmets, the eyes look out pleadingly.

*

June 30. Mt. Larissa, behind Argos. A fort: Mycenaean, Dark Age, Byzantine, Frankish, Turkish, Venetian, Turkish, Greek. Differing wall constructions tell of the various builders, from the gigantic, ingeniously fitted Cyclopean masonry of the Mycenaeans to the small mortared Venetian and later stones. The towers and battlements—what's left of them—clutch the cliff, far over the Argive plain with its orange groves and olives. Nauplion lies down there, and the whole gulf spreads softly out in the noon sun. This was the plain sacred to Hera; she renewed her virginity every year in the fountain at what's now the monastery of Agia Moni (whose fountain is now dedicated to the Eternal Life of Christ). Up on this military crag where for millennia men have bled and shouted and cursed and rallied and vomited and died, barely a cicada grates the stillness; drought and stone preside; heat clamps over us like a white cope. Out of the drought and silence, in a corner of the high inner court, a fig tree thrusts up, outrageously green. In its shadow I imagine I hear the whisper not only of leaves, but of water. And there must be water up here. A few feet away, water *is* visible down an ancient cistern. From a bough of the fig, at my approach, three little dark blue birds with narrow yellowish beaks startle up noisily and flit to the near wall, where they perch, whistling, on the stones.

POETRY READING

manibus date lilia plenis (Aeneid VI)

It is a promise they hold in their hands.
Feather waver in the ghostly crests.
Rome is an iron glint in the eyes,
a twitch at swordhilt. Down the long avenue
through silted shadow and pale leaking light
stalks the future. Power,
whispers the father, power bounded
only by the edge of earth, the rim of heaven.
The arts of peace, the rule of law:
the Capitol, aqueducts, legions, circuses.
Disorder chained in the temple. Abundant calm.
In such love you have given yourself.

But who is that young one, pallid
in armor with darkened brow
and night coming on at his heels,
scent of crushed lilies, a bruise—

Here the reading breaks off.
The Emperor's sister falls into hysterical tears,
patrons and literati disband.
Servants clear away winecups, platters of cake.
And Aeneas climbs back into daylight
through the Gate of false dreams.

Notes on Contributors

Marvin Bell is the author of thirteen books, the latest of which are *The Book of the Dead Man* (poems) and *A Marvin Bell Reader* (selected poems, journals, memoirs, and essays). He has received awards from the American Academy of Arts and Letters, the Guggenheim Foundation, and the National Endowment for the Arts, and senior Fulbright appointments to the former Yugoslavia and Australia. A longtime member of the faculty of the Writers' Workshop at the University of Iowa, he divides his time between Iowa City and Port Townsend, Washington.

Rita Dove is the author of five books of poems, including *Thomas and Beulah*, which won the Pulitzer Prize, *Grace Notes*, and *Mother Love*. Her *Selected Poems* was published in 1993, the year she was named poet laureate of the United States. She has also published a novel, a collection of short stories, a verse drama, and *The Poet's World*, her lectures given as poet laureate. She is Commonwealth Professor of English at the University of Virginia and lives in Charlottesville with her husband, the German writer Fred Viebahn, and their daughter, Aviva.

Stephen Dunn recently published his *New and Selected Poems, 1974–1994* and *Walking Light: Essays and Memoirs* with Norton. He is Trustee Fellow in the Arts at Richard Stockton College of New Jersey.

Carolyn Forché published her third book of poetry, *The Angel of History*, with HarperCollins in 1994. The preceding year, Norton published *Against Forgetting: Twentieth-Century Poetry of Witness*, her anthology of work by poets who experienced conditions of extremity during the twentieth century. She teaches at George Mason University.

Alice Fulton is currently a fellow of the John D. and Catherine T. MacArthur Foundation. She has also received support from the Ingram Merrill and Guggenheim foundations. She is the author of *Powers of Congress*, *Palladium*, and *Dance Script with Electric Ballerina*. Her fourth book of poems, *Sensual Math*, was published by Norton in 1995. She is professor of English at the University of Michigan.

Donald Hall is the author of books of poetry, essays, biography, and children's literature, which have won him acclaim and numerous awards. His *Old and New Poems* was published in 1990, followed by *The Museum of Clear Ideas: New Poems* in 1993. He lives on a family farm in Eagle Pond, New Hampshire.

Joy Harjo, an enrolled member of the Creek tribe, has won numerous awards for her poetry. Her books include *She Had Some Horses*, *In Mad Love and War*, and *The Woman Who Fell from the Sky*. She is also the author of screenplays and children's books and plays saxophone with the band Poetic Justice.

Anselm Hollo, a native of Finland living in the United States since 1967, is both poet and translator, author of more than thirty collections of poems, most recently *Near Miss Haiku* and *West Is Left on the Map*. He teaches in the writing and poetics M.F.A. program of the Naropa Institute and lives in Boulder, Colorado.

Garrett Hongo was born in Volcano, Hawaii, where he has been at work on a memoir entitled *Volcano*, published by Knopf in 1995. He is the author of two collections of poems, *Yellow Light* and *The River of Heaven*, which won the Lamont award. He is editor of *The Open Boat: Poems from Asian America* and *Songs My Mother Taught Me: Stories, Memoir, and Plays by Wakako Yamauchi*. Hongo is professor of creative writing at the University of Oregon.

Donald Justice is a native of Florida now living in Iowa. His first book was *The Summer Anniversaries* (1960); his most recent is *A Donald Justice Reader* (1991). In 1980 his *Selected Poems* received a Pulitzer Prize and in 1991 he was co-winner of the Bollingen award. His *New and Selected Poems* will be published in the fall of 1995. He is a member of the American Academy of Arts and Letters.

X. J. Kennedy's first book of poems, *Nude Descending a Staircase*, which won the Lamont award, was republished in 1994 in the Carnegie Mellon University Press's Contemporary Classics series. He has also recently published *Cross Ties: Selected Poems* and *Dark Horses*, and is the author of ten books of verse for children and the widely used textbook *An Introduction to Poetry*. Formerly a professor of English at Tufts University, he lives in Bedford, Massachusetts.

Yusef Komunyakaa won a Pulitzer Prize in 1994 for his selected poems *Neon Vernacular*. Previous collections include *Dien Cai Dau* and *Magic City*. He teaches at Indiana University.

William Matthews has published ten books of poetry, most recently *Time & Money* (Houghton Mifflin). He is also author of a book of essays and translations of the Roman poet Martial. He teaches at the City College of the City University of New York.

J. D. McClatchy is the author of three collections of poems, *Scenes from Another Life*, *Stars Principal*, and *The Rest of the Way*. His essays have been collected in

White Paper, and he has edited several other books, written four opera libretti, and taught at Yale, Princeton, UCLA, Columbia, and other universities. He is editor of *The Yale Review*, and lives in Connecticut.

Cynthia Macdonald's most recent collection of poems is *Living Wills: New and Selected Poems* (Knopf). She has won numerous awards and grants for her work. She teaches in the creative writing program at the University of Houston, a program she founded in 1979. Macdonald was formerly an opera singer and is now, in addition to being a writer and teacher, a psychoanalyst with a small practice.

Heather McHugh recently published her selected poems, *Hinge & Sign*, as well as a collection of essays, *Broken English*, with the Wesleyan University Press. She teaches part of each year at the University of Washington.

James Merrill (1926–1995) was author of fourteen books of poetry, including *From the First Nine: Poems 1946–1976*, *The Changing Light at Sandover*, *Late Settings*, and *The Inner Room*. His last book, *A Scattering of Salts*, was published in 1995. His work won many awards, including the Bollingen, National Book, Pulitzer, and Bobbitt. His memoir, *A Different Person*, was published in 1993.

Susan Mitchell is the author of two books of poetry published by HarperCollins, *The Water inside the Water* and *Rapture*, which was nominated for a National Book Award. She has won several other awards for her work, including Lannan and Guggenheim fellowships. Raised in New York City, she now lives in Boca Raton, where she holds the Mary Blossom Lee Endowed Chair in Creative Writing at Florida Atlantic University.

Lisel Mueller lives in the Chicago metropolitan area. She has published five volumes of poetry, including *The Need to Hold Still*, which won a 1981 National Book Award. Her most recent collection is *Waving from Shore*. She is also a translator of German literature, with special emphasis on the works of the twentieth-century poet and fiction writer Marie Luise Kaschnitz.

Mary Oliver has won numerous awards for her poetry, including a Pulitzer Prize for *American Primitive* and the National Book Award for *New and Selected Poems*. Her recent books include *White Pine*, *A Poetry Handbook*, and *Blue Pastures*. She is currently the William Blackburn Visiting Professor at Duke University; in 1996 she will join the faculty of Bennington College.

Liz Rosenberg has published two books of poems, *The Fire Music* (1986) and *Children of Paradise* (1994), both with the University of Pittsburgh Press. She has also published several children's books with Harcourt Brace and Putnam Books, and teaches English and creative writing at the State University of New York at Binghamton.

Peter Sacks was born in South Africa but now lives in Baltimore, Maryland, where he is a professor of English and creative writing at Johns Hopkins University. He is the author of two collections of poems, *In These Mountains* and *Promised Lands* (Viking), and of *The English Elegy: Studies in the Genre from Spenser to Yeats.*

Laurie Sheck's most recent book of poems is *Io at Night*, published by Knopf, which will publish her new book of poems, *The Willow Grove*, in 1996. She has been the recipient of a Guggenheim award, and her poems have been included in the *Pushcart Prize* anthology and *The Best American Poetry* of 1991. She lives in Princeton, New Jersey.

Charles Simic, born in Belgrade, is celebrated as both poet and translator. His most recent books include *Selected Poems 1963–1983, The World Doesn't End* (which won the Pulitzer Prize), *The Book of Gods and Devils*, and *Dimestore Alchemy*. A collection of prose, *The Unemployed Fortune-Teller*, has recently been published by the University of Michigan Press. Simic teaches at the University of New Hampshire.

William Stafford (1914–1993) was honored in his lifetime with many awards, including the National Book Award, and served as consultant to the Library of Congress. His last books included *Passwords* and *My Name Is William Tell* (winner of the Western States Book Award). A selection of his poetry, edited and introduced by Robert Bly, was recently published as *The Darkness Around Us Is Deep.*

Rosanna Warren is the author of three books of poems, *Snow Day, Each Leaf Shines Separate*, and *Stained Glass*, for which she won the Lamont award. She has also won awards from the Guggenheim, Ingram Merrill, and Lila Wallace foundations. Warren is at work on a biography of Max Jacob, recently published a translation of Euripides' *The Suppliants*, and edited *The Art of Translation: Voices from the Field*. She teaches at Boston University.